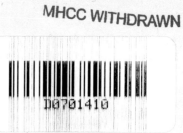

THE

DISSONANCE

OF

DEMOCRACY

THE
DISSONANCE
OF
DEMOCRACY

LISTENING, CONFLICT, AND CITIZENSHIP

SUSAN BICKFORD

CORNELL UNIVERSITY PRESS

ITHACA AND LONDON

First published 1996 by Cornell University Press.

Printed in the United States of America

Library of Congress Cataloging-in-Publication Data
Bickford, Susan, 1963–
    The dissonance of democracy : listening, conflict, and citizenship
/ Susan Bickford.
      p. cm.
    Includes bibliographical references and index.
    ISBN 0–8014–3219–7 (cloth : alk. paper)
    1. Communication in politics.   2. Listening—Political aspects.
  3. Social conflict. 4. Democracy. I. Title.
JA85.B53   1996
302.2—dc20   96–26038

This book is printed on Lyons Falls Turin Book,
a paper that is totally chlorine-free and acid-free.

B&T
NE/OS

for my mom,

IRENE RASH

CONTENTS

ACKNOWLEDGMENTS

It is a delight to thank publicly the people whose help made this book possible. My first thanks go to my teachers, Stephen G. Salkever of Bryn Mawr College and Mary G. Dietz of the University of Minnesota. Steve Salkever first taught me to love the history of political thought and the practice of political theory; without his extraordinary and compelling example, I would not be a teacher and a writer. He has always encouraged me in my efforts to engage a variety of theoretical voices, for which I continue to be grateful. I have also found it useful, over the years, to remind myself of Steve's insistence that it was better to be interestingly wrong than boringly right. I'm not sure I have always had the courage to follow that advice; luckily, Steve remains a valued mentor, and I have appreciated his comments on various pieces of this project. I am also deeply grateful to Mary Dietz for all the energy and attention she has given my work. Mary's intense support, her careful critical eye, and her willingness to disagree have been invaluable, and her own intellectual passion remains an inspiration. And Mary, simply by being who she is, taught me something essential to being a teacher: she took me seriously as a scholar from the first—and so I learned to take myself seriously, too. I can't repay her for that; I can only hope to do the same for my students.

It is a wonderful privilege to live in a family of people who have a remarkable ability to invent creative possibilities for their lives, and the boldness to pursue them. For the example they set, for their constant loving moral and material support, and for their enthusiastic interest in my work, I thank my family: my mother, Irene

Rash; my sisters, Donna Bickford and Barbara Jean; my mother's partner, James D. Lamp; and my aunts, Jean Kroflich and the late Sue Rash.

Most of the ideas in this book unfolded during my time at the University of Minnesota, and I am grateful for the challenges and encouragement provided to me there by Terry Ball, Sara Evans, Sandra Peterson, Kathryn Sikkink, Dana Chabot, Jennifer Clelland, Barbara Cruikshank, Steven Gerencser, Andrew Seligsohn, Ron Steiner, and Kris Thalhammer. I had the good fortune to complete final revisions here at the University of North Carolina at Chapel Hill, where my colleagues and students have provided a stimulating and supportive environment in which to work. I am particularly grateful to my fellow political theorists Michael Lienesch and Steve Leonard, who continue to provide invaluable attention, engagement, and support. (Mike's bottom drawerful of candy helps too.)

I thank the Conflict and Change Center of the University of Minnesota for a research grant that supported work on this project at an early stage, and the American Association of University Women Educational Foundation for a dissertation fellowship. The generosity of these institutions gave me the crucial intellectual gift of time.

J. Peter Euben gave this book a thorough and engaged reading, and I thank him for his perceptive suggestions and thoughtful criticisms. Thanks also to Roger Haydon of Cornell University Press for his warmth, candor, and commitment.

An earlier version of Chapter 1 appeared under the same title in *Journal of Politics* 58 (2): 418–441, and the material is used here by permission of the University of Texas Press. Portions of Chapter 3 and 4 were published in Bonnie Honig, ed., *Feminist Interpretations of Hannah Arendt* (University Park: The Pennsylvania State University Press), 1995, pp. 313–335. Copyright 1995 by The Pennsylvania State University and used by permission of the publisher.

In this book, I argue that friendship is not an appropriate model for political action. It is, however, a great help for writing political theory! I am particularly happy to have the chance to thank my friends Lisa Disch and John McGowan. Since the genesis of this project, I have benefited immensely from Lisa's insight and intelligence, her understanding of the work process, and her enthusiasm for talking and arguing about political theoretical matters. I am grateful for Lisa's strong friendship and for all I continue to learn from her discerning passion for thinking, for teaching, and for political engagement. It would be nice enough simply to be on the same campus as John McGowan, given his exceptional capacity for listening and for combining critical judgment with intellectual openness. But it's even nicer to be friends. With his characteristic insight and generosity, John gave this manuscript a particularly timely reading, and in a variety of ways saw me through the final stages of revisions (not least by encouraging me to trust my instincts). The warm friendship that he and Jane Danielewicz offer plays a central role in making me feel personally and intellectually at home in Chapel Hill.

Special thanks go to another exemplar of friendship, the dauntless Jennifer Clelland, who not only came to North Carolina in August to visit, but spent half her vacation reading page proof.

Merleau-Ponty tells us that "it is harder to live than to write books" (*Signs* 20). He doesn't mention how hard it is to live *while* writing books. Luckily for me, I live with Greg McAvoy, who has always exhibited unparalleled creativity in sustaining my spirit. I'm grateful to Greg for his extraordinary, instinctively generous heart, his perceptive readings (and rereadings) of these chapters, and his great homemade pasta. Greg's thoughtfulness—in every sense of the word—contributes immeasurably to my life and my work.

This book is dedicated, with love and gratitude, to my mom, Irene Rash. If it contains even a fraction of her intelligence and daring, the reader is indeed fortunate.

SUSAN BICKFORD

Chapel Hill, North Carolina

Abbreviations

ARISTOTLE

NE	*Nicomachean Ethics*
Pol.	*Politics*
Rhet.	*On Rhetoric*

HANNAH ARENDT

AJ	*Hannah Arendt Karl Jaspers: Correspondence*
BPF	*Between Past and Future*
CR	*Crises of the Republic*
EJ	*Eichmann in Jerusalem*
HC	*The Human Condition*
JP	*The Jew as Pariah*
LK	*Lectures on Kant's Political Philosophy*
LOM	*The Life of the Mind*
MDT	*Men in Dark Times*
OR	*On Revolution*
OT	*The Origins of Totalitarianism*

MAURICE MERLEAU-PONTY

PP	*Phenomenology of Perception*
PrP	*The Primacy of Perception*
S	*Signs*
SNS	*Sense and Non-sense*

THE

DISSONANCE

OF

DEMOCRACY

Not knowing how to listen, neither can they speak.
                                    —HERACLITUS

But there come times—perhaps this is one of them—
when we have to take ourselves more seriously or die;
when we have to pull back from the incantations,
rhythms we've moved to thoughtlessly,
and disenthrall ourselves, bestow
ourselves to silence, or a severer listening, cleansed
of oratory, formulas, choruses, laments, static
crowding the wires.

                              —ADRIENNE RICH,
                                 "Transcendental Etude"

Our commitments sustain our power and there is no free-
dom without some power.
                              —-MAURICE MERLEAU-PONTY,
                                 Phenomenology of Perception

Chapter 1

LISTENING, CONFLICT, AND CITIZENSHIP

As Plato's *Republic* begins, Polemarchus playfully threatens to use force if Socrates does not agree to return with him to the Piraeus. Socrates suggests an alternative: he might persuade Polemarchus to let him go. "But could you persuade us," Polemarchus challenges, "if we refused to listen?" And Glaucon responds firmly, "there's no way" (*Republic* 327c–328). Here, in one of the earliest works of political theory, Plato has his characters recognize the centrality of listening. Yet neither Plato nor his successors give explicit theoretical attention to the role of listening, and to a large degree, this theoretical neglect of listening extends to contemporary democratic theory. This omission is particularly surprising given democratic theorists' emphasis on shared speech as a practice of citizenship.

Two questions come to mind here: why is listening absent in this way? And why should we care—that is, why is listening important? My concern is with the second question. I hope to show that thinking about listening is central to developing democratic theory (and envisioning democratic practices) for our contemporary social and political context. So this book does not examine (textually or psychoanalytically) the *neglect* of listening in historical and contemporary political thought. Still, investigating the character of political listening implicitly points us to possible reasons for its disregard, reasons that have to do with the presumed character of politics. As I argue later in this chapter, the complexities of listening can be ignored in the context of certain conceptions of politics—but not others.

My remarks here are intended briefly to characterize a set of issues surrounding political listening, issues that I explore in more depth throughout this book. Let me begin by noting that my analysis is located in an understanding of politics that stresses its conflictual and contentious character. I use Aristotle, Hannah Arendt, and contemporary feminist theory to delineate political conflict in fairly specific terms: such conflict has to do with the character of political questions, the conditions under which they are asked, and who is debating them. Political questions have only uncertain answers, and yet what course of action is chosen can have immediate and profound effects on our lives and our world. Argument about these choices takes place in a context of socioeconomic inequality and the antagonisms and struggles such inequality gives rise to. And citizens themselves are willful persons with disparate interests, opinions, identities, and experiences.

What makes politics possible in the face of such discord, what keeps us from being doomed to war, anarchy, or the relentless clash of unyielding wills? I contend that what makes politics possible, and what democratic politics requires, is a kind of listening attention to one another. Political listening is not primarily a caring or amicable practice, and I emphasize this at the outset because "listening" tends immediately to evoke ideas of empathy and compassion. We cannot suppose that political actors are sympathetic toward one another in a conflictual context, yet it is precisely the presence of conflict and differences that makes communicative interaction necessary. This communicative interaction—speaking and listening together—does not necessarily resolve or do away with the conflicts that arise from uncertainty, inequality, and identity. Rather, it enables political actors to decide democratically how to act in the face of conflict, and to clarify the nature of the conflict at hand. Deciding democratically means deciding, under conditions in which all voices are heard, what course of action makes sense. Thus my goal is to develop a conception of politics as a communicative engagement that takes conflict and differences seriously and yet allows for joint action. Explicit in such a conception is listening as a central activity of citizenship, and throughout this book I mobilize a set of examples intended to illuminate the way in which listening is and can be central to our political lives. For the conception of citizenship that I am analyzing is not a romantic one, but one that is currently practiced and thought.

Let me stress also that my goal in this project is to analyze listening as a distinctive activity and *not* as a metaphor for a variety of related activities—reading, writing, or interpretation. I focus my attention on actual communicative interaction between political actors, not on the interpretation of texts or on a general "openness to being."[1] There may indeed be similarities between, for example, reading and listening; but the relation and the distinction are themselves matters for analysis, and that further analysis would itself require this project: the investigation of the distinctive features of listening as a crucial and particular political activity.

To get an initial sense of why listening is a central and difficult component of political action, let us return to the drama enacted in the opening scene of the *Republic*. Polemarchus's challenge—"do you see how many of us there are?"—points to two factors that might resolve the question here in his favor: numbers and force. Surprisingly, he skips over the possibility of using numbers without force, that is, deciding the question by majority rule. Unlike force, deciding the question by majority rule would depend on a prior agreement to abide by majoritarian decisions; the space between the Piraeus and Athens apparently was not governed by such an agreement! In any case, these options share the possibility of resolving the immediate dispute in a way that does not require communication. The third and communicative option that Socrates proposes, persuasion, is workable only if the other listens. There is a crucial distinction being made here: deciding by means other than force makes the decision rely not just on oneself but on others; we have to listen, and we are dependent on the other to listen as well. As Polemarchus is quick to point out, not listening is an effective kind of power, one he is prepared to exercise, and one against which Glaucon seems to feel there is no recourse.

Yet the scene does not end here, with Socrates and Glaucon playfully coerced to return. Immediately after Polemarchus's assertion that he will not listen, Adeimantus begins to offer reasons for Socrates to stay: "Don't you know that there is to be a torch race on horseback for the goddess tonight?" He begins, in other words, an attempt at persuasion (which Polemarchus briefly joins), an attempt designed specifically to appeal to Socrates, with his interest in novelty and in staying up talking all night. It is after this attempt,

---

[1] This focus thus has influenced whose work I find helpful (e.g., Aristotle and Arendt) and whose work I do not engage, despite apparent similarities (e.g., Gadamer and Heidegger).

with support from Glaucon, that Socrates agrees to consider the matter resolved. Socrates, who at first raises the possibility of persuading Polemarchus to let them go, ends up being persuaded to stay—because he listened to Adeimantus (as is evident by his response, "on horseback?").

Although Plato obviously intends this exchange to dramatize a political problem of some kind, it is perhaps not a fair example of conflictual communication. It is in jest, it is among friends who know one another well enough to offer quickly convincing reasons. But interestingly enough, friendship is not invoked here. Socrates is not asked to stay for love of his friends or to consider the consequences for them if he does not do as asked (the tactic Crito tries in a different context). He is offered reasons to make the decision to stay, reasons designed to get him to form a positive opinion about the desirability of staying. (Whether Socrates actually decides that he would rather stay than go is unclear; he simply implies that the decision was not his alone to make and that the question has been resolved.) This way of dealing with the conflict is possible only because Socrates is willing to listen, and because Adeimantus takes on the role of continuing the discussion. (Polemarchus, to be fair, later takes the responsibility for continuing a different argument.) What I want to stress here is that *both* speaking and listening are central activities of citizenship. Focusing on listening does not require denigrating or diminishing the role of speech, for politics is about the dynamic between the two.

It is this "dynamic between" that Polemarchus wants to avoid. He does not want to risk the possibility that Socrates will talk his way out of the situation, that Polemarchus himself will be persuaded to change his mind. He wants to control the outcome of the encounter and ensure that the solution is in line with what he now desires. Listening opens up the chance that something else will happen—a different outcome, or Polemarchus coming to think differently. To highlight the role of listening is to confront the intersubjective character of politics. Communication inherently presupposes different beings *and* the possibility of something between them; it points to both separateness and relatedness. If we automatically coincided, formed a not-very-differentiated whole, we would not need to speak or listen or argue, nor would we if we were doomed to noncommunication, to sheer unbending differences.

Communication is an effort that acknowledges a more-than-one, a separateness, a difference that may be the source of conflict, *and at the same time* foregrounds the possibility of bridging that gap by devising a means of relatedness.

But as Polemarchus realizes, it also means ceding the possibility of control and the certain achievement of one's current goals. Historically, this "quest for certainty" has driven many politicians and much political theory (Dewey 1929), and it is a quest that can have a variety of motives: the lust for power, an obsessive need for order, sheer intensity of moral purpose. We are sometimes overwhelmed by a passion for control simply because of our passion for the world, because we care so much about certain things or events (in this case, because Polemarchus and the others care so much about talking all night with Socrates). This difficulty presents one of the central challenges of politics: addressing a conflict through political interaction demands that we resist the desire for complete control, but what is behind that desire (a particular commitment) is what prompts us to political interaction in the first place.

As political theorists, we can obscure the difficulties created by this inevitable conjunction of differences and relatedness either by ignoring the conflictual conditions in which political communication takes place, or by conceptualizing politics in a way that does not require communication. Contemporary theorists have followed both these routes: those who take conflict seriously tend not to stress interaction, while those who value interaction tend to underestimate the presence and persistence of conflict. Both approaches, I contend, miss the central complexity of political life.

Consider, for example, the work of John Rawls. Rawls's theory of justice is designed to provide a social and political order that is tolerant of diverse ways of life. Rawls begins by acknowledging differences, in the form of the irreducible plurality of (sometimes conflicting) conceptions of good that individuals have. In the face of these differences, we need principles of justice to ensure the basic liberties that allow us to freely pursue our individual sense of the good and our diverse life plans, yet still enable social cooperation and the resolution of conflicting claims (Rawls 1971, esp. 3–16. See also Rawls 1985, 248–250).

Rawls grounds the principles of justice that are to govern the social order in rationality and consensus, that is, these principles must be rationally arrived at and mutually agreed upon. He achieves this through the well-known device of the original position in which individuals are covered by a "veil of ignorance" regarding their own social and economic circumstances, racial and gender identity, psychological tendencies, and so on. (They do know, however, that such differences among people exist and that, whoever they are, they want more rather than fewer "primary goods": "rights and liberties, powers and opportunities, income and wealth" (Rawls 1971, 146–147, 136–137, 62).[2] Thus constrained, participants deliberate about the content of the principles of justice that will guide their political, social, and economic institutions. In this initial situation, because "everyone is equally rational and similarly situated, each is convinced by the same arguments" (1971, 139).

The original position, then, is a theoretical device for creating agreement on the principles that are to order our social institutions. In actual argument about such principles and institutions, the original position remains the normative guide; citizens are to replicate the original position by placing certain constraints on deliberation in a way that simulates the formal conditions of that initial situation. Concerns that arise from knowing personal information cannot be invoked in arguing about just political, economic, and social arrangements.[3] The kind of arguments that can be proposed in political interaction are those that are rational for persons who do not know any personal characteristics about themselves to propose (1971, 138).

Rawls's justification of these constraints on deliberation (and political identity) is based on his understanding that individuals in a society have interests that coincide as well as interests that conflict. For Rawls, our conflicting interests come from our diverse conceptions of good plans of life. What we share, though, is an interest in public institutions designed to enable us to pursue those

---

[2] Rawls later (1971, 178–179, 396) adds self-respect to the list of primary goods.

[3] As issues of increasing specificity arise, more knowledge is gradually permitted; e.g., when it comes to arranging specific economic institutions, participants are permitted a "full range of general economic and social facts." It is only at the stage of "the application of rules to particular cases by judges and administrators, and the following of rules by citizens generally"—that is, after all liberties are decided upon and all institutions are in place—that full knowledge is permitted (Rawls 1971, 195–201, esp. 199).

plans of life and still live together in a peaceful and productive society. That shared interest is what is specifically political for Rawls, and it is only agreement on these political questions that makes possible the harmonious pursuit of differing conceptions of the good (1971, 4; 1985, 230 and passim). Thus, to preserve a just and pluralistic society, our political selves—who we are when we engage in political decision-making—must resemble participants in the original position, that is, appear beyond or apart from our personal or social identities. For our political identity can include only those things that we have in common (reasonableness, a concern for primary goods) and not the individual attributes or circumstances that affect our differing conceptions of the good.

It is this understanding of identity that communitarian critics of Rawls have taken exception to. The difficulty with Rawls's theory, Michael Sandel argues, is that it relies on a notion of the self that can know itself as separate from, and that has the capacity to act rationally prior to, knowing its "values and ends" (1982, 11–13, 20–23). On a Rawlsian view, "what is most essential to our personhood is not the ends we choose but our capacity to choose them" (Sandel 1982, 19). Sandel offers by contrast a vision of the self whose self-understanding is deeply constituted by its ends, which ends come not from a universal capacity for reason, but from the specific communities of which we are a part. The activity of such a self is best characterized not by *choice* (of ends, and means by which to pursue them) but by *self-knowledge*: discovering what, "in this clutter of possible ends," is central to my identity as a particular kind of person and a member of particular communities.[4]

Alasdair MacIntyre argues similarly that the communities or "traditions" to which we belong define in an important way who we are. Determining what is good for us is not a matter of weighing personal desires and calculating how to maximize them, but rather depends on understanding ourselves as "bearers of a particular social identity. . . . I am someone's son or daughter, someone else's cousin or uncle; I am a citizen of this or that city, a member of this or that guild or profession; I belong to this clan, that tribe, this nation. Hence what is good for me has to be the good for one who in-

---

[4] For a discussion of how we are constructed to *be* members of particular communities—in other words, how subjectivity is formed in a context of power—see Chapter 4 below.

habits these roles" (1981, 204–205. For a similar statement, see
Sandel 1982, 179). Public identities here are rooted in communal
affiliations, and the corresponding conceptions of what is good.

Rawls has dismissed these criticisms of the character and significance of the Rawlsian self, arguing that his view of persons in
the original position does not assume that "the essential nature of
persons is independent of and prior to their contingent attributes,
including their final ends and attachments." His is not a metaphysical notion of the self at all, but rather a description of free citizens—free in that, among other things, "their public identity as free
persons is not affected by changes over time in their conception of
the good." Accepting the constraints of the original position "no
more commits us to a metaphysical doctrine about the nature of
the self than our playing a game like Monopoly commits us to
thinking that we are landlords engaged in a desperate rivalry, win-
ner take all" (1985, 241, 238–239).

But this simile is unconvincing, because the constraints of the
original position (unlike the rules of a game we casually engage in)
delineate the shape and content of our basic social institutions.
Thus who we are in the original position, even if not a "metaphysical
doctrine about the nature of the self," surely must reflect something
important about the kinds of social and political creatures we are.[5]

What it centrally reflects, in Rawls's theory, is that we need a
public identity that is constituted by what enables us to agree—our
capacity for reasoning our way to the principles of justice that ensure we can cooperate socially and yet pursue our divergent conceptions of the good. More complex conceptions of the good
cannot be part of political identities because that would open up
to question one's status as a citizen whenever one's understanding
of the good—say, one's religious values—changed. So Rawls would
not disagree that one's conception of the good is connected to
one's communities. His point is that conflicts about these concep-

[5] In a later formulation, Rawls alters the simile from landlords in a game of Monopoly to tragic actors in a play: simulating the original position "no more commits
us to a particular metaphysical doctrine about the nature of the self than our acting
a part in a play, say of Macbeth or Lady Macbeth, commits us to thinking that we are
really a king or a queen engaged in a desperate struggle for political power" (1993,
27). My criticism still holds, though; if someone argues that our basic institutions
should be based on a Shakespearian tragedy, then surely they must think that the
play indicates something central about who we are as political actors.

tions are precluded from politics not because they are "unimportant or regarded with indifference" but rather because "we think them too important and recognize that there is no way to resolve them politically" (1985, 230).

The result (however unintended) of these constraints on public identity is not merely that citizens do not argue about the good in the political realm, but that they do not argue at all. Recall Rawls's point about the identical reasoning process that all in the original position share: "Therefore we can view the choice in the original position from the standpoint of one person selected at random." The rationality that guides political decision-making is oddly isolated and uniform. In Rawls's theory, plurality in the political realm must give way to protect the plurality of private lives (1971, 139).[6] Sandel contends that this version of politics and identity is incoherent; people cannot be identically situated and still be distinguishable persons, so in that original position there are no others with which to choose, to deliberate, to reason (1982, 131–132; see also Benhabib 1986b, 413). Yet Sandel's own version of the thinking activity of distinguishable persons is strangely private as well, a matter of "self-discovery." What contrasting conception of politics underlies Sandel's and MacIntyre's commitment to understanding the good as a public matter, inextricably tied to the communities and traditions to which one belongs? Commentators have noted that neither Sandel nor MacIntyre gives us much of a sense of what communitarian politics would look like (Gutmann 1985, 318–319; Wallach 1987, 596–601). The examples that Sandel uses to counter the primacy of justice are private ones: love, personal friendship. MacIntyre explicitly gives up on the idea of politics in contemporary Western societies, which he argues lack a moral consensus. Without that consensus, modern politics is just "a set of institutional arrangements for imposing a bureaucratized unity on a society." (He does, however, mention that we can still experience political community in projects like "schools, hospitals, and philanthropic organisations" [1981, 236–237, 146].)

For MacIntyre, then, conflict among differing conceptions of the good for the most part precludes the possibility of meaningful

[6] This is particularly ironic, since Rawls criticizes a rival theory, utilitarianism, for imaginatively "conflating all persons into one" and not taking seriously "the distinction between persons" (1971, 27).

politics at all. Although he describes a healthy tradition as one that is partially constituted by conflict about what it ought to be, conflict is considered only within a tradition and in the context of loyalty to that tradition (1981, 206). This notion does not take into account the conflict that happens when a deep rupture with tradition takes place, when its meaning is profoundly recast from within in a way that shatters the moral consensus, or when it is questioned from outside its own terms.[7] The latter might be a conflict *between* traditions or communities. Neither MacIntyre nor Sandel confronts what happens when the selves constituted by different communities clash—that is, what this thicker conception of identity means for politics. MacIntyre indicates only that such confrontation is dangerous to still-coherent traditions; it cannot result in any moral consensus, and it erodes a community's commitment to its own traditions. He suggests that the only reasonable thing for still-coherent communities to do is to stop "shoring up the imperium"—that is, stop entering into public debate—and withdraw, creating enclaves of the virtues that might survive our barbarous times (1981, 234–235, 244–245). But both MacIntyre and Sandel acknowledge that people belong to more than one community and have more than one "role." How can this communitarian understanding do justice to the complexity of identity? What am I to do if "the good" of the various communities I belong to conflict?

This question of "what to do" points to the lacuna common to Rawlsian liberalism and this version of communitarianism. The Benedictine withdrawal that MacIntyre recommends is simply not a luxury that many communities have; most communities—or rather, people from those communities—ignore public debate at the peril of their health, their lives, and their freedom. Strikingly absent in both approaches is any conception of communicating and taking action. For Rawls, institutions "coordinate" citizens who "follow rules" that allow them to pursue their preferred way of life. Rawls's theory evokes an image of citizens as traffic, and politics as a kind of traffic control that steers us away from interfering with each other's journey. Alternatively, from the communitarian point of

---

[7] Jane Smiley's novel *A Thousand Acres* provides a stunning account of rupture from within, as her protagonist comes to realize that the tradition of communal spirit and family farming of which she is a part is intertwined with a tradition of exploitation, violence, and abuse.

view, there is a sort of turning inward, either to sustain communal
enclaves (MacIntyre) or to explore, alone or with our friends, "the
clutter of possible ends" (Sandel).

These theories provide us with too limited an understanding of
human togetherness. What divides us and connects us, I will argue,
is much more complex than can be mapped onto a distinction between the right and the good. We are defined by both our situatedness and our capacity for choice. And politics is not simply about
shared interests or shared conceptions of the good; it is how we decide what to do in the face of conflict about all these things. Politics
in this sense is constituted neither by consensus nor community, but
by the practices through which citizens argue about interests and
ends—in other words, by communication. It is through such communicative practices that we come to understand our interests and
our identities in ways that inform our decisions about what to do.

This conception of politics will not sound unfamiliar to those
who have read theorists of "participatory democracy."[8] And the
stress on communicative action will evoke the work of Jürgen
Habermas. Let me situate my argument in relation to these litera-
tures. Theorists of participatory democracy explicitly stress the action of citizens. In Benjamin Barber's words, political action is
"doing (or not doing), making (or not making) something in the
physical world that limits human behavior, changes the environment, or affects the world in some material way" (1984, 122). Although democratic participation can take a variety of forms,
political "talk" among citizens is central to political action in
"strong democracy"; citizenship is not merely a legal status, but a
practice that involves communicative engagement with others in
the political realm. In this realm, Barber argues, public actions are
taken and public choices made "in the presence of conflict, and in
the absence of private or independent grounds for judgment"
(1984, 122, 132). Verbal exchange in public settings must under-
gird other modes of participation, for it is through such engagement that we sort through conflicting claims about various

[8] E.g., Pateman 1970; Barber 1984; Cohen and Rogers 1983; Green 1985; Evans
and Boyte 1986; Boyte 1989; Wolin 1981 and 1985; Fishkin 1991. Although I cite primarily political theorists here, other social scientists give citizen participation a central role, e.g., economists Bowles and Gintis (1986), urban theorist Stephen Elkin
(1987), and planning educator John Forester (1989).

alternatives and come to a better understanding of the consequences of particular actions. There is no private reasoning process
that is adequate for making these judgments; we need communicative interaction to help ourselves think publicly about the power we
exercise and the decisions to be made (Barber 1984, 178–198;
Fishkin 1991, 1–4, 58–59, 91–92; Lasch 1990).

For Barber, democratic talk functions to "transform" conflict.
This communicative interaction transforms both how participants
see their interests and who they think they are, for it is through acting politically together that citizens become conscious of the ties
between their own self-interest and the good of the political community, and of how these ties affect what public decisions should be
made. Through political interaction, "the *I* of private self-interest
can be reconceptualized and reconstituted as a *we* that makes possible civility and common political action" (1984, 190, and chap. 8
generally). This is Tocqueville's "self-interest properly understood":
taking an active role in public affairs creates a kind of "reflective patriotism," as citizens realize how their own interest is bound up with
the interest of the whole (1969, 235–237, 525–526). It is also
through participation itself that citizens develop the skills and psychological qualities necessary for democratic participation, and the
sense of efficacy that ensures continued participation.[9]

Since this transformation happens through communicative
interaction, that interaction cannot involve simply talk but must
require a particular kind of attention to one another. Barber provides the fullest account of the functions and possibilities of democratic talk, so it is not surprising that he is (as far as I can
determine) the first contemporary democratic theorist explicitly
to discuss listening.[10] But it is precisely in his discussion of listening
that the troubling consequences of the ideal of transformation begin to appear.

The values that govern democratic talk for Barber are the values inherent in Michael Oakeshott's understanding of "conversa-

[9] See Barber 1984, chap.7; Pateman 1970, chap. 2; Evans and Boyte 1986. These
points also underlie Green's discussion of the democratic division of labor (1985,
chap. 5) and Cohen and Rogers's discussion of autonomy and social structure (Cohen and Rogers 1983, 151).

[10] More recent analyses of the role of listening in politics can be found in
Forester 1989 and Boyte 1989; I include these in my discussion in Chapter 5.

tion": civility, empathy, and respect toward equals (Barber 1984, 222–223). These values find expression in listening: "Listeners . . . feel that an emphasis on speech enhances natural inequality in individuals' abilities to speak with clarity, eloquence, logic, and rhetoric. Listening is a mutualistic art that by its very practice enhances equality." Listening understood in this way involves neither strategic analysis nor mere toleration of another's utterance. Rather, listening means "I will put myself in his place, I will try to understand, I will strain to hear what makes us alike, I will listen for a common rhetoric evocative of a common purpose or a common good." The effort of listening is directed toward figuring out what unites us, and we accomplish this through the exercise of empathy (Barber 1984, 175).

For Barber, speaking and listening together are oriented toward a "creative consensus" that transforms the conflict that is at the heart of politics. This transformation is not always successful, but it is always sought after: "The strong democrat regrets every division (though there may be many) and regards the existence of majorities as a sign that mutualism has failed" (1984, 224, 207). Barber distinguishes this ideal of consensus from what he calls a unitary one; the latter is assumed to be "the organic will of a homogeneous or even monolithic community." He understands democratic consensus as neither natural nor spontaneous, but as actively achieved through civic participation (1984, 148–151, 224). There seem to be two types of consensus at play here. Communicative action requires a "procedural consensus" on how to deal with conflict, or as he says, "agreeing *how* to disagree" (1984, 128–129). But the strong democratic method of dealing with conflict is to transform it so that we share in a "common ordering of individual needs and wants into a single vision of the future" (1984, 151, 224). The implication here is that procedural consensus—that we will disagree by speaking and listening to one another with empathy and civility—results in more substantive consensus.

Although Barber provides an often compelling vision of public life, I suggest that his version of strong democracy has more unitary aspects than he acknowledges. In other words, the distinction between assumed and achieved consensus cannot do all the work he wants it to do. In describing strong democratic politics, Barber consistently uses the language of neighborliness, community, conversation, empathy, and common consciousness (e.g., 1984, 119, 183, 189, 202, 224). But, as Hanna Pitkin has argued in her critique of Oakeshott, the politeness and civility that "conversation" connotes seem at odds with the conflict and purpose that are central to politics (Pitkin 1973, 518). There is a continual tension between Barber's rhetoric of commonness and caring, and his insistence that strong democracy takes into account heterogeneity and conflict. Both conflict and heterogeneity must be transfigured, as citizen action "serves to transform interests and to reorient identity" (1984, 209).

This reorientation makes the identity of citizen "sovereign" over other roles, other aspects of identity. Barber's resolution of the conflict that Sandel and MacIntyre overlooked hinges on the "civic and psychic integration" by which "multiple identities . . . can be ordered and made consistent with political judgment." But Barber's own powerful description of the tensions in one imaginary individual make this resolution unconvincing (1984, 208–209). And he later struggles with what citizenship means with respect to those other aspects of identity in an uncharacteristically blurry formulation: "The civic role here is not omnicompetent or exclusionary, but neither is it merely one among many roles. It is primus inter pares. Citizenship is not necessarily the highest or the best identity that an individual may assume, but it is the moral identity par excellence" (1984, 224).

My argument in this book is that in a general context of socioeconomic inequality, conflict, and diversity, it is inappropriate and potentially dangerous to frame communicative interaction in this way. Jane Mansbridge's distinction between unitary and adversary democracy helps locate the flaws in this transformative and consensual vision of politics. Her definition of unitary democracy differs from Barber's, for she supposes neither homogeneity nor "self-abandonment" to a collective will (Barber 1984, 148–149). For Mansbridge, a unitary democracy is simply one that assumes there are common interests among citizens and thus stresses friendship, equal respect, and decision by consensus. An adversary democracy understands citizens' interests to be in conflict and takes as its purpose equal protection of those interests. The decision-making procedure is not one of face-to-face interaction, but generally involves private voting and majority rule (1983, 3–5, 8–10).

In Mansbridge's terminology, "interests" refer to a much wider range of concerns than those of narrow self-interest—concern for others, for example, or commitment to a principle (1983, xii).[11] Adversary procedures are ones that we turn to when we expect to disagree on these matters. By contrast, consensus is "a form of decision-making in which, after discussion, one or more members of the assembly sum up prevailing sentiment, and if no objections are voiced, this becomes agreed-on policy. . . . The consensual process differs in form from a strict unanimity rule in that no vote is taken, and it differs in purpose from a strict unanimity rule in that people usually adopt it when they expect to agree, not when they expect to differ" (1983, 32).

Democracies are rarely purely unitary or purely adversary. Mansbridge argues that most polities include both interests that conflict and interests that are shared among all; thus both adversary and unitary procedures are legitimately part of democratic politics. We need neither exclude conflicting interests from the political realm nor assume that they will be transformed into common interests, but rather recognize that different forms of decision-making are appropriate to each.

Failing to distinguish between unitary and adversary situations can in fact erode the democratic nature of the interaction, as is evident in Mansbridge's further discussions of consensus. Her understanding of consensual decision-making is similar to Barber's in emphasizing active creation rather than organic unity or identical reasoning. A commitment to this process of decision-making can, on one hand, ensure that all views are taken seriously before acting. But on the other hand, Mansbridge points out, formally consensual decision-making in situations in which interests conflict can also work to suppress conflict. Her analyses of political interaction in a town meeting in "Selby," Vermont, and in the Helpline crisis center show the dangers inherent in using consensus as a standard. Unitary procedures and assumptions of common interest create a communicative situation in which it is particularly difficult for people to *disagree*; the result can be a "false or managed consensus." The norm of common interest can "mask real conflicts of interest," and such masking usually works "to the detriment of citizens who are already at a disadvantage" in socioeconomic terms (1983, 32–33, 35, 263,

[11] See also Ball (1979, 201) for a discussion of interests as "morally complex wants" that provide "reasons for undertaking a course of action." Further references to "interest" are meant in this sense.

295). In other words, as feminist theorists have argued, appeals to the "shared purposes" or "common interests" of a community are not neutral; they often falsely universalize the perspectives of the powerful, while the concerns of those not part of the dominant culture are marked out as particular, partial, or selfish (Young 1990, Fraser 1992). An orientation toward consensus can thus undermine the very purposes of democratic participation, for the benefits of thinking things through together are lessened when some voices are not heard. And for participants marked out in this way, participation can be deeply alienating rather than empowering.

For Mansbridge, it is crucial for citizens to develop a sensitivity to the need to shift between adversary and unitary modes. In mostly unitary contexts, participants need to be careful not to suppress conflicting interests, while primarily adversary assemblies need to be able to discern what common interests they have (1983, xi, 289–290, 300). Mansbridge calls for "a single institutional network that can allow us both to advance our common interests and to resolve our conflicting ones" (1983, 7). But it seems to me that the necessity for shifting back and forth calls rather for a conception of communicative interaction that allows both—that does not suppress conflict for the sake of consensus, but provides opportunities to figure out commonalities as well. In other words, participants could make a judgment about whether adversary or unitary decision rules are appropriate only by communicating together. But such interaction must be regarded as adversarial to avoid the inequalities that result from an orientation to consensus. Although Mansbridge distinguishes between "deliberative" and "adversary" procedures (see also 1990, 14–22), her own insights call for a conception of deliberation that is explicitly adversarial, that is, that takes place among citizens who do not necessarily feel friendship toward one another or recognize a common interest.

My argument for the importance of adversarial deliberation is not meant to preclude adversarial procedures such as voting; precisely because a consensual model can be undemocratic (not to mention the constraints of time and energy), the move to voting is certainly necessary, and I find Mansbridge's argument for proportional outcomes persuasive (1983, 265–268; see also Guinier 1994). But such a decision rule needs to be placed in the context of an adversarial mode of democratic communication, which is precisely what is missing from most contemporary accounts of democratic deliberation.[12]

An adversarial mode is also missing from Habermas's understanding of communicative action. His work is connected to a much broader set of concerns about society and rationality, concerns rooted in the desire to furnish a rationally defensible basis for critical theory and practice. That is, he wants to provide philosophical justification for normative claims about society and practical judgments about what to do. This justification, he argues, is provided through a particular conception of communicative action.

Communicative action, for Habermas, is interaction in which all participants are motivated solely by the desire to reach understanding and are "oriented to achieving, sustaining, and renewing consensus." The exclusion of "all motives except that of a cooperative search for the truth" means that the consensus that is eventually reached is based only on the "force of the better argument" (1984, 17–25, 35–40, 84–86; 1990, 57–59).

Making rational and normatively justifiable practical judgments thus requires a distinction between communicative action and what Habermas calls strategic action: "Whereas in strategic action one actor seeks to *influence* the behavior of another by means of the threat of sanctions or the prospect of gratification in order to *cause* the interaction to continue as the first actor desires, in communicative action one actor seeks *rationally* to *motivate* another by relying on the illocutionary binding/bonding effect of the offer contained in his speech act" (1990, 58). This "offer" has to do with the validity claims that Habermas argues are inherent in the very act of speech: claims to rightness, truth, and truthfulness which can be "redeemed" through more communicative action (or, in the case of truthfulness, consistent behavior [1990, 58–59; 1987, 121–122]). Redemption is achieved and action is rationally justified when consensus on the

---

[12] Conversely, Fraser's analysis of inequality and conflict seems to lead her to reject the notion of deliberation in favor of "contestation" (1992, passim). Contestation is certainly part of deliberation, but it cannot encompass the entire meaning of political communication, for it leaves out the sense of working together (in the face of contention) that is necessary. In developing this conception of communicative interaction, I will continue to use Mansbridge's distinction between unitary and adversary situations to describe the regard citizens are assumed to have for one another in each, as well as to point to the absence or presence of shared substantive interests.

part of all involved has been reached. The suspension of all motives except the search for understanding makes it possible to achieve consensus that is also normatively justifiable (i.e., not distorted by power). This rational/moral consensus is thus not about negotiating compromises or balancing conflicting interests; it is instead a cognitive transformation that clarifies common interests (1990, 70–76; 1984, 35–40).

Like Rawls, Habermas says such consensus is about norms of action, not substantive judgments of the good life; like Barber, he insists that it can be achieved only through communicative action (1990, 66, 104–109). (Here again, though, the lines between a procedural and a more substantive consensus blur.) One's first reaction may be to say that in excluding strategic action, Habermas does not describe specifically political interaction, in which people come together clearly to "cause" and "influence" as well as understand, and have no guarantee of reaching consensus. Yet Habermas certainly agrees that strategic action exists: "The pattern of consensual conflict resolution is by no means the dominant one. The means of reaching agreement are repeatedly thrust aside by the instruments of force" (1990, 106). So although both strategic and communicative action are part of practice in the world, they are not equally valid normatively, and communicative action is always at risk of being polluted or overwhelmed by strategic action.

It is this normative valuation, this attempted purification of social action, that I find unjustifiable; it seems to me no more helpful or defensible an approach than idealizing communal affiliations. Denigrating strategic action only obscures the difficult complexity of actual political interaction, in which strategic and communicative action are intertwined, and I am not convinced that this intertwining should be regarded with regret. Trying to purify this mix of motives leaves us unable to appreciate the complexity of human interaction, and reinforces a romantic ideal both of politics and of who we are as citizens. My claim is not that such an ideal is irrelevant; on the contrary, the problem is that the orientation toward this ideal can have distinctly undemocratic consequences (Mansbridge 1983; Benhabib 1986b; Young 1990; Fraser 1992).

This book is an attempt to theorize democratic communicative interaction that depends not on the possibility of consensus but on the presence of listening. Such listening does not require the purification of motives or abstracting from our identity, nor does it involve empathy for one another or a strong sense of community. It is a constitutive element in the process of figuring out, in the face of conflict, what to do. Listening—as part of a conception of adversarial communication—is a crucial political activity that enables us to give democratic shape to our being together in the world.

To explicate and defend a conception of citizen interaction that relies on adversarial communication, I turn first to Aristotle. Aristotle has often been understood as a theorist of unitary politics, and it cannot be denied that he stresses the role of community and friendship in politics. But Aristotle helps us extend our understanding of adversary procedures because for him it is precisely the presence of conflict that makes communicative interaction among citizens necessary. Aristotelian political deliberation is a messy and turbulent practice that takes its very meaning from the inevitable presence of conflict (which revolves around the socioeconomic interests of citizens and the uncertainty of political questions). Yet deliberation is also the practice through which practical reason is collectively exercised. For Aristotle, what governs and makes possible such adversarial and communicative interaction is not necessarily friendship, but a kind of attention to others that does not rely on the bonds of civic friendship or on a strong sense of substantively shared interests.

Although Aristotle provides a valuable analysis of the political role of attention to others, in the end I find unsatisfactory his discussion of who citizens are, for their public identity seems to be centrally defined by their place in the socioeconomic order. To address this limitation, I examine the political thought of Hannah Arendt. Arendt recasts the meaning of political communication by arguing that the fact of human plurality (with its particular Arendtian meaning) means that citizens' perspectives cannot be predicted based on their physical or material conditions. Humans are uniquely opinionated and active beings, characterized by the capacity to "start anew"; thus political speech and action are profoundly unpredictable in their meaning and consequences, since we are acting among others who are equally capable of action. I argue that this understanding of action is deeply democratic. It also requires a kind of attention to others that Aristotle does not discuss (and whose concern is not necessarily glory or immortality, as

Arendt readers have surmised). The exercise of such attention is central to the human capacity to make our presence felt in the world. I analyze the nature of this "presence" and the character of the attention required; such analysis makes it clear that listening is constitutive of political action for Arendt, and thus shares in action's unpredictable nature. Although she never explicitly analyzes listening as a political practice, we can get a preliminary sense of what it might involve by looking at her accounts of opinion formation (i.e., representative thinking and judgment) and her distinction between interests and opinions.

Although these accounts are suggestive, they suffer in the end from a tension in Arendt's work that prevents her from investigating the forces that screen political attention, deflecting it from some voices and opinions, focusing it on others, and in the process establishing particular ways of hearing. In Chapter 4, I contend that the forces which underlie socioeconomic inequality can block or distort attention in ways that prevent democratic listening. We begin to get a sense of this distortion by looking at the connection between bodily-social existence and the opinions that we speak. The two are connected not by an equation between social position and opinions, but by the means of political action itself: speaking. I use feminist and sociolinguistic theory to argue that although the content of speech is distinctive on an individual level, different *ways of speaking* are associated with different social groups. Further, different ways of speaking are taken more or less seriously in a pattern that tends to reflect social inequality. However, this connection between social existence and the means of political communication is not deterministic in any sense; people associated with a particular way of speaking may not in fact speak that way or may speak in a variety of ways, and what way of speaking is prized depends on the context. The indeterminacy of this connection does not prevent it from having political effects, which means that political listening must be of a particular kind and must somehow integrate the Arendtian and Aristotelian conceptions of citizens.

Gloria Anzaldúa's work on rethinking the connection between identity and politics is especially fruitful here. Her metaphor of "making face" is particularly apt because it brings together (rather than regards as contradictory) our embeddedness in the socially constructed givens of our existence, and our capacity to present

ourselves self-consciously in ways that engage but do not simply reflect those givens. Anzaldúa and other feminist writers share with
Arendt the insight that appearing in public depends upon the regard of others. Yet they do not examine the difference between the
systematic distortion of certain voices and the inevitably uncontrollable character of joint action.

What *is* the difference between distorted listening and simply
active listening? What kind of effort or action is "genuine" listening? Let me sketch out a preliminary approach to listening, a
promissory note for the more detailed analysis in Chapter 5. I rely
here on the work of Maurice Merleau-Ponty, whose analysis of perception is particularly suggestive for political listening. For him,
perception has a particular character, shaped by the fact that humans are both *situated* in a particular physical, social, and historical setting, and are *subjects*, creative forces not limited to what that
setting prescribes. How do such creatures perceive, and how might
they perceive each other?

Not surprisingly, for Merleau-Ponty, our perception is neither
an exclusively mechanical process, nor is it a matter of disembodied
consciousness. The physical reception of sensory impressions is not
separable from a particular orientation of *attention* to the world.
When we see an object, it is because we turn to it (or it comes before us) and we focus on it; we pick it out of the general field of
things to perceive (*PP* 29–34). On one level, this attention is not directed by consciousness—we do not will our two eyes to present us
with a single vision, we do not command our ears to discern a
melody in a set of sound waves. Such focusing of attention is somehow inherent in the structure of perception, part of our general
human orientation to the world.

But beyond this generally shared orientation, we are directed
toward the world in more specific and diverse ways; my perception
is always a perception from a particular perspective. Yet that perspective is not flat or isolated. "My point of view is for me not so
much a limitation of my experience as a way I have of infiltrating
into the world in its entirety" (*PP* 329). My perspective points toward other perspectives by virtue of being in a field that indicates
other dimensions of, and other ways of gaining access to, the object: "When I look at the lamp on my table, I attribute to it not only
the qualities visible from where I am, but also those which the chim-

ney, the walls, the table can 'see' " (*PP* 68; see also 330). To say that I perceive an object in a field is to say that I do not perceive it as having only the face it shows to me; rather, I perceive it as a wholeness, part of which is hidden from me and yet still present.

The perceptual relation between the object and the field is what Merleau-Ponty calls the "object-horizon" or "figure-ground" structure of perception. We can perceive something only because it is distinguished from that which surrounds it; we do not experience the world as a massive blur of being, but as a space in which discrete objects appear. The figure-ground structure is the "means whereby objects are distinguished from each other, [and] it is also the means whereby they are disclosed" (*PP* 68). Objects appear when we concentrate or focus on them, and the surrounding world becomes the background or horizon that allows that object to stand out. The crucial point here is that the figure-ground structure is not one in which the ground is invisible or absent; it remains present and is perceived as present, part of a "unique totality" (*PP* 137–138, 68).

Without this preconscious orientation of attention that allows a figure to appear against a ground, we could not perceive at all. But we can also direct our attention consciously. As we transfer our gaze, for example, from one object to another, the first object becomes part of the field, the ground for the second. It "recedes into the periphery." Each object has the potential to be the sole focus or to be part of the ground that allows another object to appear (*PP* 68, also 102). The very act of focusing, of paying attention, of creating the figure-ground structure, itself refers to other possibilities. The perception of horizons indicates that it is possible "to bring about a new articulation of [the horizons] by taking them as *figures*" (*PP* 30).

The act of focusing or concentrating that is inherent in our perception does not hold out the promise of a singular reality underneath appearance. On the contrary, we exist in a context of indeterminacy and ambiguity, a context in which figure and ground are not unalterable or fixed. We are not uncovering some true reality through perception; rather, we are *giving meaning*. We give meaning to phenomena by placing them perceptually in the world, by bringing into focus their characteristics and boundaries, by relating and locating them with respect to other objects.

The world is both given, and given *to us* (*PP* 360). Existence—the meaning-giving perceptive process of being in a world—is an act "by which man takes up, for his own purposes, and makes his own a certain *de facto* situation" (*PP* 172n). We enter into relationship with the world through perception; by giving meaning to phenomena we shape the contours of that relationship. But this meaning is not absolute, for the world "outruns" our perception, our perspective always points toward more than we can see. "Ambiguity is of the essence of human existence, and everything we live or think has always several meanings" (*PP* 169).[13]

This indeterminate existence is full not only of objects, but of other people. And precisely because my perception shows me my own perspectivity, it points to the perspective of those others: "Insofar as I have sensory functions, a visual, auditory, and tactile field, I am already in communication with others taken as similar psychophysical subjects. No sooner has my gaze fallen upon a living body in process of acting than the objects surrounding it immediately take on a fresh layer of significance: they are no longer simply what I myself could make of them, they are what this other pattern of behaviour is about to make of them" (*PP* 353). Existence, "the very process whereby the hitherto meaningless takes on meaning" (*PP* 169), is indeterminate because I can actively construct various figure-ground relations *and* because those relations are also constructed by others whose presence and perspective I am aware of. Other people reflect our own way of taking up the world and require from us a particular kind of attention—it is language that plays "a crucial role in the perception of other people" (*PP* 352–354).

Perceiving others through language means, of course, listening. Although Merleau-Ponty does not say so, I will argue that we can think of listening as having the same structure of perception as does vision; that is, the figure-ground structure can be used to describe the other-self relationship in political listening. This conception is significant because it treats listening as an activity that does not require self-abnegation or a radical suspension of my own perspective. Rather, in listening I must actively *be with* others. Listening as an act of concentration means that *for the moment* I make myself the background, the horizon, and the speaker the figure I concentrate on. This action is different from trying to make of oneself an absence that does not impose on the other. Just as it is only by appearing against a background that an object has shape and mean-

[13] Or as Merleau-Ponty protested when accused of being ambiguous, "One is always ambiguous when one tries to understand others. What is ambiguous is the human condition" (*PrP* 41).

ing, it is only my presence as ground that lets the other figure exist at all, in the world or in my mind. But just as we cannot focus on two separate objects with equal levels of concentration, neither can we hold two people equally in our minds. That is, we cannot hear our inner voice and the other's voice at the same volume.[14]

Listening is, as Merleau-Ponty says about vision, "an act with two facets"; we create the background as we take up and focus on the speaker (*PP* 168). Listening is not passive, nor does it require the assumption of substantive shared interests or the suspension of strategic motives. Rather, it involves an active willingness to construct certain relations of attention, to form an "auditory Gestalt" in which neither of us, as parts of the whole structure, has meaning without the other. Listening to another person cannot mean abnegating oneself; we cannot hear but *as* ourselves, against the background of who we are (*PP* 395). But without moving ourselves to the background, we cannot hear another at all. Listening involves the willingness, in other words, to play a particular role in the forming of figure-ground, which role and which action are central to perception.

This interdependence, in which speaker and listener are different-but-equal participants, seems particularly apt for describing listening as a practice of citizenship. It makes listening, and not simply speaking, a matter of agency. In Chapter 5, I explore further what the activity of listening requires from the point of view of the listening subject, and I address the question of how listening can *appear* in public. I then argue for a particular understanding of the interaction between speaker and listener, one that takes into account Arendt's and Merleau-Ponty's understanding of what it means to act in a common world. Since this interaction is often deeply conflictual, it does not necessarily take its meaning from, or its purpose to be, consensus; these theorists' analyses suggest a different normative goal that can better guide communicative political action in a diverse and inegalitarian social order. I conclude by identifying cultural phenomena that threaten to undermine listening, and by considering what practices and institutions might provide further space for the worldly exercise and development of this kind of citizenship.

[14] Ihde's phenomenological experiments convincingly demonstrate this auditory difficulty (1976, 143–145, 161), which has its visual analogue. When I try to look at two objects equally at the same time, I find I can do so only by diminishing the level of attention; I have to draw back and stare at a point somewhere in between.

Chapter 2

BEYOND FRIENDSHIP

ARISTOTLE ON CONFLICT, DELIBERATION, AND ATTENTION

■ Aristotle's vision of politics is often invoked as an alternative to contemporary political culture (the latter characterized by alienation and antagonism, the former involving friendship and civic virtue).[1] These interpretations focus primarily on Aristotle's concern with friendship and community, and in so doing they unnecessarily limit his usefulness for thinking about political practice in our large, diverse, and often divided polity. In this chapter, I argue that Aristotle's analysis of deliberation demonstrates the centrality of (often deep) conflict in political interaction, and has two important contributions to make to our contemporary understanding of politics. First, Aristotle's analysis of deliberation extends and enriches our understanding of adversary procedures, for it is precisely when conflict is present that communicative interaction among citizens is most necessary. Second, this conception of political practice does not require the bonds of civic friendship underneath conflict, or a strong sense of shared interests. What governs and makes possible such adversarial communicative interaction is not, for Aristotle, friendship or concord, but rather a quality of *attention* inherent in the very practice of deliberation. To further examine the characteristics and consequences of this attention, I argue that it is necessary

[1] For a particularly prominent example, see MacIntyre 1981; see also Beiner 1983, 75–82, which emphasizes the importance of friendship and harmonious thinking in Aristotle's understanding of politics. MacIntyre's odd claim that Aristotle did not address the problem of moral and political conflict has been remarked upon by Bernard Yack (MacIntyre 1981, 153; Yack 1993, 6). For other examples of what I am calling the unitary perspective, see Yack's extended discussion (1993, 10–18).

to link Aristotle's discussion of deliberation in the *Nicomachean Ethics* and the *Politics* to his consideration of rhetoric.

DELIBERATION

The significance of deliberation in Aristotle's understanding of politics is evident from the very beginning of his discussion, for he understands politics to be an associative practice grounded primarily in citizens' capacity for deliberation. It is the power of speech itself that makes humans political animals. Speech here is not "mere voice," but rather the capacity to share an argument about "the expedient and the inexpedient, and therefore also the just and unjust" (*Pol.* 1253a).[2] What role does this argument—the very practice of deliberation—play in politics? What sort of conflict is involved?

Deliberation (political or otherwise) is for Aristotle a highly distinctive activity; it is both about specific subjects and for particular purposes. Thus there are certain things about which we simply do not deliberate: those that are eternal or unchanging, such as the processes of nature (whether the sun will rise) or the principles of mathematics (whether the angles of a triangle add up to 180 degrees) [*NE* 1112a].[3] Nor do we deliberate about matters of fact, "whether this is a loaf of bread, or whether this loaf has been properly baked" (*NE* 1113a). There are two reasons why such subjects—the eternal and the empirical—are undeliberable. First, they are matters that can be resolved with certainty, one by scientific demonstration, the other by sensory perception. Aristotle does not say that we would not *disagree* about whether a given object is a loaf of bread or, to give a more public example, whether a ship coming into the harbor is a merchant vessel or an enemy warship. It is just that this sort of disagreement can be settled with assurance by a kind of discernment that does not involve deliberation: eating a piece of the

---

[2] Aristotle's "therefore" is significant: politically speaking, considerations of justice and of expediency or interest are intertwined; arguing about interests necessarily leads to arguing about justice. In other words, as Salkever puts it, "conceptions of justice are not to be treated as expressing commitment to a moral or ethical realm separate from self-interest, but as embodying different judgments about our long-term interests, about how we ought to live" (1990, 75).

[3] Aristotle gives a different mathematical example here, as well as offering "the order of the universe" as an example of eternal and thus undeliberable subjects. Contemporary scientists would surely challenge the latter claim! As I note below, however, such a challenge can itself be part of deliberation.

purported bread, or looking to see if the ship is equipped with weapons. Disagreements about scientific principles or processes can be concluded with similar certainty through demonstration (*NE*, Book 6, chap. 3).

We deliberate, then, about uncertain things. In the category of "uncertain things," Aristotle does not include "irregular phenomena" like droughts or "chance events" (like winning the lottery, to update Aristotle's example of discovering a treasure [*NE* 1112a]). Such events are not subjects for deliberation because, like scientific principles and matters of fact, we can have no effect on them, and we only deliberate about "things that are in our power and can be realized by action" (*NE* 1112a–1112b, 1141b). We deliberate in order to act; hence the primacy of deliberation in ethics and politics, which are concerned with action (*NE* 1179a–1179b).

Deliberation may be about whether something *is* in our power, or, in Aristotle's words, "what is possible or impossible for us to do" (*Rhet.* I.4.3). In the same way, we might deliberate about whether the matter at hand is merely factual. Note that Aristotle gives two different examples of factual questions in the passage cited above: whether a given object is a loaf of bread, and whether the bread has been "properly baked." But why is the quality of the bread (whether it has been "properly baked") a matter of sense perception rather than, say, of taste? I may think good bread has a crisp crust, while you think the crust should be chewy. Pressed to justify our preferences, we might argue on grounds of nutritional value, aesthetic appeal, or other attributes. This situation seems to require a prior piece of deliberation on what qualifies as good, or properly baked, bread. If, to take a modern example, a printing collective decides to buy a vehicle for transportation purposes, clearly they would prefer to buy a good vehicle—but what is to count as good? A van, because of the room for hauling? A subcompact, because of the good gas mileage? A car made at a plant governed by a form of workplace democracy? It is only once this judgment is made that the "goodness" of a vehicle can be confirmed through sense perception, just as once we decide what counts as a good loaf of bread, we can perceive whether it has been properly baked.

But deciding "what counts as good" sounds suspiciously like determining the end, which Aristotle is often thought to have said deliberation is not concerned with (*NE* 1112b). The famous claim here is that "we deliberate not about ends, but about the means to attain ends."[4] Contemporary commentators have agreed, however, that Aristotle does not restrict the scope of deliberation merely to determining instrumental means. In Martha Nussbaum's rendering of the relevant phrase, she asserts that we deliberate "about what pertains to the end," and thus deliberation certainly encompasses "what is to count as the end." So even if a citizenry agrees that one of its ends is justice, they do not simply deliberate about ways to reach a given state of justice, but about what would count as having acted justly (1990, 61–62). Similarly, David Wiggins points out that deliberation about "what is toward the end" surely includes deliberation about the constituents of that end (1980, 224; see also Irwin 1985, 318). That is, there may be certain ends that we always aim toward, but the content and meaning of those ends (and not simply how to achieve them) may vary in different situations, and thus be subject to deliberation.

Still, not everything can be up for deliberation at the same time. Aristotle notes that there must be some agreed-upon or assumed factual background for deliberating, for "if we continue deliberating each point in turn, we shall have to go on to infinity" (*NE* 1113a). But he also—and this would support the more restrictive notion of deliberation—seems to indicate that the background for deliberation is the end: "No physician deliberates whether he should cure, no orator whether he should be convincing" (*NE* 1112b). We can imagine, however, a physician deliberating whether to take extraordinary measures to prolong a patient's life, or an orator deliberating about whether she should speak in a particular situation. As Wiggins points out, there is a distinction between "intrinsically undeliberable ends" and "ends held constant for the situation" (1980, 226; see also Sherman 1989, 89). A particular piece of deliberation may require grounding in some combination of factual knowledge and assumed ends, but the content of such grounding depends on the context, on what action is being deliberated about. Thus the background for one instance of deliberation may be precisely what is at issue in a different set of deliberations. "The purpose of a physician is to cure" may be the end taken for granted when a physician is deciding on an appro-

---

[4] I use Ostwald's translation (1962), except where otherwise noted.

priate course of treatment for a sick patient. In a different case, however, the physician may be deliberating whether to take extreme measures in a case with an uncertain probability of success. Here it is precisely the simple end of curing, and the physician's purpose, that are in question. In such a case, the physician must come to a more complex understanding of her purpose: is it to prolong life at any cost? to spare pain? to allocate society's resources in a particular way? simply to make clear the various options and consequences and let the patient decide? Aristotle notes that even when doctoring cannot bring perfect health, it is still possible to "treat well" (*Rhet.* I.1.14). The issue subject to deliberation is what is to count, in this instance, as "treating well." My point here is that there are assumed backgrounds to various instances of deliberation—"ends held constant"—but those ends may be at issue later, or in another set of deliberations, as the background shifts. So the need for a temporarily stable background does not mean that we do not (ever) deliberate about ends.

Conflict in deliberation can then stem from discordant understandings of the context in consideration and from differing evaluations of ends. But deliberation is also intrinsically conflictual, in that conflict stems from the very nature of the questions at hand. We deliberate only about uncertain things, and ends that can be achieved through human agency. Thus deliberation is a certain kind of figuring out that is neither sensory perception nor scientific proof. And it is figuring out an answer to a specific question: not "what is?" but "what should I (or we) do?" or "how should I (or we) act?" Deciding on this question becomes particularly difficult and contentious because answers to such uncertain questions lack the precision of scientific demonstration, and citizens have differing opinions about the right answer (*NE* 1094b, 1112b). Moreover, because we deliberate about what is in our power, it is not merely an academic exercise; we are deciding what to do (*NE* Book 3, chap. 2, and 1113a). Conflict is heightened by the importance of figuring things out right when we are not simply wishing for particular ends to be accomplished but are deciding, among differing opinions and in a context of uncertainty, how to act.[5]

[5] The distinction between "deciding" and "wishing" is made explicit in *NE* Book 3, chaps. 2–4; see also Irwin's helpful commentary (1985, 392).

Deliberation, then, *is* the exercise of practical reason. Practical reason is the figuring out of things that are not susceptible to demonstration; it is concerned with the "good attainable by action," or, as we might say, with the right thing to do (*NE* 1140a–1140b, 1141b). Practical reason is a "capacity of seeing," an ability to perceive, which is exercised in deliberation: "That man is good at deliberating who, by reasoning, can aim at and hit the best things attainable to man by action" (*NE* 1141b, 1140b, 1142a). Thus deliberation is the active use of perception—a coming to perceive, through the exercise of practical reason, what particulars are the "relevant features of a situation" and how seriously to consider each in determining a course of action (Wiggins 1980, 236; Nussbaum 1990, esp. 66–75). In other words, deliberation is a paying-attention-to. What specifically do those engaged in deliberation need to pay attention to? Aristotle gives us more specific guidance on what to attend to than merely "the relevant particulars"; that is, he tells us what must, in the political realm, count as relevant particulars. Identifying this guidance requires further consideration of what specifically political deliberation entails.

WHO GOVERNS?

It is not simply the uncertainty of the questions being addressed that makes deliberation a process of conflict. In political deliberation, conflict also stems from something about the very people who are involved. A deliberative polity, for Aristotle, includes people whose interests, needs, and opinions conflict, and the primary conflict he noted was between the rich and the poor, as central but opposite parts of the state.[6]

The political conflict between the rich and the poor centers on the question of who should rule, and on what grounds. Both sides, in answering these questions, make claims about what kind of political power is just. Justice is, Aristotle says, "a sort of equality." But in assigning political power, "there still remains a question: equality or inequality of what?" (*Pol.* 1282b). Clearly some qualities should play no role: "the complexion or height of a man" should not entitle him to "a greater share of political rights" (*Pol.* 1282b). A well-

---

[6] Aristotle also notes the possibility of personal quarrels between members of the wealthy class, but he contends that "no dissension worth mentioning arises among the people themselves" (*Pol.* 1302a).

born flute player does not, by virtue of his nobility, deserve a better flute, because nobility is not an essential characteristic of the art of flute-playing. And neither an excellent flute player nor a swift runner should, by virtue of their musical talent or swiftness, have more political power, for neither of these qualities are central to political practice (*Pol.* 1282b–1283a).

It is easy enough, in these examples, to see the political irrelevance of such qualities. But it is more difficult to identify the qualities that are central to political practice, with respect to which political power might be justly distributed. There are two problems here. First, because a state is made up of diverse elements, there are several conflicting qualities by virtue of which citizens might claim to rule. Wealth is certainly essential to a state, and freedom is a necessary constituent as well. So is excellence, since the purpose of a state is not merely to live, but to live well (*Pol.* Book 3, chaps. 9–13). Aristotle seems to have resolved in favor of excellence on at least two occasions (*Pol.* 1281a and 1283a), but he continues as if dissatisfied with this answer. For if only the good rule, "everybody else, being excluded from power, will be dishonored" (*Pol.* 1281a). Living well, for Aristotle, importantly involves reasoned decision-making; can a just state really restrict the possibility of a flourishing life to the excellent few?[7]

Even if it could—if the conflicting claims to power could be resolved in this way—Aristotle's second problem remains: how to address citizens' perceptions. Both the rich and the poor, Aristotle argues, misunderstand the nature of political equality (and thus what constitutes just political power). The wealthy think that because they are unequal—that is, superior—with respect to wealth, they should be unequal (superior) in all other respects as well (e.g., with respect to political power). Similarly, the poor, because they are equal to the rich in terms of freedom, think they should be equal to them in all other respects (*Pol.* 1280a; see also 1281a). These per-

---

[7] A different answer to this problem of valid but conflicting claims would be to take seriously Aristotle's notion of proportional justice. On this view, each group—the wealthy, the poor, the excellent—might have political power in proportion to their contribution to the state. See Von Leyden 1985, however, for an exhaustive account of the difficulty of measuring contributions and assigning proportions. Such a solution, even if possible, would still have to confront the second problem (discussed below).

ceptions complicate the problem of adjudicating between conflicting claims to rule. Even if a philosopher or a political scientist *could*
resolve these claims, there remains to be taken into account the citizens' own belief in their right to exercise political power.

Taking into account such beliefs is a political necessity, for the
stability of the state rests on "the general willingness of all classes
in the state to maintain the constitution" (*Pol.* 1294b, 1270b). A
state cannot merely rely on having abstractly good laws, for "good
laws, if they are not obeyed, do not constitute good government"
(*Pol.* 1294a). Laws must be judged also by the citizens' willingness
to obey them; to determine the best laws in a given circumstance,
one must consider the citizens' feelings toward those laws. Thus
Aristotle argues for the value of a "mixed" constitution. By combining democratic and oligarchic institutions and procedures, a state
can take into account both the many's desire for equality and the
wealthy's desire for superiority. "In a well attempered polity," Aristotle tells us, "there should appear to be both elements and yet neither" (*Pol.* 1294b and Book 5, chap. 8).[8]

Unfortunately, both rich and poor ignore this necessity when
they come into power: ". . . whichever side gets the better, instead of
establishing a just or popular government, regards political su-
premacy as the prize of victory, and the one party sets up a democracy and the other an oligarchy" (*Pol.* 1296a). And thus, as Aristotle
points out in Book 5, revolutions happen; states end up alternating
between democracies and oligarchies (not to mention tyrannies).
This kind of faction could be avoided, he argues, if constitutional
arrangements took into account all citizens' perceptions of their
needs and interests (which involves their sense of justice as well). "In
democracies the rich should be spared; not only should their prop-
erty not be divided, but their incomes also . . . should be protected."
In oligarchies, the poor must be taken care of and given some mea-
sure of involvement in the offices of the state. Further, "if any of the
wealthy classes insult them, the offender should be punished more

[8] One of the reasons a large middle class is central to the best practicable state
for Aristotle is that it results in a constitution that is a mean, and does not exclusively
favor either the poor or the rich (*Pol.* 1296a). The implication here is that a mid-
dling constitution is best not just because of the better character of those in the middle, but because it will to some extent take into account the interests of both
extremes.

severely than if he had wronged one of his own class" (*Pol.* 1309a). All rulers must "never wrong the ambitious in a matter of honour, or the common people in a matter of money" (*Pol.* 1308a–1308b).

A central element in politics, then, is the ability to attend to citizens' perceptions of their needs and interests, their evaluations of current circumstances, and their interpretations of others' actions.[9] Aristotle's argument here is not a narrowly instrumental one about how to stay in power, nor a simply conservative one about the value of stability. Rather, he is making an argument about what is necessary to preserve the conditions for politics, about how to keep the conflict between rich and poor a political (rather than mortal) conflict, by exercising a particular kind of *attention* in legislation and in general interaction.

The attentive legislator, for Aristotle, will ensure that deliberation takes into account the variety of perspectives in the state. This recommendation is evident in Aristotle's argument for inclusiveness in deliberation, that is, in his notable defense of the participation of "the many" in deliberation. There is some ambivalence here; he does assert that leisure is necessary to develop the political skills and excellence of character that contribute to good deliberation, and he acknowledges the popular opinion that the wealthy, because they have more leisure, are most excellent (*Pol.* 1273a, 1329a). But he cautions against simply equating wealth with merit, for then "the whole state becomes avaricious" (*Pol.* 1273a). A comfortable life does not lead automatically to virtue: "Men do not become tyrants in order that they may not suffer cold" (*Pol.* 1267a).

Although individual members of "the many" may not possess a sufficient degree of excellence by themselves, Aristotle contends that collectively they end up with a decision that is generally "quite good enough" (*Pol.* 1281b). Each individual has "a share of excellence and practical [reason]" and thus at least a partial understanding of the matter at hand. Combining their perspectives yields an understanding "as good or better" than that arrived at by "those who

---

[9] I will generally use "perspectives" to denote this variety of perceptions which need to be attended to. I am not suggesting that Aristotle thinks knowledge is always bounded by perspective, nor that he values equally all perspectives, as will be made clear below. My argument here is that, for Aristotle, the perspectives of citizens are constituents of the specifically political knowledge that can be gained through the exercise of practical reason.

have special knowledge" (*Pol.* 1282a). There are then no dangers in including the many, and in fact there are benefits. Aristotle argues that the perspective of all those to whom the laws apply is uniquely valuable and in some senses superior to the perspective of those who style themselves political "experts." The "users" of the law may in fact be the better judges, "just as the pilot will judge better of a rudder than the carpenter, and the guest will judge better of a feast than the cook" (*Pol.* 1282a). In these examples, "better" seems to have a particular meaning, for the way a pilot can "judge better" has to do with how well a rudder performs its intended function. The carpenter may still be better able to judge how to amend or improve that rudder. Aristotle's analogy seems designed to show that every citizen has a perspective that is important in different ways, and thus should be included in political deliberations.[10]

Aristotle does not claim that everyone's capacity for practical reason is equal. Rather, he argues that every citizen's capacity is good enough to justify their participation in politics, and he contends that "they will advise better if they all deliberate together, the people with the notables and the notables with the people" (*Pol.* 1298b). As the discussion above indicates, "advise better" has more than one meaning. One is almost an epistemological point: in uncertain matters that concern a diverse collectivity, a full understanding requires taking into account a variety of perspectives. As citizens with particular places in the social structure, we each have some *knowledge* to contribute. Further, including a variety of perspectives is important for preserving the conditions for politics itself. For making political decisions requires taking into account citizens' perceptions of their interests, which interests and opinions may conflict. The best way to ensure that citizens feel their perspectives are taken into account, Aristotle seems to be saying, is to include all citizens in deliberative decision-making. At *NE* 1141a, he says, "Each particular being ascribes practical wisdom in matters relating to itself to that thing which observes its interests well, and it

---

[10] One might think that Aristotle could use this argument to extend citizenship to the disenfranchised. Women, for example, were certainly subject to the laws and thus could, on Aristotle's own terms, have a valuable perspective as well. As is well known, Aristotle instead justifies the limits he places on inclusiveness in deliberation (i.e., on citizenship) by contending that slaves and free women, in different ways, lack sufficiently developed capacities for practical reason (*Pol.* Book 1, chap. 13).

will entrust itself to that thing." So each citizen has something to offer *politically* as well: our commitment to the polity, not in terms of
patriotism or loyalty to a particular state, but rather in terms of a
commitment to politics as the way to solve public problems.

So the capacity for paying attention that is central to deliberation has a special characteristic in political deliberation; it includes
paying attention to the perceptions of one's fellow citizens. In other
words, an important part of what counts as the "relevant particulars" of a political situation is the perspectives of others. Such attention serves as a kind of bond that draws citizens together in
political argument. Thus what characterizes the political *koinonia*—
what members of a specifically political community have in common—is the practice of deliberation together and the attention
that makes it possible.[11] But such attention need not, and in most of
Aristotle's political examples *does* not, arise from the bond that
scholars most commonly cite: friendship. I will argue for this in
some detail, since friendship is often taken to be one of the necessary characteristics of Aristotle's account of politics.

FRIENDSHIP, COMMUNITY, AND CONFLICT

As most translators note, the Greeks used *philia* to denote a wider
range of relationships than does our ordinary understanding of
"friendship": relations between business partners, family members,
citizens, fellow travelers, and personal friends, among others (Ostwald 1962, 214, n. 1; Irwin 1985, 403). Aristotle distinguishes these
relationships by considering not who they are among, but the purpose for which they are formed: they may be based on the pleasure
friends give one another, on the utility or advantage they have for
one another, or on the virtue or character they possess. These relationships share two distinguishing characteristics. First, friendship
involves goodwill; friends are mutually well-disposed toward one another. One wishes one's friend good for the friend's own sake (*NE*
1156a, 1157b).[12] But friendship is not merely an emotion; it re-

[11] See Ostwald's discussion of *koinonia* as involving a "bond" whose nature varies
depending on what kind of group is involved (1962, 309–310).

[12] As Cooper notes, our feelings need not be totally altruistic here; we may also
have self-interested reasons for wishing a friend well. But a genuine friendship requires that "the friend's own sake" be reason enough for acting, whatever other reasons we may have (Cooper 1980, 334n).

quires "actual social interaction," active engagement in one another's lives (*NE* 1157b, 1171b–1172a, and *Pol.* 1280b).[13] In John M.
Cooper's apt phrase, it involves "mutual well-wishing and well-
doing" (1980, 302; see also *NE* 1167a).

Not surprisingly, this conception of friendship is central for
those who read Aristotle from a unitary perspective. But the difficulty here, as some commentators have noted, is that Aristotle just
does not fill us in much on the specific characteristics of political
friendship (e.g., Cooper 1977, 645). This omission is surprising because of his own estimation of its importance: "Friendship we believe to be the greatest good of states and what best preserves them
against revolutions" (*Pol.* 1262b; also *NE* 1155a). But what kind of
bond is political friendship, and what role does it play for Aristotle?
How is it compatible with his understanding of politics as deeply
conflictual?

One of the most insightful commentators on Aristotle and conflict, Bernard Yack, argues that Aristotle's appreciation of conflict
and his emphasis on friendship are not in opposition. Rather, the
character of the political *koinonia*—what citizens share—gives rise
to both conflict and mutual concern. Friendship itself is "a source
of conflict as well as a means of promoting greater cooperation"
(1993, 110). Yack's analysis of the Aristotelian political *koinonia* thus
involves more complexity and conflict than most interpretations,
but it is still limited, I argue, by the exclusive reliance on friendship
as the bond.

Yack's argument that political conflict is both rooted in and me-
diated by friendship has taken two different forms, both of which
rely on the presence of "mutual concern" in Aristotelian politics. In
a 1985 article, Yack contends that political friendship spawns conflict precisely because it is a difficult mixture of advantage friendship
and character friendship. Claims of advantage lead to discussions of
justice because claims to advantage conflict and we need to adjudi-
cate those disagreements. "The argument about advantage thus
leads to an argument about who shall decide what collective advantage is," which in turn leads to the question of how justly to decide
on who should rule (1985, 101–102). What we share in a political
community is thus an *argument,* about what we should do and about

---

[13] The phrase "actual social interaction" is Ernest Barker's (1959, 236).

what is just and what is not (1985, 94, 96–97). What holds the community together in the face of this conflict—what keeps the thing shared an argument rather than a war—is political friendship. Despite its importance, political friendship does not magically resolve conflict; it is itself prone to conflict and distrust. We expect our fellow citizens to be receptive to appeals of justice and thus be virtuous, yet we suspect appeals to justice that do not take our own interests into account. An Aristotelian political community, in Yack's imaginative simile, is "more like a family business, than like either a family or a business" (1985, 109, 104–106).

But the conflict involved in this version of political friendship is not the only kind of political conflict. Sharing in the running of a family business means that despite the existence of individual self-interest, there is an important way in which members have common interests, standards, goals, and traditions. Such a collective resembles a unitary polity, one in which a sense of common interests underlies interaction. Mansbridge would confirm Yack's argument that certain sorts of conflict are particularly likely in such a situation, and Aristotle himself discusses the kinds of conflict that happen between friends (*NE* Book 9, chaps. 1 and 2; Mansbridge 1983, xi). But what is also possible and in fact expected in unitary situations is the existence of what Aristotle calls concord. Concord is a "friendship among fellow citizens," a relation in which citizens "have the same judgment about their common interest" in matters of action (*NE* 1167a–1167b). Aristotle gives some examples of what one translator calls "thinking in harmony": "There is concord in a state when all citizens decide that the offices should be elective, or that an alliance should be concluded with the Spartans, or that Pittacus should govern them at the time when Pittacus himself was willing to do so." The concord is broken here by Pittacus's dissenting opinion, for concord is found only "in those matters in which it is possible for both partners or all partners to attain their goals" (*NE* 1167a; see Ostwald 1962, 256–257n). This does not preclude argument (concord is not simply "an identity of opinion," *NE* 1167a); but it does require that all can come to share a judgment about what action in this particular context is to their common advantage.

In a diverse and adversarial polity, however, the communal structures of argument that bring citizens together may not resolve the conflicts between various interests, needs, and senses of justice. The sources of conflict in a state can stem not simply from the tension between interest and virtue, or from concern about whether others will live up to a shared tradition. Conflict can also be—and often is, in a large, diverse polity—about how multiple "family businesses" with their attendant interests and virtues can coexist politically. For this latter conflict to be a political conflict does indeed require that citizens have something in common that makes them part of the same political thing—but it need not be substantive interests or identical characters. The thing in common can simply be the practice of decision-making in a conflictual context, along with a sense of the justice of the practice. (This, however, does not preclude criticizing that practice, or the possibility of the practice being distorted.)

In his more recent work, Yack redefines political friendship and revamps his "family business" metaphor. Yack contends that political friendship is exclusively advantage friendship, and that sharing an advantage relationship leads to both the mutual concern that characterizes friendship and the sense of reciprocity that characterizes justice. It is a mistake to construe political friendship as involving shared virtue; attempts to "intensify" political friendship in this way are likely to produce severe recriminations, deception, and especially bitter conflict (1993, 110–115, 133–140, 117–121).

The metaphor more suited to describe a specifically political *koinonia*, Yack says, is that of fellow travelers who are "all in the same boat." He qualifies this image: "Because the goals of political action are not nearly as clear as the destination of a ship, the sense of sharing obstacles and dangers is not as certain to develop among citizens as it is among fellow travelers. Moreover, because these goals, unlike fellow travelers' destination, are always in the distance, this sense often dies as the result of resentment and disappointment. Nevertheless, however fragile it may be, participation in political community, Aristotle would argue, does dispose us to developing a fairly extensive and powerful sense of mutual concern" (1993, 125). But this insistence on the development of mutual concern precludes recognition of particular and prevalent forms of political conflict. Let us grant that all persons in a boat have a shared interest in the boat not sinking (or at least not sinking in a way that will cause them harm). Sharing this goal seems likely to coexist with other potentially severe conflicts, and thus is not likely to dispose us to "mutual well-wishing and well-doing." We may disagree on the destination, the route, and the speed; safety and weather predictions; who should be at the tiller, who gets the best seat or the best room, who has to clean the cabins or bail the water, or if it's fair for some people to have to do all the cleaning or bailing; how to treat people who are seasick; what to do if there are only ninety-five life jackets but one hundred people; and how to make all these decisions. Certainly we share an interest in the boat staying afloat, and not letting our conflict swamp or overturn it. My point is that, with this level of "sharing," I am as likely to make an argument for pushing some people overboard (say, the people who will not give up the best cabins) as I am to develop for everyone "a fairly extensive and powerful sense of mutual concern."

Yack intentionally makes Aristotelian friendship as "lukewarm" as he can, but it still relies on mutual concern (1993, 124–127). But we may be together in a boat or a "regime" (to use Yack's earlier language) without having any effective sense of well-wishing and well-doing, that is, without Aristotelian friendship.[14] Insisting on the presence of friendship in all political communities means ignoring the conflicts that are prevalent in adversarial communities—a mistake that Aristotle himself does not make. For Aristotle, deliberation is a practice that can enable citizens who do not perceive themselves to have substantive common interests, and are not bound by friendship, to interact politically. As the previous discussion of deliberation indicates, Aristotle stresses the importance of

---

[14] I do think that Yack was right the first time, when he identified political friendship as a mix of advantage and character friendship. In defense of his later view, Yack argues that although the polis exists for the sake of the good life, this does not mean that "sharing in political community amounts to sharing in the good life. It merely implies that the political community is a necessary means to the end of good living or human flourishing" (1993, 114). But one of the activities that comprises human flourishing—the exercise of practical reason in deliberation—is the central activity involved in sharing a political community. In other words, the activity of sharing a political community can be seen as partially constitutive of human flourishing. The bond at hand may be that complicated mixture of advantage and character friendship, or, as I am arguing, it may be a kind of attention inherent in the practice of deliberation. It is perhaps the lack of focus on deliberation as an activity that leads Yack, in his laudable attempt to save Aristotle from the civic republicans, to conjure up such a deep chasm between advantage and character, interest and virtue.

citizen interaction not only under conditions of friendship, but particularly in conditions characterized by a lack of goodwill. The relations between rich and poor citizens in the *Politics*—the former, say, striving for increased political power, the latter for land redistribution and the forgiveness of debts—hardly seem to involve being mutually well-disposed toward one another in the way that friendship requires.[15] There is no hint here of joy in each other's company (*NE* 1158a) or providing for another's good for the other's sake. And it is not common interests that they share, but rather the same interest—in land, for example—in a way that brings them into conflict. For Aristotle, then, deliberation is a practice that allows for deeply adversarial political relationships and not only ones that involve mutual concern.

Any serious theory of political participation has to confront the existence of both kinds of relationships, both kinds of conflict. And Aristotle, I think, has done so. It seems clear that friendship, as a bond of mutual well-wishing and acting, is an important characteristic of the best states for him (and Yack's argument that the friendship bond also chafes and should not be romanticized seems quite right to me). But I suggest that Aristotle actually gives us two alternatives for the bond that holds citizens together in the face of conflict, and that the nature of that bond varies according to the kind of state (and even in the same state over time). In some states, there are conflicts among people who do not necessarily feel goodwill toward one another and quite possibly do not perceive any commonality. In the absence of friendship, there is still a kind of attention to one another that makes political interaction possible. For Aristotle, we have the capacity to try to see from other people's perspectives, to imagine their perceptions, not to be selfless or morally good, but because we are creatures who are capable of politics and not simply warfare. Despite enmity, inequality, and conflict, Aristotle tells us, citizens can feel committed to politics as a means of addressing problems if they feel that as a practice it pays attention to their needs and interests. "Paying attention" in this way does not erase conflict; we may still have clashing needs, serious conflicts of inter-

---

[15] "Debt bondage" and "land hunger" were two central sources of political conflict in ancient Greece; see Finley 1983, 104–114, and Austin and Vidal-Naquet 1977, 24–25.

ests, and other disagreements. But attention works as a bond because it keeps such conflict political.

There are two connotations to "attentiveness," which correspond to the two different ways in which we might pay heed to others politically. The first connotation involves an emotional orientation, in the sense of being considerate or caring toward the object of attention—an attentiveness that springs from friendship and is present in unitary contexts. The second understanding of attentiveness is rather a sense of focused awareness, of being mindful or observant of something or someone. For the second sense of attentiveness, we need not feel a strong commitment to our partners in deliberation, but rather a less demanding commitment to the process of public problem solving, that is, to politics. Attention need not be kindly, then; it can be strategic or grudging. But even so, it creates and sustains the conditions necessary for politics and for the expression of political conflict.

It may be the case that such mindfulness can lead to friendship, that participating attentively in the practice of deliberation can help us realize common interests with those to whom we thought ourselves opposed. Yet this cannot be presumed, nor does it undermine the need for a mode of political interaction that does not require friendship or the recognition of strong common interests. This need is underscored by the fact that Aristotle himself undertook to describe such a mode of interaction as part of his science of politics. In fact, he tells us more about what I am calling "attention" than he does about political friendship, through his analysis of the art of paying attention to the perspectives of others in order to persuade—that is, the art of rhetoric.

RHETORIC AND REASON

My argument that Aristotle stresses the political importance of attention to others has thus far drawn primarily from the *Nicomachean Ethics* and the *Politics*, but it will come as no surprise to readers of Aristotle's *Rhetoric*. The need for attention to others is the very grounding of rhetoric; as Aristotle points out, "the persuasive is persuasive to someone," that is, to some particular one or ones (*Rhet.* I.2.11). Part of Aristotle's concern in the *Rhetoric* is to show that this sort of attention is not merely sleazy—a means for demagogic manipulation—but that it is essential to rhetoric as a legitimate and rational political art. This conception of rhetoric has undergone a renaissance in contemporary political thought (Arnhart 1981; Beiner 1983; Nichols 1987). Although recent commentators portray Aristotle's conception of rhetoric as proceeding from or productive of a unitary notion of the political community, I suggest two ways in which this in an incomplete account of Aristotelian political communication. First, it overlooks the fact that Aristotle defines political phenomena in ways that encompass the many different kinds of political communities that exist. And second, it fails to consider the relationship between rhetoric and deliberation. Investigating these issues gives us a fuller, more complex understanding of what political attention might involve, but it also locates some of the tensions in Aristotle's own account (which might lead us to be cautious in reclaiming rhetoric as the primary model for political communication). I conclude by pointing to what we might learn from probing the limits of Aristotle's account.

Rhetoric is an art whose function is "to see the available means of persuasion in each case" (*Rhet.* I.1.4). There are three available means, and all involve perceiving particular relevant features of one's listeners. The first mode of persuasion is that exerted by a speaker's *character*, as exhibited in his speech (and not necessarily "from a previous opinion that the speaker is a certain kind of person" [*Rhet.* I.2.4]). The qualities of character that Aristotle believes are persuasive are practical reason, virtue, and goodwill.[16] The demonstration of these three qualities gives the audience reason to believe that the speaker has formed a right opinion and is giving what he perceives to be the best advice (*Rhet.* II.1.5–7). But how a speaker can communicate these qualities is influenced by the char-

---

[16] In *NE* Book 9, chap. 5, Aristotle tells us that goodwill is not the same as friendship because it is a somewhat mild feeling of well-wishing, as when at athletic contests, "a spectator may come to have good will for a competitor and side with him without giving him any active assistance." To think of this feeling as "lacking in intensity," as Aristotle does, may seem surprising to those of us accustomed to watching fans at contemporary sporting events. But Aristotle's point is that such a feeling is "superficial" because it does not involve knowing an athlete and wishing for her or his well-being in general, nor does it involve any interaction with the athlete. Since goodwill can be "the beginning of friendship," the point for rhetoric seems to be that one way for speakers to be persuasive is to show that they are open to the possibility of establishing a friendship with the audience. So it seems possible for Aristotle that friendship could be part of the "character" exhibited, but it is not a necessary component.

acter—in a different sense—of the audience. Aristotle suggests paying attention to the ends of the constitution under which one is arguing, for there are characters distinctive to each form of constitution (*Rhet.* I.8.5–6). There are, further, personal and socioeconomic characteristics that determine the character of the audience, such as age, wealth, position (*Rhet.* II.12–17).

Thus, in analyzing the means of persuasion, a speaker tries to discern how his listeners—as particular "types"—will hear words designed to demonstrate his own trustworthy or believable character. Aristotle recommends the utility of appearing like one's audience, for "all people receive favorably speeches spoken in their own character and by persons like themselves" (*Rhet.* II.13.16). But it would seem that the diverse types present would make it impossible to exhibit all these characters at once; perhaps this mitigates against the unscrupulous use of such mimicry. Moreover, Aristotle argues for the persuasiveness of devices that challenge an audience. One strategy he recommends is to contradict common opinion, but in a way that shows one's own moral qualities (*Rhet.* II.21.13–14). He also suggests using language in strange and surprising ways, for it is pleasing to the listener to learn to see something in a different way. Metaphor is particularly useful here, for "metaphor especially has clarity and sweetness and strangeness" (*Rhet.* III.2 and 11). Finally, Aristotle asserts that "fairmindedness" is the quality whose exhibition makes a speaker most worthy of credence (*Rhet.* I.2.4). These points indicate that a speaker does not simply, chameleonlike, take on the character of his audience in considering the way in which his listeners will hear.

The second factor that affects how an audience hears is their emotions; speakers persuade by causing their listeners to feel in particular ways (*Rhet.* I.2.5). Thus listeners are not just narrowly self-interested "rational actors." Aristotle understands humans as passionate beings, moved by anger, pity, fear, generosity, and other emotions. But as the *Nicomachean Ethics* makes clear, humans are also capable of feeling those passions "at the right time, toward the right objects, toward the right people, for the right reason, and in the right manner" (*NE* 1106b). "Disposing the listener in some way" (*Rhet.* I.2.3) is not a matter of mere demagoguery or manipulation, because emotions are not simply irrational. The art of rhetoric involves knowing what state of mind emotions induce, against whom they are felt, and for what reasons (*Rhet.* II.1.9). So speakers can move listeners only by supplying convincing reasons for why a particular emotion is appropriate in this case and why it should guide their decision. As Aristotle says in the *Nicomachean Ethics*, decision "is either intelligence motivated by desire or desire operating through thought, and it is as a combination of these two that man is a starting point of action" (*NE* 1139b; see also *NE* 1113a).

Reason is central to rhetoric in another way, for the third means of persuasion is the "logical argument" itself (*Rhet.* I.2.3). This emphasis on reason is what Aristotle believes distinguishes his *Rhetoric* from other treatises on "the arts of speech," and what distinguishes rhetoric from sophistry and other dishonorable uses of speech (*Rhet.* I.1.3–6).[17] The form that rhetorical argument takes is the enthymeme: a sort of syllogism, but one that generally begins from and demonstrates probablistic statements (what is true for the most part), and whose premises are often left implicit (*Rhet.* I.2.11–15). Such argument draws from common opinion, which in some way "resembles the true" (*Rhet.* I.1.11). But as Mary Nichols points out, common opinion can be quite diverse, as is evident in both the *Rhetoric* and the *Politics* (1987, 660–661, 669). The examples that speakers choose to move and persuade their audiences, and the premises that they draw on, reveal something about the speakers' characters. Hence this final means of persuasion is not separable from the other two; that is, one does not demonstrate character and incite emotion except through reasoned argumentation (*Rhet.* I.1.3–10).[18]

To exercise these three means of persuasion—to communicate his character, dispose his listeners properly, and reason effectively—a speaker has to perceive his listeners as the kind of creatures Aristotle thinks they are: socially grounded, passionate, reasonable beings. Understanding the psychology of citizenship that underlies Aristotle's account of rhetoric is what enables a speaker to be persuasive. The speaker attends to his listeners in order to see how to lead them to a particular judgment, in effect, to persuade them that his opinion is correct.

---

[17] See Lord 1981 (esp. 336–338) for a useful commentary on Aristotle's intention in writing the *Rhetoric*; also Arnhart 1981, 22–23.

[18] See also the commentary in Arnhart 1981, 21–23, and Nichols 1987, 664–665.

These features of rhetoric, two contemporary analysts argue, give it a particular political function. The result of rhetoric is not simply persuasion or agreement about a particular decision, but a richer shared sense of community. Nichols argues that rhetoric is a "means for statesmanship" that provides "a comprehensive position that is both rooted in common opinion and able to go beyond common opinion." By clarifying and integrating heterogeneous common opinions into a "consistent whole," the rhetorician conveys a coherent account of the community itself (1987, 661, 668–669).[19] For Ronald Beiner, too, rhetoric promotes community: "One affirms one's membership in a given community, confirming one's commitment to it, by adjusting one's speech to the opinions and sensitivities of one's fellows. . . . In taking cognizance of the particular needs and aspirations of his audience, the orator expresses his community with them" (1983, 101). Rhetorical speech, as Nichols puts it, "point[s] to the connection between speaker and listener" (1987, 664).

But what is the nature of this connection? As Nichols notes, the speaker is constrained by his audience, the statesman is "limited by citizens and by the law that regulates their joint participation in rule" (1987, 662–671; 1992, 8). But the constraints derive from the audience's character(s) and their tendency to react in fairly predictable ways. It is in some sense the nature of the audience, rather than their action, that limits the speaker. Although Aristotle does equate "being persuaded" with "judging" (*Rhet.* II.1.2, II.18.1), it seems a pretty passive sort of judgment, and the connection between speaker and listener does not exactly seem to be that of peers and equals. In fact, as Nichols asserts, the statesman's actions "reveal not only the restraint imposed by others but the control he exercises." Even though he operates under contextual constraints in trying to influence others, the statesman is less limited by citizens than they are limited by him (1992, 122, 8).

Understood in this way, rhetoric as political communication seems oddly unidirectional. The speaker engages in some sort of prepolitical or private act of deliberation, and that "seeing" involves investigating possible ends, as well as sifting through common opinions, to see how to persuade others to aim at and hit the right target. As both Beiner and Nichols note, deciding on the right course

[19] For her more detailed analysis of the work of statesmanship, see Nichols 1992.

of action is not separable from considering particulars about who is to take that action.[20] So that prepolitical deliberation does in some way involve attention to others. But this kind of deciding is not the same as collective deliberation. In other words, there is a difference between political deliberation (as an inclusive, collective figuring out) and deliberative rhetoric (which involves persuading others to the already figured out).

Nichols notes that Aristotle's word for deliberative rhetoric was *demegorike*, literally "speaking to the *demos*" (1987, 662n). We might suspect that Aristotle's argument for including the many was not exactly a defense of their abilities after all, given the apparent quality of that inclusion. The exercise of the art of rhetoric can be seen as providing a way to convince the many that they are involved in ruling, and to confine their involvement to that of a pliable audience, while wiser or wealthier heads do the actual deliberating. Aristotle may have persuasively defended rhetoric against its ancient critics, but can he overcome this more contemporary democratic complaint about the unequal relationship implicit in such a version of political attention and communication?

I offer two Aristotelian answers to this problem. Neither of these answers denies the existence of political elites in Athenian politics or Aristotelian states. They do, however, show that political communication for Aristotle involves more than the somewhat mechanical mode of rhetoric in which a speaker leads an audience to a judgment or neatly integrates opinions into a consistent whole. The first response to "the problem of rhetoric" requires us to take seriously the implications of Aristotle's assertion that the function of rhetoric is "not to persuade but to see the available means of persuasion." This does not mean that rhetoric is unconcerned with the moment of communicative action, with speaking effectively. Rather, Aristotle likens the art of rhetoric to that of medicine, adding that "neither is it the function of medicine to create health but to promote this as much as possible; for it is nevertheless possible to treat well those who cannot recover health" (*Rhet.* I.1.14). Aristotle's point seems to be that properly exercising either art does not depend on achieving abstractly ideal results. Rhetoric does not always produce persuasion and concord any more than medicine always

[20] Beiner 1983, 85, 95; Nichols 1987, 668–670; Nichols 1992, 86–90.

produces perfect health, because in particular contexts neither health nor concord may be possible. It is still possible for the skillful exercise of each art to promote its ideal end as much as circumstances allow.

What exactly is rhetoric promoting in such circumstances; what is the rhetorical equivalent of "treating well"? It is not clear what it would mean to promote persuasion as much as possible—to persuade as many as one can, or to get the many as close to concord as one can? And rhetoric as part of politics itself has other ends: the advantageous, the just, the praiseworthy.[21] These ends, too, are what must be promoted "as much as possible." I think for Aristotle promoting these ends—rhetorically "treating well"—means something like giving good advice. (He refers to deliberative rhetoric as "the ability to persuade and give good advice" at *Rhet.* I.8.1).[22] Even when an assembly has decided upon (what seems like) a misguided course of action, a speaker may still offer advice to shape that action in a way that mitigates bad consequences, or suggest modifications that steer that action as close as possible toward "the good."

An Athenian example of just such treatment occurs in Thucydides' account of the Peloponnesian War, when Nicias at first tries to persuade the Athenian assembly to abandon the proposed campaign against Sicily. Having failed to do so, he proceeds to argue for the necessity of a large and heavily armed force, "thinking that he should either disgust the Athenians by the magnitude of the undertaking, or if obliged to sail on the expedition, would thus do so in the safest way possible." Then, when the Athenians' enthusiasm for the campaign continues unabated and they press Nicias for a more exact accounting of the necessary forces, he reluctantly provides some provisional numbers (*The Peloponnesian War*, Book 6, chaps. 9–25). The example of Nicias, who continued

---

[21] These ends are at first said to correspond respectively to deliberative, judicial, and epideictic rhetoric. But Aristotle notes that deliberative rhetoric may involve all three ends and says later that the "good" is advantageous (*Rhet.* I.3.5–6, I.6.1–2). See Nichols's example of how deliberative rhetoric addresses both justice and advantage (1987, 662–663).

[22] In the Athenian assembly, discussion was opened by the president asking the ritual question, "Who of the Athenians has advice to give?" (Ober 1989, 133, 296). Ober notes that orators were often referred to—and referred to themselves—by the term "advisor" (*sumboulos*) (107).

to offer his best advice even when he could not sway the assembly as he had hoped, can help us see that rhetoric is not simply a matter of controlled persuasion. Yet Aristotle would, according to the criteria above, still count this as an exercise of rhetorical skill. (The reader of Thucydides can see why; without some rhetorical skill on Nicias's part, his advice might simply go unheard.) By defining rhetoric in the way he does, Aristotle acknowledges that the role of the audience is not simply passive. Listeners are unpredictable, resistant, and active in a way that forces the rhetor continually to regroup and rethink how to promote, through speech, the appropriate ends.[23]

This conclusion points us toward the second Aristotelian answer to "the problem of rhetoric." It is not only that rhetoric involves more than persuasion, narrowly understood; deliberation itself involves more than rhetoric. Aristotle tells us that both rhetoric and deliberation are concerned with matters that can be other than they are (*Rhet.* I.2.12–14, *NE* 1140a), but he does not tell us very much about the relationship between the two.[24] Obviously, persuasion is an important part of deliberation; citizens do not simply come together and wonder aloud, "What do you think we should do?" "I don't know; what do you think?" And both rhetoric and deliberation involve intellectual qualities necessary for living well, for both are central to "acting for reasons and having and giving reasons."[25] But these intellectual qualities—or capacities of seeing—are somewhat different. Whereas rhetoric tells us how to give reasons to others, deliberation (public and private) is how we come to have reasons and take reasonable actions. This does not mean that the two are totally separate activities, but that rhetorical concerns are not the only concerns

[23] Ober's study of the Attic orators further demonstrates the extent to which elite speakers were constrained by the mass public through the latter's heckling and restlessness, encouragement of intraelite conflict, and the threat of legal action against those whose advice was deemed bad (1989, esp. chap. 3).

[24] Nor do his recent commentators. Nichols and Arnhart, in their concern to demonstrate that rhetoric is a form of political reasoning, neglect to work out its relationship to the form of reasoning that is deliberation (Nichols 1987; Arnhart 1981). Beiner discusses both practices, but does not address how they work together, and sometimes seems to blur the two (1983, esp. 95).

[25] This enormously helpful formulation of the human *ergon* (the "typical and characteristic activity of people") is Peterson's (1992, 96).

in deliberating.[26] In other words, there is more to figuring out how to act than producing or promoting agreement. Citizens—and statesmen—come to deliberation with particular opinions (they "have reasons") and specific outcomes they want to bring about, but those opinions are shaped and reshaped in the conflictual process of deliberation, which encompasses more communicative acts than merely persuading.

In the *Rhetoric*, Aristotle supplies many examples of different topics and tactics, but no detailed account of a set of deliberations through which we could consider the nature of the various exchanges. He does tell us, though, what concrete matters political deliberation is concerned with, one of which is "finances" (*Rhet.* I.4.7; the list at *Pol.* 1298a is similar). Let us look closely, then, at a contemporary set of deliberations about finances, in order to get a sense of the range of communicative phenomena involved in deliberative figuring out. I return here to Mansbridge, and her detailed description of a town meeting in "Selby," Vermont. The issue at hand is whether the town will fund the pro-zoning Regional Planning Commission (RPC).[27]

The deliberations begin with a detailed presentation prepared by the RPC. This is clearly an attempt by the head of the RPC to persuade the town to fund the commission and institute zoning. After this presentation, however, the contributions are many and varied. Resident A questions the RPC's sincerity ("who wrote that up for you?"); Resident B asserts that zoning violates the rights of prop-

[26] A different way to proceed here would be to consider the relation of rhetoric as an art (and therefore concerned with production) to deliberation, which is concerned with action. There are two reasons why I do not make this distinction. First, the distinction between action and production is a vexed problem, one not clarified very much by Aristotle's assertion that action, unlike production, is done "for its own sake" (*NE* 1140b). See Ackrill 1980 for a sense of the problems here, and the argument that Aristotle just does not say what an action is. Second, I do not think that rhetoric was an art for Aristotle in the technical sense the *Nicomachean Ethics* describes. (If it were, it would have been an uncharacteristic act of omission for him to neglect the relationship between rhetorical production and political action implied in "deliberative rhetoric"). Lord 1981 outlines some ambiguities in the text of the *Rhetoric* that might indicate that Aristotle did not in fact think rhetoric was an art but possibly something like "a non-teachable knack." This interpretation does not seem very likely to me because it undermines the argument for the rationality of rhetoric. It seems most likely that rhetoric is (as Lord concludes) some unspecified kind of rational tool to be used in the service of politics (338–339).

[27] My brief account here does not do justice to Mansbridge's original description; the reader should refer to Mansbridge 1983, 55–57.

erty owners in a way reminiscent of communism. (The RPC apparently did not study Aristotle's advice about conveying character and attending to the constitution under which one argues.) The RPC repeats its case. Resident C argues that the RPC's notion of zoning would not protect the town against really undesirable developments: "What good does your zoning do if it allows a Howard Johnson to move in?" Resident D wonders whether the state has the authority to zone because of environmental control laws, to which an RPC representative says no. Someone else raises the question in a different form and is strongly affirmed by Resident B. Another resident insists, "You take money from the state, and they tell you what to do." This statement is vocally supported by others.

As the discussion continues, it includes name-calling, repetitions, threats, expressions of frustration, assertions of interest, and a motion to vote by secret ballot (not to mention two recounts requested by residents). In this example, there are both attempts at persuasion and other contributions to collective figuring out. People ask questions, request clarification, affirm others' statements, raise related issues, and express feelings. There may be some sense in which all these contributions could be said to involve persuasion, for example, asking "who wrote that up for you?" might be seen as an attempt to persuade others of the RPC's insincerity. But to treat them all as efforts to lead others to a particular judgment assumes that all those who spoke had already made up their minds on how to vote (this seems unlikely from Mansbridge's text, which shows that during the secret ballot citizens continued to argue among themselves about the issues brought up in discussion). To reduce all communicative acts to persuasion is to unnecessarily flatten out the complexity of deliberation, for deliberation is also expressive and investigative in important ways, and is characterized by the interaction of a variety of communicative components. Rhetorical communication is only part of making collective judgments, not the whole of deliberation.[28] If this is so, then the atten-

---

[28] For a Homeric example of deliberation that supports this point, see Schofield 1986, 22–26 (I am grateful to Sandra Peterson for this reference). It is clear here that Diomedes' eventual recommendation, to which he persuades the others, has been informed by the expressions of fear, factual information, and arguments that have gone before. Nichols's model of statesmanship, I would argue, neglects the way in which deliberation involves this *collective* figuring out.

tion that a speaker gives to his audience in an attempt to persuade them is not the only kind or moment of attention necessary for deliberation. Participants must also pay attention in order to understand and judge others' contributions, reshape their own opinions, and determine their own responses. This kind of listening is central to collective figuring out, to the communicative exercise of practical reason.

CONCLUSION

Since it is Aristotle who helps us develop an understanding of deliberation as a conflictual communicative practice that involves attention to others, we might wish in the end that he had provided more detail about (or more examples of) how listening works as part of this expressive and investigative practice. Of course, we do get implicit advice about specifically rhetorical listening by reading the *Rhetoric* in reverse. For example, since Aristotle advises speakers to consider carefully the kind of character they want to convey, we might gather that the listening involved in being persuaded requires paying attention to the character displayed in the giving of reasons. At one point, Aristotle calls character the most important proof (*Rhet.* I.2.4), and perhaps one of the reasons that rhetoric is so important for him—one of the reasons he wants to reclaim it for politics—is because it preserves political space for character, for those who are particularly excellent and wise to engage effectively in ruling. (And it is this strain in Aristotle that Nichols's analysis of statesmanship does justice to.) The role of rhetoric in deliberation might be larger in states fortunate enough to include those particularly gifted with practical reason. Presumably it is the "few best" who could come to deliberation having already discerned the correct end and the correct way to go about achieving it. These true arguments will be persuasive to the many because all citizens have some share of practical reason; the art of rhetoric shows the *phronimos* how to guide and engage that practical reason, so that the many too will come to see the correctness of the proposed action (*Rhet.* I.1.12). If they are not glaucoma-ridden, *phronesis*-wise, the many can share in the exercise of reason with the *phronimos* as they actively judge his character and arguments. Thus "being persuaded," even in ideal states, need not involve simply the passive recognition of right reasons (as our suspicious democrat charged earlier).

The comparison to medicine and treating well might alert us that Aristotle thinks such concord about the advantageous and the just is possible only in glowingly healthy or ideal states where there are strong shared interests. Yet his own interest in "what is" (and improving what is) leads him to define rhetoric and deliberation so that they can still play a role in the more tumultuous, antagonistic politics of imperfect states. What Aristotle tells us is that diverse, unequal, and conflictual states require a kind of interactive attention that, even if unfriendly, serves as a political bond. I certainly do not deny that Aristotle valued concord, and the kind of community and ethos it requires. But in our contemporary world, we have no such culturally common resource, and whether and how we share what interests is often what is in dispute. Rather than regard this dissension as a sign of civic disarray, we can put aside Aristotle's ideal of the "few best" and of friendship, and take seriously his enthusiasm for understanding politics as a realm of conflict and interaction among imperfect, diverse, and sometimes unequal citizens. Such politics has its own challenges and normative demands, and figuring out in practice and in theory what these mean for citizen action is, I submit, one of the central tasks facing citizens and democratic theorists. In undertaking this task, we would do well to remember Aristotle's emphasis on the political and epistemological need for communicative interaction in the face of conflict.

But we might also question Aristotle more closely on his understanding of public identity, on who is paying attention to whom, or to what. In Aristotle's "best" states, the practical reason of the many is engaged through listening. But it is not clear if it is necessary for the many to be *listened to*. Perhaps the *phronimos*, armed with Aristotle's recommendations in the *Politics* and the information in the *Rhetoric* about the characters of various types, can know the perspectives of others without ever actually listening to them.[29] For citizens' perspectives are, in Aristotle's discussions, rooted primarily in their socioeconomic positions; a citizen's perspective is

---

[29] And perhaps this is why Aristotle uses primarily visual metaphors to denote the kind of perception necessary (e.g., *NE* 1140b). Arendt finds a wonderful quote from Aristotle on the importance of hearing for gaining knowledge, but as she tartly remarks, "he seems never to have remembered this observation when he wrote philosophy." The reference is to Aristotle's *On Sense and Sensible Objects* 437a, cited in Arendt, *LOM* I 277n.

that of the rich, or the poor, or the well-born. This is not to argue that Aristotle was a crude determinist or that he was a secret elitist, but that he took seriously the importance of material conditions—not simply the weather and location of cities, but also the occupations (and body types) that structure human lives (e.g., *Pol.* Book 7 passim, and Book 1, chap. 5). But the consequence for deliberation might be that reasoned attention to material conditions and structural effects can, in the best states, replace listening.[30]

I am left uneasy about this Aristotelian possibility, which points us toward the need to think more deeply about the public identities of citizens. To do so, I turn in the next chapter to Hannah Arendt, who wrestles with these questions of citizenship in the material world. Arendt is deeply suspicious of any focus on material conditions that would lead us to obscure the political expression of distinctively human capacities, for it is these capacities that are central to political identity. She in the end provides us with a more complex understanding of who citizens are, and recasts the meaning of political communication. In so doing, she gives us powerful normative reasons for why it would not necessarily involve concord, and tells us more about the role that attention plays in citizen interaction.

[30] Aristotle also shows us the dark consequences of his stress on material conditions. For him, the "kinds and conditions of labor" (Nussbaum 1980, 420) affect not only one's interests and needs, but one's character. Artisans and tradesmen, by virtue of the labor they perform, cannot develop the excellence central to citizenship (despite their possession of practical reason) and thus in the best states must be denied a share in ruling (*Pol.* 1328b–1329a, 1278a). Presumably the excluded would not create unrest as long as they felt their interests were taken into account by the rulers. Nussbaum points out that Aristotle honestly confronts this "dark spot," unlike Plato (for whom such laborers did not have practical reason) or theorists of liberalism (who ignore the effects of material conditions on equality). She further argues that this exclusion is a matter of regret for Aristotle (1980, 420–421). There is regret, perhaps, because that exclusion violates his own understanding of distributive justice—such laborers contribute to the state at one level, yet receive no compensation in the form of power. (I owe the rendition of this last point to an anonymous reviewer.)

Chapter 3

WHERE WE LISTEN AND ARE LISTENED TO

HANNAH ARENDT ON PLURALITY AND PUBLIC APPEARANCE

*. . . because being here means so much, and because all
that's here, vanishing so quickly, seems to need us
and strangely concerns us.*
—RILKE, *Ninth Elegy*

■ Arendt's work is centrally motivated by a concern for human
plurality, a condition of human existence that is essential and yet
somehow fragile. Although her vision of politics has much in common with Aristotle's, it is around this crucial concept that the difference between them lies. When Aristotle tells us that a state is by
nature a plurality, he seems to mean primarily that a state is composed of different parts with different purposes, all of which are
necessary for the state's self-sufficiency (e.g., *Pol.* 1290b–1291a).
But Arendt means something quite different. For her, plurality and
political action are inextricable from each other and require a kind
of attention to others that Aristotle does not discuss. This attention
is necessary not for reasons of glory or immortality, but to make
real the human capacity to make our presence felt in the world. In
the first sections of this chapter, I analyze the nature of this "presence" and the character of the attention it requires. This discussion
makes it clear that listening was central for Arendt, although she
herself never explicitly analyzed it as a political practice. In the last
section of the chapter, I argue that we can get a preliminary sense
of what Arendtian listening might involve by looking at her accounts of opinion formation. (Thus one role that attention plays in
Arendt's thought has to do, as in Aristotle, with figuring things

out.) What is distinctive about Arendt's account is that she emphasizes both subjectivity and worldliness, a worldliness in part constituted by the presence of others. Her analysis leads her to an understanding of politics in which subjectivity and intersubjectivity—our sense of self and the presence of others—are profoundly yet paradoxically enmeshed. For Arendt, the character of political attention is shaped by the necessity of preserving this tension, and thereby maintaining a world with space for the exercise of distinctively human capacities.

POLITICS AND PLURALITY:
REVEALING THE UNIQUE "WHO"

Politics for Arendt is the "acting and speaking together" of equals (*HC* 198, 41, 24–25). The Greek *polis* was one of the primary models she drew upon to flesh out her vision of politics, but there are other, more historically recent ones: the Parisian Commune, the original Russian soviets, the French underground resistance to the Nazis during World War II, the U.S. movement against the war in Vietnam, and Thomas Jefferson's idea of the ward system. What unites these examples is that they create space where participation in public affairs can be enacted through word and deed. Word and deed—that is, speech and action—are intertwined; they are often the same activity, since "many, and even most acts, are performed in the manner of speech" (*HC* 178; see also *HC* 26). Politics is thus, as it was for Aristotle, rooted in public human communication.

Human plurality is intimately connected to politics, for plurality, Arendt says, is "the basic condition of both action and speech" (*HC* 175). What Arendt means by plurality is precise and complex—she herself called plurality "paradoxical"—and analyzing this conception discloses something integral to her thinking about politics and the way it is intertwined with attention. She explains plurality by delineating its two characteristics: equality and distinction. "If men were not equal," Arendt claims, "they could neither understand each other and those who came before them, nor plan for the future and foresee the needs of those who will come after them" (*HC* 175). If equality here is something that helps us to understand each other—the meaning of our past and the needs of our future—it seems at first to refer to some respect in which we are all the same. (Benhabib calls it a "generic equal-

ity of the human constitution" [1988, 32]). But when Arendt elsewhere addresses equality as sameness, it is clear that such equality
can have no specifically political significance. There is an equality
that springs from human bodily processes, the needs of life and
the certainty of physical death. But "from the viewpoint of the
world and the public realm, life and death and everything attest-
ing to sameness are nonworldly, antipolitical, truly transcendent
experiences" (*HC* 214–215). This physiological sameness is nonworldly because it cannot appear, literally, in the sense that our
human form is meant to cover such internal processes (*LOM* I
28–29). Although "the need for food has its demonstrable basis of
reality in the life process itself," my hunger pangs are unavoidably
my own; no one else can testify to their reality (*HC* 56–57). They
are therefore "shielded against the visibility and audibility of the
public realm" (*HC* 112).

So this kind of equality cannot possibly be characteristic of plurality as a condition for speech and action, the very activities that
constitute a public realm. If equality is a central element of plurality, then it must be a kind of equality that can appear in public.[1] For
Arendt, one kind of "equality attending the public realm" is political equality. Political equality is an equalizing of unequals; it gives
equal standing to those who may otherwise be unequal (e.g., in
wealth, talent, occupation). Political equality makes peers out of
those who are different (*HC* 215; *OR* 30–31).

Why is this kind of equality central to plurality? Why do we
need equal *standing* in the public realm to understand each other,
plan for the future, grasp each other's needs? We need this equal
standing because it alone makes speech and action possible. It creates a realm of peers, where we are neither ruling nor being ruled,
but engaging with one another in joint speech and action. In equalizing us, political equality creates a space where we "are listening
and can be listened to" (*LK* 40). Occasionally Arendt says this the
other way around, as though speech and action created equality: we
are equal by virtue of our commitment to a joint enterprise, that is,

---

[1] Arendt refers to another sense of equality as sameness, but it cannot be part
of plurality either, for it is the "conformism inherent in every society" (*HC* 39). "This
modern equality" results from society imposing equally the requirements of "normal" behavior on its members (*HC* 39–41). For Arendt, behavior is antithetical to action (see below).

"the joint effort equalizes" (*OR* 174–175, 278). But to be part of that joint effort already requires a certain standing. It is our shared standing that establishes us all as voices to be listened to, yet that political persona allows our own individual voices to "sound through" (*OR* 106–107).

It may seem odd for plurality as a central characteristic of the human condition to rely on something as artificial as political equality. But artifice too is part of the human condition, because humans do not merely exist on earth but live in a world, the result of human making and acting (*HC* 52–53). For Arendt, "in order to be what the world is always meant to be, a home for men during their life on earth, the human artifice must be a place fit for action and speech" (*HC* 173). Political equality is an important part of this "fitness," as is evident from Arendt's analysis of totalitarian regimes. In these regimes, the destruction of the "juridical person" was an essential step in creating "living corpses," that is, in destroying human plurality (*OT* 447–451).

For Arendt, then, humans are "unequals who stand in need of being 'equalized' in certain respects and for specific purposes" (*HC* 215). But what is the source of this need (as opposed to its purpose, which is speech and action)? In other words, why is inequality between humans something to be corrected for, why is speech and action necessary between those who share the world? There is a deeper sense of equality here, that underlies inequality of condition and gives rise to the need for political equality. This sense of equality is related to the second characteristic of human plurality: distinctiveness.

It is our distinctiveness that creates the need for our own voice to sound through, the need for speech. We would not need speech, or a space in which to speak to each other, if each of us were not distinct from "any other who is, was, or will ever be." Here Arendt is not referring to sheer bodily existence; rather, plurality means that *who* we are is unique. If humans did not have this quality of uniqueness, "signs and sounds to communicate immediate, identical needs would be enough" (*HC* 175–176). Speech and plurality are mutually interdependent because humans are more than needful creatures. Our unique identity is something that appears through speech and action, even when that speech is not aimed at such a manifestation: "Men disclose themselves as subjects, as distinct and unique persons, even when they wholly concentrate upon reaching an altogether worldly, material object" (*HC* 183).

The paradox of plurality lies in the fact that each human being is a unique "who"—yet every human being shares this quality of uniqueness. So this paradox is not one between levels of existence; Arendt is not pointing to the fact that we are all the same on some material or physiological level, yet on another level we are all different. Rather, human plurality means that we are both undeniably distinctive, and inescapably more than one. In Arendt's words, "We are all the same, that is, human, in such a way that nobody is ever the same as anyone else who ever lived, lives, or will live" (*HC* 8; see also *OR* 175).

Plurality is a central condition of human existence, and yet it is fragile; it can disappear under conditions of tyranny, mass society, or anytime the public realm and its attendant political equality is supplanted or destroyed (e.g., *HC* 40–41, 58). What kind of uniqueness, what kind of identity is it that is so crucial yet so circumstantial? What is the content and meaning of the plural, unique "whos" that we reveal in public action? The "who" that is our unique self cannot be described, Arendt cautions: "The moment we want to say *who* somebody is, our very vocabulary leads us astray into saying *what* he is; we get entangled in a description of qualities he necessarily shares with others like him . . . with the result that his specific uniqueness escapes us" (*HC* 181). My identity is not captured simply by describing the qualities I possess, the interests I have, or the sociological categories I belong to. These are all components of how we might describe someone, but in that they are also characteristic of others, they do not help locate or point to the unique identity that is "me." This unique self is not something like personality, or inner self, either. It is precisely the sameness of our "inner psychic ground" that makes possible a science of psychology, Arendt argues, and contrasts such inner sameness to the "enormous variety and richness of overt human conduct" (*LOM* I 29, 34–35; see also Young-Bruehl 1982, 320).

To try to get a fix on this "who"—to try to figure out what public identity is for Arendt—let us look at what it means to reveal that "who" in public. This "who" is revealed only in speech and action; it is "implicit in everything somebody says and does" (*HC* 178–179;

also *BPF* 263).[2] When I speak in public—when I say "it seems to me"—I am not simply relaying sensory information; I am revealing my *opinion* about some worldly concern. Unlike qualities, interests, or personality traits, opinions belong, for Arendt, "exclusively to individuals" (*OR* 227). But it is not just a string of disconnected opinions that can be said to be "me." Rather, this speech as action, or any other action, is part of my "unique life story." It is precisely stories, "the result of action and speech," that "reveal an agent" (*HC* 184). A story "is the only medium in which the originally intangible manifestation of a uniquely distinct 'who' can become tangible *ex post facto* through action and speech. *Who* somebody is or was we can know only by knowing the story of which he is himself the hero" (*HC* 186). This emphasis on the story of which speech and action is part would seem to indicate that my identity arises not simply from what I say or do, but from the circumstances in which I do it and the history of what I have done. The actions of characters in a story are given meaning by the context in which they are embedded. For example, both Jesus of Nazareth and Plato's Euthyphro refused to give their own families special consideration; yet readers may see in one story a genuine expression of love for humanity and in the other a confused sense of self-righteousness. Thus it is not only the content of my opinions that reveals my distinctiveness, but the context. That I act, and say particular things in specific situations with respect to particular issues, shows me to be a certain "who," a certain public self—or rather becomes part of the story through which my identity takes shape.

Implicit in this account of identity, with its stress on appearance, is the need for a particular kind of attention on the part of others. It is significant that in the passage quoted above, Arendt does not say that by listing "what" someone is, we simply have not addressed the question of "who" he is. Rather, focusing on the "what," the qualities shared with others, "entangles" us and "leads us astray." So it is not merely that whoness cannot be put into "unequivocal verbal expres-

[2] When Arendt contrasts this meaningful speech to signs (*HC* 176), she cannot have been thinking about the sign language used by people who are deaf. The expressiveness of a sign language like ASL, for instance, makes it clear that such language does (like speech) make "who" the speaker is audible and visible in the public realm. The public realm, however, has to be constructed in such a way that such language can be "heard" (e.g., equipped with sign language interpreters for the hearing).

sion," but that such attempts misdirect us, actively obscure "whoness." It is for this reason that Arendt sees positive possibilities for public identity in the device of "the mask." She invokes the Latin *persona*, which originally "signified the mask ancient actors used to wear in a play . . . it had to hide, or rather to replace, the actor's own face and countenance, but in a way that would make it possible for the voice to sound through." In the same move, the public persona of legal equality conceals politically irrelevant qualities and enables our voices to be publicly heard (*OR* 106–107). The mask does not itself constitute our public identity; rather, it is a device that permits the appearance of a "who" whose interlocutors are not misled by "what."[3]

But this device does not, for Arendt, let us define for ourselves "who" we are; we cannot control how our public identity, revealed through word and deed, is perceived by others. We do make attempts at self-presentation: humans "indicate how they *wish* to appear, what in their opinion is fit to be seen and what is not. . . . *Up to a point* we can choose how to appear to others" (*LOM* I 34, 36). But we are neither "author nor producer" of our stories; the disclosure of who we are "can almost never be achieved as a wilful purpose" (*HC* 179). Our identity relies in a sense on others, who see us as we cannot see ourselves.[4] And such others may not see us in the same way, for "to appear always means to seem to others, and this seeming varies according to the standpoint and perspective of the spectators" (*LOM* I 21).

It seems odd that an important part of our fully human identity should rely on publicness in this way. Why should I be so dependent on the perceptions of others? What if they are wrong, what if they misunderstand me? Our dependence on others comes from the connection between the human mode of being, which is plurality, and the human mode of reality, which is appearance.

"Appearance" for Arendt is inherent in the human condition because of what she called "the world's phenomenal nature": "The world men are born into contains many things . . . all of which have in common that they *appear* and hence are meant to be seen, heard, touched, tasted, and smelled, to be perceived by sentient creatures

[3] I discuss the quite different ways feminist writers have used the metaphor of the mask in Chapter 4.

[4] See also *HC* 180, 183, 186, 192, 243. Arendt obviously believed this with respect to her own public identity, as is evident in the discussion in Hill 1979, 326, 336.

endowed with the appropriate sense organs. Nothing could appear, the word 'appearance' would make no sense, if recipients of appearances did not exist—living creatures able to acknowledge, recognize, and react to—in flight or desire, approval or disapproval, blame or praise—what is not merely there but appears to them and is meant for their perception" (*LOM* I 19). The "worldliness of living things" (humans and animals) is characterized by their dual role as "subjects and objects—perceiving and being perceived—at the same time" (*LOM* I 19–20). Reception and appearance presuppose each other; they are the phenomenal result of the fact that we live in a world characterized by plurality, by more than one. As experiences, reception and appearance feed into each other: "*Whatever can see wants to be seen, whatever can hear calls out to be heard, whatever can touch presents itself to be touched*" (*LOM* I 29). This urge to actively present one's self is for Arendt an urge to consciously answer "the fact of one's own appearingness . . . to respond by showing to the overwhelming effect of being shown" (*LOM* I 21).[5] But as the passage above indicates, this reception is not merely a passive taking in, but is itself active. In fact, self-display (as opposed to "the sheer thereness of existence") is possible only because of the active perceiving presence of others, who acknowledge, recognize, approve or disapprove (*LOM* I 19–22). This account suggests, then, that we are "who" we are not just in the act of showing, but in the act of perceiving what is shown.

For Arendt, to be deprived of the possibility of appearance before others is "to be deprived of reality, which humanly and politically speaking, is the same as appearance. To men the reality of the world is guaranteed by the presence of others, by its appearing to all" (*HC* 199). Without others to testify to what seems to them, what we know can only have a private, sometimes nightmarish quality; we cannot even trust "immediate sensual experience" (*OT* 475–476). For "the presence of others who see what we see and hear what we hear assures us of the reality of the world and ourselves" (*HC* 50).

---

[5] Kimberley Curtis has argued that not only speech, but this elemental urge, "the aesthetic provocation of multiple, distinct, appearing beings," is central to achieving a common world. Our ethical challenge is thus "to cultivate . . . our *pleasure* in the feeling of reality intensified through the presence of particular others and the recalcitrant and plural quality of the world thus engendered" (forthcoming; emphasis added).

The very survival of a common world relies on "men willing to testify to what is and appears to them because it is" (*BPF* 229). If I hear one morning on the radio an announcement of a newsworthy event, yet no one I talk to that day knows of it, I am likely to wonder if it was a dream. This bewilderment would dissolve upon reading about it in the paper the next day; such a report can reassure me that it was not a dream precisely because it provides evidence that others besides me know of the event.

In other words, we depend on the perceptions of others for the very quality of realness that the world has. (This is evident in our everyday language, as we ask one another, "did you see that?" or "do you hear that noise, too?" or "did you think she seemed more subdued than usual?") It is not that a multiplicity of perspectives lets us perceive a reality that is beyond perspective or beyond appearance; rather the multiplicity of perspectives on what appears is what *constitutes* reality. And realness comes not necessarily from others seeing *as* we see, for Arendt stresses that the public realm is always composed of a variety of perspectives. Reality—the quality of realness—derives from knowing we are talking about the same thing; it is enough to know that our perception is oriented toward a common object of discussion (*HC* 57–58). In saying "it seems to me," I am communicating my perspective to others to whom the world also "seems"; the reality of our common world arises from the very exercise of trying to fit our perceptions of appearance together.

When I "actively make my presence felt, seen, and heard," I appear as part of that common world. I display my uniqueness "as an individual" (*LOM* I 29); I show "who" I am before others who are equally unique and equally capable of commitment to a joint enterprise. It is through speech and action that uniqueness is disclosed, but this very disclosure requires more than one, *before whom* one discloses. Hence Arendt constantly equates plurality with "the presence of others" (*HC* 237; *LOM* I 74; *OR* 175). Reception and appearance are bound up together, as acts of unique humans, as the constituents of worldly reality. So the further unarticulated paradox of plurality is that the appearance of individuality in the world requires togetherness. This togetherness, this "presence" of others that makes real my distinctive public self, involves not the mere existence of other human beings, but their active attention. Plurality, after all, is not characteristic of either the private or the social realm, although other human beings exist there. We may see such human beings—say, together on a subway car—but they do not necessarily meaningfully *appear* to us. Meaningful appearance requires that we actively *make ourselves present* to each other through what we say and do (*LOM* I 29; *HC* 198–199 and 212; *OR* 19).[6]

It seems odd to think of this "presence" as our identity because we tend to think of our uniqueness as something private and intimate. For Arendt, who we are *can* be "intimately and exclusively our own"; in fact, in the absence of a public realm, it is only in the realm of intimacy that distinction and difference can exist (*HC* 199, 41). Love, Arendt tells us, possesses "an unequaled clarity of vision for the disclosure of *who*" (*HC* 242). But for Arendt, love is an essentially private matter that cannot withstand the "much harsher light of the public realm" (*HC* 51–52). Love lacks a kind of worldly reality because it focuses with passionate intensity on the individual "to the point of total unworldliness" (*HC* 242); but the public realm "simply cannot afford to give primary concern to individual lives and the interests connected with them." In politics, "not life but the world is at stake" (*BPF* 156). It is not that politics somehow does not require living, breathing human beings. But politics itself is concerned not with the maintenance of individual life, but with what is between individuals: the world (*HC* 52, 182). Politically speaking, I enter this world of things and people as one among many. I am entering a realm where my individual life is not a central care and focus in the way that it is among my family and friends, and where my own perspective does not have the special standing it does among those who love me.

But despite the lack of control and the lack of intimacy, this public "who" is no less me, no less real, than the "who" that my intimates know. For Arendt, the multiplicity of perspectives in the public realm

[6] Jennifer Ring's apt example makes precise the distinction between existing together and appearing to one another: "Shopping malls are not public spaces in Arendtian terms because nothing truly public has ever transpired at a shopping mall. Side by side, but not collectively, people there purchase consumer items for their private dwellings and their private bodily needs. Neither speech nor reasoning takes place at a shopping mall" (1991, 439). As Mary Dietz pointed out to me, this is true only in a general sense, for a shopping mall can be a place for political action, as can a subway car (for example, either might be the site of a demonstration, or the meeting place of a group of dissenters). So speech and action can happen in places designed for other activities (consumption, transportation).

is what constitutes reality for the kinds of creatures we humans are. In other words, the "me" that I disclose when I am *with* other humans in speech (and neither for them as in charitable giving, nor against them as in criminal activity) is the worldly manifestation of "who" I am (*HC* 180). This manifestation is significant—that is, this "who" is me—*because* the world (and not simply my private abode) is my home.

I cannot help but disclose "me" even if I "wholly concentrate upon reaching an altogether worldly, material object." This disclosure has worldly consequences of its own: "the physical, worldly in-between along with its interests is overlaid and, as it were, overgrown with an altogether different in-between which consists of deeds and words and owes its origin exclusively to men's acting and speaking directly *to* one another . . . for all its intangibility, this in-between is no less real than the world of things we visibly have in common. We call this reality the 'web' of human relationships" (*HC* 182–183). When we disclose the "who" through action and speech, we establish relationships and produce a certain narrative meaning. But the actor is not the author; the fact that this disclosure is neither predictable nor wholly controllable is simply one piece of the general unpredictability of action. Because action takes place in an "already existing web of human relationships, with its innumerable, conflicting wills and intentions," it is unlikely to achieve its original purpose (*HC* 184, 190). No one can simply impose his or her will "under human conditions," that is, among other beings who also have the capacity to act (*BPF* 164–165). "Since action acts upon beings who are capable of their own actions, reaction, apart from being a response, is always a new action that strikes out on its own and affects others" (*HC* 190). The fact that we cannot control how others see us act and hear us speak confirms that listening itself is active and unpredictable, part of the response that is always also a new action. In communicative action with other unique beings, we "start new unprecedented processes whose outcome remains uncertain" (*HC* 231).

So political action is not efficient, is perhaps hopelessly inefficient—it "almost never achieves its purpose" (*HC* 184)—precisely because it takes place under conditions of human plurality. Politics requires individuals who feel the need and responsibility to speak and act from their unique perspective (*BPF* 229). Yet politics also requires accepting that my perspective cannot prevail or remain unaltered by virtue of the very presence of others, for no individual can control or impose actions on a body of unique individuals (except through violence). Freedom then has not to do with being at liberty to achieve one's goal, but with the activity of meeting with others in word and deed (*BPF* 148, 152).

The ability to deal with the inevitable messiness and unpredictability of politics, the willingness to take the risk of action is, as theorists like Tocqueville and Dewey have recognized, part of the democratic character (Tocqueville 1969, esp. 92–95, 244; Dewey 1929, chap. 1). It is this interlacing of individuality, uncertainty, and togetherness that makes Arendt's understanding of action profoundly democratic (despite strains of elitism in her work) and distinct from Aristotle's. For Aristotle, the uncertainty in political matters came from the fact that they could be other than they are. Political situations are ones in which more than one action is possible, and although it is not immediately clear which one is right, citizens have a perceptual process (deliberation) that allows them collectively to determine the right course of action. But for Arendt, uncertainty is rooted in the very condition of the kinds of beings that we are; her understanding of politics is inextricable from her conception of plurality because the very activity of communicating requires that we be unique, and more than one.

THE "WHO" IN ACTION: PERFORMANCE AND COMMUNICATION

The plurality that political action requires and expresses is interwoven with another politically relevant human condition: natality. To be human is to be born into the world, a "newcomer," and we carry with us this impulse and capacity to start anew: "Because they are *initium*, newcomers and beginners by virtue of birth, men take initiative, are prompted into action" (*HC* 177, 9). This understanding of political action and actors contrasts with a view of the world as strictly governed by an inevitable process that guarantees certain results, for "the new always happens against the overwhelming odds of statistical laws and their probability . . . the fact that man is capable of action means that the unexpected can be expected from him, that he is able to perform what is infinitely improbable" (*HC* 178). It is in this performance that the meaning of action lies: "Motives and aims, no matter how pure or how grandiose, are never unique; like psychological qualities, they are typical, characteristic of different types of persons. Greatness, therefore, or the specific meaning of each deed, can lie only in the performance itself and neither in its motivation nor its achievement" (*HC* 206). The way in which "greatness" reveals something about the nature of all action is that it is uncommon enough, or unexpected enough, to be remembered.

Although this general point is evident on a first reading of Arendt, I do not think I really grasped its significance until it "shone forth" in a fairly recent worldly example. The story of Israeli-Palestinian relations in this century has been one of violence and hatred, and the leaders of the two peoples have been among the most uncompromising—have, in fact, sworn to destroy each other. And yet, when I was working on an earlier version of this chapter in September 1993, Israel and the Palestine Liberation Organization (PLO) had just signed peace accords recognizing each other diplomatically and establishing limited Palestinian self-rule. The specific moment that perhaps encapsulated the meaning of this action was at the signing ceremony, when Israeli prime minister Yitzhak Rabin and PLO chairman Yasser Arafat shook hands. The resulting gasp (and subsequent cheers) from the assembled dignitaries testified to the "startling unexpectedness" of that action and the accord it symbolized. The greatness of this action—and who it revealed Rabin, Shimon Peres, and Arafat to be—is independent of motives or aims; it would not matter if their motives included, say, self-aggrandizement or the desire to undercut political opponents, and it does not matter if in fact Rabin and Arafat (not to mention Rabin and Peres) disliked each other. (As Rabin himself snapped when asked by reporters how he felt about the handshake, "I don't believe this is the place to speak about personal feelings. We are talking about major decisions.")[7] And the remarkable, luminous character of this act will not be changed by what happens to relations in the future, even if the meaning of the story changes because in five years the accords have fallen apart. The greatness of this act—improbable, and thus worthy of remembrance—is that it displays the human capacity to disrupt the automatism of the cycle of vengeance (*HC* 240–241), and the human capacity to care, not

[7] See the report in the Minneapolis *Star Tribune*, September 14, 1993, 1A, 7–8A.

just for one's self, but for the world in which one lives with others. Rabin quoted from the Book of Koheleth (Ecclesiastes) in saying there is "a time of war and a time of peace." An Arendt reader might be reminded of another quote, strangely enough (for this accord between Jews and Muslims) from the gospel of Luke (Arendt's translation): "And if he trespass against thee . . . and . . . turn again to thee, saying, *I changed my mind*; thou shalt *release* him" (*HC* 240n). In releasing one another from their past deeds, Israelis and Palestinians turned again toward one another to establish new relationships—what Arendt might see as a rebuilding of the web of human relationships that "overlays" and "overgrows" the specific part of the world that is the Middle East.

Arendt's stress on greatness, appearance, and display (e.g., *HC* 41, 196–198) has been criticized as valorizing a peculiarly Arendtian model of the Greek hero, but I think this example shows that there is more to action than, as in Hanna Pitkin's unforgettable image, the posturing "of little boys clamoring for attention ('Look at me! I'm the greatest! No, look at *me*!')" (1981, 338).[8] Although Arendt often uses language that conjures up the stereotype of a warrior-hero, it is important to note that for her, the capacity at issue is inherent in being human (for it is through speech that we distinguish ourselves). As Arendt herself notes, the "hero" a story discloses need not have what we think of as typically heroic qualities; "In Homer, the word *heros* has certainly a connotation of distinction, but of no other than every free man was capable" (*HC* 186n).

But what makes the human condition of plurality fragile is that "every free man" is also capable of not distinguishing himself. The quality that is essential for politics (beyond the shared capacity to start anew) is courage. Many examples remind us that physical courage is still a part of the courage necessary to disclose one's self in public: occurrences of "gay bashing," the history of the civil rights movement in this country and labor movements worldwide—and now, unhappily, I have to add to this list the assassination of Yitzhak Rabin. But in making peace the former warrior Rabin revealed far more than physical courage. The mem-

---

[8] See also Jennifer Ring's analysis of "the pariah" as an alternative model of the political actor in Arendt's work (1991).

orableness of Rabin's actions does not rest on his subsequent vul-
nerability to extremist violence, but on his exemplary display of
the human capacity to make politics, not war, with his enemies. It
is this capacity that is given further worldly reality as Palestinians
and Israelis continue their joint building of specifically political
institutions.

The courage to take political action always goes beyond physical courage, beyond "a willingness to suffer consequences." Since
we can never know the consequences of action, "courage and even
boldness are already present in leaving one's private hiding place
and showing who one is, in disclosing and exposing one's self" (*HC*
186). In exposing myself to the attention of others, I "act into" a
web of human relationships that may entangle me in unforeseen
ways. This is why the meaning of action and of "who" I am is not dependent on having achieved certain results or having possessed certain motives. But there is a kind of conscious aim that is still
important; insofar as I perform, I do so to communicate in some
way to those others whose active presence is so central to my ability
to appear in the world. This unavoidable intertwining of performance and communication is for the most part neglected in contemporary debates about Arendt. Some theorists stress the
communicative or dialogic nature of Arendtian public action (e.g.,
Habermas 1977; Benhabib 1988). By contrast, other theorists,
rather than criticizing her model of glory, want to reclaim precisely
this aspect of her work, and argue for understanding the political
self and the public realm as agonal and performative (e.g., Villa
1992a, 1992b; Honig 1992).[9]

It seems clear that Habermas is mistaken in assuming that
Arendt's understanding of communicative action was one that resulted in consensus (1977, 4–6). The tangled "overgrown" web of
human relationships is characterized by "innumerable, conflicting
wills and intentions" (*HC* 183–184). There is no guarantee of a harmonious or consensual outcome; the most Arendt will ever say is
that "many" can come to an agreement on how to act. When we act
into the web of human relationships, we do not necessarily create
a nice mesh, but may instead ricochet off each other, deflecting or

[9] Benhabib 1992 finds both strains in Arendt, but maintains that the performative mode undermines the communicative, and hence limits Arendt's usefulness.

entangling each other, unexpectedly creating or disrupting relationships, leaving threads knotted or sheared off.

However, Villa's notion that "agon" is primary for Arendt and
needs somehow to be "tamed" to enable joint (i.e., communicative)
action is not quite right either (1992b, 276).[10] Communication and
performance do not need to be *reconciled*; like appearance and reception, they presuppose one another, for "no one in his right
mind would ever put on a spectacle without being sure of having
spectators to watch it" (*LK* 62). What makes a performance a performance, rather than a series of unrelated gestures and nondis-
closing words, is that it is directed toward spectators with the
purpose of communicating something about common "worldly objective reality" (*HC* 182). This is why action establishes relationships
rather than just dissolving into air. But because appearance and reception partake of the same character—because we are active and
unpredictable in listening as well as speaking—speaking and listening do not work smoothly together to produce wise or consensual decisions.[11] Surely this is a central source of agon in Arendt; we
attempt to present ourselves and communicate our thoughts in a
particular way, but this very presence depends on others who will
judge and interpret the performance for themselves. Despite this
conflict and disorder, actions still have performative meaning; the
meaning of the original performance between Rabin and Arafat
was precisely that it established a relationship that was a communicative one rather than one of violence and warfare.

This example points us toward another question about
Arendt's understanding of action. Readers have wondered what *besides* peace and war would be talked about in the public realm,
given Arendt's pointed distinction between the public realm of appearances on one hand and the private and social realms on the
other (e.g., Pitkin 1981; Hill 1979, 315–316). This is a crucial question to address for my purposes, for it reopens the question of who
citizens are, and thus of how we pay attention to one another.

---

[10] Nor does his distinction between Habermasian seriousness and a presumably
Arendtian playfulness ring true. Arendt clearly regarded acting as a serious enterprise (although not necessarily a humorless one); hence the need for courage.

[11] See also Canovan's criticism of Habermas and Isaac's response to Villa
(Canovan 1983, 108–109; Isaac 1993). Although Isaac's concern is with historically
situating Arendt, his criticism of Villa is similar to mine.

WHAT ABOUT THE SOCIAL QUESTION?

As is well known, Arendt sharply distinguishes the private and public realms in terms of the activities that go on in each. In Arendt's schema, the private realm is where the needs of the body—for food, shelter, and the like—are met. Thus the private realm is characterized by necessity, the irresistible demands of somatic needs and processes. The public realm, by contrast, is the space of freedom, and public action is free precisely insofar as it is not driven by necessity. "The mastering of the necessities of life in the household was the condition for freedom of the *polis*"; one had to be free from the needs of the body in order to exercise care for the world (*HC* 30–31).

The different purpose and character of each realm means that there are particular problems distinctive to each. Arendt's concern about the contemporary public realm is that it has been taken over by "the social," a hybrid realm where the needs of the household appear in the realm reserved for freedom: "Society is the form in which the fact of mutual dependence for the sake of life and nothing else assumes public significance and where the activities connected with sheer survival are permitted to appear in public" (*HC* 46).[12] Arendt elsewhere describes the "social question" as "the problem of poverty," or the deprivation of the necessities of life (*OR* 60).

That such a problem is not political and should not be public is a startling claim, and commentators have been sharply critical of it. Sheldon Wolin argues that Arendt, in trying to maintain a distinction between "the social" and "the political" ignores the extent to which the social has political consequences: "Society contains important distinctions of wealth, birth, and education that are typically extended into political power." The Greeks themselves recognized this, he contends; Arendt's distorted version of the Greek *polis* disregards the class conflicts and push for socioeconomic equality that characterized the Greek political scene (Wolin 1983, 3, 7–8).[13] Hanna Pitkin points out the dangerous possibilities

---

[12] See also *HC* 35, 38–45. It is important to remember that for Arendt the public and private realms require the existence of each other in order to maintain their specific characteristics. The "rise of the social" erodes not simply the public realm but the private as well (*HC* 58–78).

[13] See also Salkever's argument that Arendt distinguishes the purposes of the public and private realms in a distinctly un-Aristotelian way (1990, chap. 4).

that Arendt's conceptual scheme can give rise to: "the exclusion of 'everything merely necessary or useful' from political life means simply the exclusion of the exploited by their exploiters" (1981, 336). Adrienne Rich, too, reads oppression into Arendt's consigning to invisibility the "activity of world-protection, world-preservation, world-repair," which has traditionally been women's work (1979, 205–206).[14]

These criticisms indicate that there is much to be cautious of in Arendt's strict separation of the private and public realms and her apprehension toward "the social." But rather than dismiss Arendt as a perhaps inadvertent accomplice in oppression, I want here to take her concerns seriously in order to discern their importance for thinking about politics, in particular the interconnected nature of politics and plurality. I argue that the incompatibility that Arendt sees between the public and the social (or, to put it another way, between questions of freedom and questions of poverty) does not come simply from a romantic loyalty to a possibly misunderstood Greek ideal or from a thinly veiled elitism. For Arendt, there are two related and dangerous problems when poverty becomes a political issue. First, it changes who the participants are—or rather, changes them from "whos" to "whats." Instead of being plural, unique individuals, they are interchangeably alike, with identical and predictable needs—in effect, a mass. And so, second, the activity appropriate to the social realm is not action or speech, but administration—the bureaucratic process by which we find efficient means to already determined ends.

Why for Arendt does this change happen, and what makes it so pernicious? It is not because poverty—the absence of sufficient food or decent housing—is unimportant, but rather because its importance cannot be denied. When Arendt says that poverty demands attention (*OR* 112, 60) she means it literally; the urgency of life processes commands us insofar as we are biological creatures. (Even geniuses, she asserts, would have difficulty thinking properly if they were hungry [*CR* 73n].) Clearly, for Arendt, there can be no disagreement that people should be fed and housed properly, and she is not indifferent to the fact that "public life obviously was pos-

---

[14] For a discussion of Rich's and other feminists' responses to Arendt, see Dietz 1991 and 1995.

sible only after the much more urgent needs of life itself had been taken care of" (*HC* 65). Such necessities, then, should not be subject to political power and processes. The right to these necessities of life are "prepolitical rights that no government and no political power has the right to touch and to violate" (*OR* 109). Arendt's claim is in fact a radical one: that everyone should have the needs of life met is a certainty not subject to debate, and no political aims can override it.

So Arendt excluded "the social question" not because she did not want to hear about it, but because she thought, for deeply principled reasons, that there was nothing to say. It is precisely the unarguability of "questions" of poverty that make them apolitical or rather antipolitical. For Arendt, there can be no unique opinion about whether we need to eat, for "the cry for bread will always be uttered with one voice. Insofar as we all need bread, we are indeed all the same" (*OR* 94). Regarding participants in the public realm from the perspective of poverty destroys human plurality, for it reduces us to the physiological level at which we are all alike.[15]

There is no need for speech in this social realm, for humans do not need speech to communicate "immediate identical needs and wants" (*HC* 176). So politics ("the twofold process of decision and persuasion") gives way to administration (the management of things), once concerns are reduced to necessary ones in the face of which we can have only one opinion and one common interest (*OR* 91; also *OR* 272–274). The conformism that Arendt sees as characteristic of modern society is "ultimately rooted in the one-ness of man-kind" (*HC* 46), that is, our physiological sameness (rather than our distinctiveness). Thinking in terms of automatic or necessary processes destroys the possibility for action, for words and deeds that communicate a unique self; as creatures subject to hunger, cold, and weariness, as part of "the animal species mankind," we can all be expected to *behave* the same (*HC* 40–46).

Interestingly, however, when Arendt is pressed on this issue, she says that it is not exactly the case that certain questions or issues cannot be permitted in the public realm. It is rather that every question or issue has a "double face," one political and one social.

---

[15] This reduction to identical physical reactions was precisely what the concentration camps accomplished (*OT* 438, 454–456).

She takes the example of housing: "There shouldn't be any debate about the question that everybody should have decent housing" (i.e., this is the social face, in which she later includes the question of "how many square feet every human being needs"). But whether housing will be integrated, and whether people who live in what has been designated inadequate housing will be forced to move—these are the political questions (Hill 1979, 318–319). On the political side, then, there is some room to debate what counts as decent housing (integrated or not?) and how to achieve it, that is, what to do about it. If we apply this principle to the example of eating, we might say that the human need for food, and the amount and variety of food the human body needs to remain healthy can (in Arendt's terms) be determined by nonpolitical means. But whom we will eat with, or who decides whom we will eat with, is a political question.

Although Arendt seems to think it is clear which aspects of each question are which, both examples reveal the difficulty of trying to make this precise distinction. One could certainly argue instead that integration is beyond debate, and that there is in fact disagreement over the food humans need—whether ketchup is a vegetable (as the Reagan administration claimed) or whether the new "pyramid" of nutrition is a superior guide to eating compared with the old "four basic food groups." Arendt might respond that we can scientifically know about nutrition, and disagreement arises not from uncertainty about the questions, but from the meat industry's interest in opposing the pyramid, or the Reagan administration's interest in cutting the costs of school lunch programs. So this disagreement is somehow inauthentic, a meaningless debate. But by what standards do we distinguish between authentic and inauthentic disagreement? For here in the late twentieth century, it is clear that scientists produce contradictory research and discover previously unknown consequences, and that the human body has the capacity to astonish and flummox even experts.

Raising these questions points to precisely what Arendt's division between the public and social realm would preclude: questioning whether something *is* political, whether it is an uncertain matter or not. Arendt's unyieldingness on this matter comes from her understanding that humans both create their own conditions and are conditioned by them (*HC* 9). Discussing in public ques-

tions that reduce participants to their biological processes can condition us to regard ourselves in this way—that is, to think of citizens
as beings defined by the urgency of life's necessities. By being public, this vision of citizenship can take on an unfortunate kind of reality, because how we can appear has everything to do with how we
regard one another. In Arendt's view, "the trouble with modern
theories of behaviorism is not that they are wrong but that they
could become true" (*HC* 322).

Yet Arendt herself believed that humans were never wholly conditioned (*HC* 9), and she used examples that make clear that economic issues and political purposes can be combined. She regards
as exemplary the early labor movement because "they were the only
group on the political scene which not only defended its economic
interests but fought a full-fledged political battle." In other words,
Arendt says, they spoke "*qua* men—not *qua* members of society"
(*HC* 218–219). Note that Arendt does not compare speaking "as
men" to speaking as members of a class; that is, it is not their identity as workers that she contrasts to their public identity. To speak as
a member of society is to speak as a being under the sway of necessity, so Arendt's point is that they spoke as humans capable of forming unique opinions. But the implication here is that defending
their economic interests was interwoven with the "full-fledged political battle" that was the fight for public freedom—the freedom to
participate in shaping the world that was their home, too.

A similar discussion suggests that the "transformation of the social question into a political force" is possible for Arendt (*OR* 62).
The early Marx did this, she argues, in his discussion of "exploitation." Poverty could be understood as a political question once it
was seen as a result of "an economy which rested on political
power and hence could be overthrown by political organization
and revolutionary means." To make this argument, Marx had to regard the poor as *not* bound by necessity, as capable of a "spirit of
rebelliousness" that came not from necessity but from being persuaded "that poverty itself is a political, not a natural, phenomenon" (*OR* 62–63). To do anything about this phenomenon, the
poor must regard themselves as capable of action as well. Compare
Arendt's view of the men of the French Revolution, whose mistake
was to regard *les malheureux* as wholly driven by necessity (and thus
"the new body politic" was founded on the "right to 'food, dress,

and the reproduction of the species', that is, upon his right to the necessities of life" [*OR* 109]). And yet these "men of the Revolution" had originally been motivated "to found a space for public freedom," to participate in public affairs (*OR* 124–125, 132–133). The implicit comparison between the early Marx and the French revolutionaries shows that the conflict between the need for bread and the desire for public participation (in other words, between necessity and freedom) results only partly from the urgency of the needs of the body. The conflict also stems from the tendency to regard those driven by the needs of the body as incapable of being free or caring about freedom; the men of the French Revolution did not attribute to *les malheureux* their own desire for public happiness. Perhaps, as Pitkin ends up arguing, "it is not a particular subject-matter, nor a particular class of people, but a particular attitude against which the public realm must be guarded" (1981, 342).

Because political action is inherently an appearing to others, this is an issue of regard or attention in more than a metaphorical sense. The importance of how citizens regard themselves and one another is evident in Arendt's discussion of compassion, which is intended to demonstrate a way of paying attention to people that is antithetical to political action. This may at first seem odd, for compassion in Arendt's view can be concerned only with a particular person and thus might seem particularly well-suited for discerning the unique "who" (an attitude suited, in other words, to the human condition of plurality). But compassionate regard is (like love) unworldly. Arendt defines compassion as "cosuffering," as identifying with and feeling the suffering of others (*OR* 85, 81). Compassion thus erases any distinction between people, it "abolishes the distance, the in-between which always exists in human intercourse." Because of this capacity of compassion to erase the space between people, it can be perverted into pity, which is antipolitical because it treats all the suffering as one mass (*OR* 85–86, 94). Neither pity nor compassion is concerned with persuasion and discussion, the essence of politics: "Such talkative and argumentative interest in the world is entirely alien to compassion, which is directed solely, and with passionate intensity, towards suffering man himself" (*OR* 86).

Arendt may be wrong about the character of compassion (we may disagree that it necessarily involves erasing the distance between persons in this way), but Wolin is wrong that Arendt does not allow "fellow-feeling" to enter politics (Wolin 1983, 3). She does, but although "it may be aroused by suffering," she avoids calling it "feeling." It is rather "a principle that can inspire and guide action": solidarity. The difference between solidarity and compassion is that the former establishes "deliberately . . . a community of interest with the oppressed and exploited" (*OR* 88–89). What distinguishes a community of interest is precisely that its concern is with what *inter-est*, what is between us in the world, and not simply our individual sufferings (*OR* 86; also *HC* 182). Solidarity in this sense treats the oppressed as actors and equals, not merely as victims. Solidarity means regarding others as capable of taking an interest in the world and speaking for themselves, capable of political action, and therefore meant to be listened to and not simply cared for.[16] In other words, the action that solidarity guides is how we pay attention to one another; the public realm is characterized both by certain ways of talking, and certain ways of listening. And being equals means that it is not only the oppressed poor for whom being regarded in this way is essential; solidarity "comprehends the strong and the rich no less than the weak and the poor" (*OR* 89). The rich and the poor, to be able to establish a community of interest, must both be guided by solidarity.[17]

If I regard others as capable of joint political action because it is a distinctively human mode of taking an interest in the world, then I must regard myself as equally capable and equally interested.

---

[16] Interestingly, a similar argument appears in another essay concerned with revolution, Martha Nussbaum's analysis of James's *The Princess Casamassima*: "What is being said [in the story] is that politics must not address the problems of human life entirely from the bottom up, so to speak, thinking of the spirit only at a time when the needs of the body have been completely satisfied. . . . Food has point only as food for something, and if the sense of this something is lost, feeding will be a feeding of animals" (Nussbaum 1990, 211).

[17] It is instructive in this regard to recall Arendt's discussion of suffering in *The Human Condition*. Here "doing" and "suffering" are "like opposite sides of the same coin": "Because the actor always moves among and in relation to other beings, he is never merely a 'doer' but always and at the same time a sufferer" (*HC* 190). The human condition of plurality makes doing and suffering inevitable results of each other, so sufferers can of course be doers, but only if humans regard one another with the kind of attention adequate to plurality.

If I do not, excessive concern for the private can overwhelm the public even when sheer necessity is not at work. Arendt contends that "the social question interfered with the course of the American Revolution no less sharply, though far less dramatically, than it did with the course of the French Revolution." Here, the concern for public happiness "yielded" not to the passion of compassion but to the desire for economic abundance—what Arendt calls "the fatal passion for sudden riches" *(OR* 137–139).

To avoid being driven by, or yielding to, economic needs does not mean to disregard them; the political side of needs is interests, with which all action is concerned (*HC* 182). Interests are the political side of needs because part of what is between us in the world is related to those needs—houses, grocery stores, restaurants, manufacturing plants. This is why integrating a housing project can be for Arendt a political question, about some "worldly material object" even though that object is also concerned with meeting nonpolitical needs. It is important to remember here that a concern for the world is not set against concern for human lives; the world is one not merely of things, but of other people. It is just that our action in this world must be the kind that will enable the human artifice to remain a place "fit for action and speech," the domicile of human beings engaged in argument and persuasion.

It is certainly true that Arendt generally presents the need for bread and the desire for participating in public affairs as antithetical (e.g., *OR* 139, 245). The existence of "poor people's movements" (welfare-rights movements in the United States, base communities in Brazil) shows that this need not be the case. (Pitkin argues that it was not in fact the case in Arendt's own example, the French Revolution [1981, 342].) Homeless activists have also shown that one need not have private needs met to be capable of public action. Although Arendt insists that "every attempt to solve the social question with political means leads into terror" *(OR* 112), the above discussion shows that the split between the social and the political is more complicated, ambivalent, and less clear—in Arendt's own thought—than many commentators suppose. My reading here is meant to suggest that on Arendt's own terms the social "overwhelms" the political only to the extent that the cry for bread is all that is uttered, *or heard.*

On this reading, Arendt and Aristotle share an understanding that human needs and the burden of labor present a problem for citizenship. For Aristotle, the burden is borne by certain people who are thus without the leisure necessary to develop the kind of character citizenship requires. In other words, socioeconomic conditions determine people in relatively predictable ways, and in the best-guided state those who are governed by need would perhaps be excluded from politics. Arendt's alternative is to exclude those sides of the question that reduce humans to need-governed creatures, precisely as a way to keep the people (in all their humanness) in. Yet Arendt's own inability to provide very persuasive criteria for what is social and what political reminds us of the value of Aristotle's understanding that the uncertainty of political matters means that what counts as uncertain (i.e., political) is itself a possible subject for deliberation. Arendt might have applied to this question the lesson she says Lessing taught: that no scientific conclusion, no matter "how convincingly proved," is worth sacrificing the opportunity for humans to talk together and thus "humanize" the world (*MDT* 23–30).[18]

In any case, Arendt does tell us more about the kind of attention that citizens must direct toward one another; she describes this explicitly political regard as respect. Not surprisingly, the quality of respect plays an important role in her understanding of how human plurality makes action so uncertain. What makes the boundlessness and unpredictability of political action bearable, Arendt says, are our faculties of forgiving and promising (*HC* 236–247); our possession of these faculties is what makes political courage humanly and not just heroically possible. Promising provides a grounding, some stability out of which to act, "an island of certainty in an ocean of uncertainty" (*HC* 244). But such promises are, as John McGowan puts it, extravagant, risky, and fragile: "If humans try to overcome unpredictability by offering each other promises, forgiveness must embody our awareness that human action can never fully succeed in such an effort" (McGowan, forthcoming). The irreversible and ultimately uncontrollable

---

[18]See Honig 1992 for an astute interpretation of Arendt's understanding of action that allows us to question the line between the political and the social, even though Arendt herself did not.

character of action, and the fact that we can never undo what was done, require forgiveness, which acts by "releasing men from what they have done unknowingly" (*HC* 240) and, presumably, what they did knowingly but later regret. In the private realm, love has the power to forgive, because love sees the "who" and thus forgives what was done for the sake of who did it (*HC* 241–243). Interestingly, for Arendt "what love is in its own, narrowly circumscribed sphere, respect is in the larger domain of human affairs. Respect, not unlike the Aristotelian *philia politike*, is a kind of 'friendship' without intimacy and without closeness; it is a regard for the person from the distance which the space of the world puts between us, and this regard is independent of qualities which we may admire or of achievements which we may highly esteem" (*HC* 243). Respect, like love, enables us to see through *what* a person is to *who* they are. The significant difference between the two is that loving (or compassionate) attention erases the world. Through respect, however, we see from "across the distance the world puts between us," acknowledging others as different from us yet, like us, a unique who. This seeing comes not out of liking or "esteem" for their particular personal qualities, nor because they personally resemble us. Although Arendt does not say so, it must come from and express the principle of solidarity: viewing another as (like us) capable of action, "that talkative and argumentative interest in the world" (*OR* 86). We make the effort to see the unique who, we "regard" them, through the faculty of respect, which is central not merely to forgiveness but to politics itself, for it is that regard which enables speakers of words and doers of deeds to appear in the world.

Since speech and action are the activities that go on in the public realm, this respect must have something to do with not merely seeing (as the word "regard" would seem to suggest) but also hearing. It is striking that, despite its importance in her understanding of action, Arendt does not analyze the phenomenon of listening explicitly. Some perplexities about what listening might involve in an Arendtian public realm can be discerned by looking at her analysis of the activities which for her center on attention to others—that is, at her discussion of representative thinking and opinion formation, which is connected thematically to her work on judgment and common sense.

TRAVELING THE DISTANCE THE WORLD PUTS BETWEEN US: OPINIONS, JUDGMENT, AND COMMON SENSE

Opinions are the content of speech in the public realm; my opinions—how "it seems to me"—are a central part of my unique identity. Opinions belong "exclusively to individuals" (*OR* 227), and "there are few things by which men are so profoundly distinguished from each other as by these" (*BPF* 247). Opinions are "inspired by different interests and passions" and grounded in fact, yet opinions about the same facts can "differ widely" (*BPF* 238). Differing opinions are always characteristic of "men in the plural," as unanimity of opinion is characteristic of mass society and tyranny (*BPF* 235; *JP* 182; *OR* 225–226).

Not surprisingly, then, opinion requires the presence of others. "No one is capable of forming his own opinion without the benefit of a multitude of opinions held by others" for "opinions are formed and tested in a process of exchange of opinion against opinion" (*OR* 225, 227; also *BPF* 247). Our opinions are thus affected by the others with whom we live together in the world. My own thinking is influenced by the "possible judgments" of others: "The thinking process which is active in judging something . . . finds itself always and primarily, even if I am quite alone in making up my mind, in an anticipated communication with others with whom I know I must finally come to some agreement" (*BPF* 220).[19] Arendt's point here and in the later lectures on Kant is that "no thinking and no opinion-formation are possible" without the public expression of other opinions. Although Arendt argues that thinking itself requires privacy, she agrees with Kant that publicity plays an important role: "Unless you can somehow communicate and expose to the test of others, either orally or in writing, whatever you may have found out when you were alone, this faculty exerted in solitude will disappear." Thus, she concludes, "critical thinking implies communicability," the possibility of conveying our thought to others. And this stress on communicability and publicity "obviously implies a com-

[19] It is significant in this context that Arendt equates the Greek *phronesis*, the excellence most central to politics, with "the ability to see things not only from one's own point of view but in the perspective of all those who happen to be present" (*BPF* 221).

munity of men who can be addressed, and who are listening and can be listened to" (*LK* 40).

But if a community is "implied" and communication is "anticipated," these others need not be literally, immediately present. Because I have the ability to re-present others in my mind, opinions can be arrived at "by discursive, representative thinking" (*BPF* 247). This conception of representative thinking is more complicated than it first appears, and I think Arendt herself was not always consistent or careful in working through its meaning. In the following discussion, I argue that there are two kinds—or perhaps two subjects—of Arendtian representative thinking, and that in neither is Arendt necessarily talking about actual interaction. Let me begin by quoting at length the often-cited passage in "Truth and Politics":

> Political thought is representative. I form an opinion by considering a given issue from different viewpoints, by making present to my mind the standpoints of those who are absent; that is, I represent them. This process of representation does not blindly adopt the actual views of those who stand somewhere else, and hence look upon the world from a different perspective; this is a question neither of empathy, as though I tried to be or to feel like somebody else, nor of counting noses and joining a majority but of being and thinking in my own identity where actually I am not. The more people's standpoints I have present in my mind while I am pondering a given issue, and the better I can imagine how I would feel and think if I were in their place, the stronger will be my capacity for representative thinking and the more valid my final conclusions, my opinion. (*BPF* 241)

What can it mean to "be and think *in my own identity* where actually *I* am not"? This "exertion of imagination" requires "liberation from one's own private interests" (*BPF* 242; see also *LK* 43), so when I put myself in another's place, it is actually some modified version of myself, for I leave my worldly interests behind. The "I" that is left behind must be something like "me-in-terms-of-my-interests." But Arendt clearly does not believe that representative thinking requires selflessness, or a total stilling of one's own concerns, for such thinking is not empathy or taking on another's feelings—"my own identity" is still central. What's left about myself—"my own identity"—that I bring along to another's place must be the "me" that is not determined by my interests, me insofar as I am a unique and opinionated human. It is important to notice that both terms—both "me"s—are preserved in representative thinking. So although my traveling self may be "liberated" from private interests, those interests are still present as a sort of comparative self; in other words, there is still a connection, or perhaps a communication, between the "I" left behind and "my own identity" that goes traveling.

The model we have for understanding how this can be so comes from Arendt's understanding of the duality of the thinking ego. For Arendt, the thinking consciousness is always "two-in-one," for thinking is a "dialogue . . . between me and myself." It is precisely "this *duality* of myself with myself that makes thinking a true activity, in which I am both the one who asks and the one who answers" (*LOM* I 185). Arendt herself makes the connection between this two-in-one, and human plurality in general: "Nothing perhaps indicates more strongly that man exists *essentially* in the plural than that his solitude actualizes his merely being conscious of himself, which we probably share with the higher animals, into a duality during the thinking activity" (*LOM* I 185; see also 187).

The recognition that as a thinking self we are more than one makes it possible for us to be divided in thought without losing our selfhood; in representative thinking, just one of the partners in the dialogue assumes the standpoints of others. We do not exactly leave ourselves behind; rather, we let others in in order to be with them—not in a way that assumes identity, but in a way that gives voice to difference. We mimic—through the activity of thinking as a dialogue—the conditions of communication among plural beings, which is to say that we think as individuals in something like a public space.

But *where* are we traveling to in this space? What precisely is another's "standpoint"? It is here that Arendt gives two kinds of answers. The long passage quoted above is introduced by saying that political (representative) thinking involves "taking into account other people's *opinions*" (my emphasis), and in the passage itself Arendt seems to use "viewpoint" and "standpoint" interchangeably. However, in other discussions of the plurality of perspectives in the public realm, Arendt seems to mean something more embodied by "standpoint." She elaborates the notion of standpoint by describing it as "actually, the place they stand, the conditions they are subject to, which always differ from one individual to the next, from one class or group as compared to another" (*LK* 42–43). The spatiality of this concept is underscored by her discussion in *The Human Condition*. There Arendt describes the public realm as relying for its very existence on "the simultaneous presence of innumerable perspectives and aspects in which the common world presents itself . . . for though the common world is the common meeting ground of all, those who are present have different *locations* in it, and the location of one can no more coincide with the location of another than the location of two objects" (*HC* 57, my emphasis). Location seems to mean literally one's relation to the worldly things that make up the common world.

In trying to make clear what Arendt might mean by "the place we stand in relation to worldly things," consider her understanding of what gives a thing its "worldly character." The worldly character of a thing is constituted by its "location, function, and length of stay in the world" (*HC* 94). My relation to worldly things thus might mean something like where I live, what I own, or do not, or can never own or have access to (location); the tasks a thing is used to accomplish and whether it is to my benefit or disadvantage to achieve those goals (function); and whether I want to get rid of it or maintain it (permanence or length of stay). We might refer to these concerns as our *interests*—and so would Arendt. It is the physical "world of things" that gives rise to our "specific, objective, worldly interests." Such interests "constitute, in the word's most literal significance, something which *inter-est*, which lies between people and therefore can relate and bind them together" (*HC* 182). The fact that our interests relate us does not necessarily mean that we have common interests—a thing may relate us precisely because we are fighting over it—but that we communicate about them. "Most action and speech is concerned with this in-between . . . most words and deeds are *about* some worldly objective reality in addition to being a disclosure of the acting and speaking agent" (*HC* 182).

One version of representative thinking, then, is that I am imagining myself with a different set of interests. (This seems to make sense because my own interests are precisely what I left behind.) I have left behind my location—my relation to the world of things—for someone else's. This understanding of representative thinking is supported by Arendt's example of reflecting upon a slum dwelling (which comes from an unpublished lecture of Arendt's, quoted in Beiner 1982). I try to imagine "how I would feel if I had to live there, that is, I try to think in the place of the slum dweller." This does not mean that I canvass the slum dwellers for their opinions, or that I think I can imagine what slum dwellers actually feel and thus empathize or "conform my opinions to those of others." To return to the distinction made above: this "I" that is relocating is actually "my own identity" (rather than the interest-bound me); the me that is a unique thinking being is imagining that its location in the world is the slum. My concern is not so much with what others actually feel, but with how my own self would feel: "I still speak with my own voice" (Beiner 1982, 107–108).

The opinion that I form is "enlarged" by leaving behind my location in the world and imaginatively entering someone else's. This enlargement gives my opinion the political validity that Arendt calls impartiality. Impartiality does not mean being separate from the world and its conflicts, "above the melee," nor does it subsume the plurality of perspectives on the world "under one aspect" (*LK* 42; *HC* 57–58). Rather, an enlarged view is not partial (more than just a part) in the sense that it is reached precisely by "going through" the many particular perspectives of those related and separated by that world (*LK* 42–44; *BPF* 241).[20]

But "perspectives" can be spatial or mental; that is, "it appears to me" has more and less literal meanings. This dual meaning corresponds to the fact that it is not simply interests that are expressed in the political realm, but opinions that are communicated. The other version of representative thinking is that we take into account others' *opinions*. It is important to distinguish the two versions of representative thinking precisely because interest and opinion cannot be collapsed; for Arendt they are "entirely different political phenomena" (*OR* 226–227). Yet the two are related in some way, for action is always about some worldly interest, the web created by talking to one another grows over the world of objective things. They are connected as "speech is to the existence of a living body" (*HC* 182–183); although speech must issue from a living body, that body does not determine the content of speech. Similarly, our opinions, though they may be about and thus related to our interests, are ir-

---

[20] Disch's felicitous term for this Arendtian notion is "situated impartiality." See Disch 1994, esp. chap. 4, for a detailed discussion of the significance of this concept for contemporary debates about knowledge and experience.

redeemably individual and cannot be reduced to those interests anymore than to the needs of the body. To imagine that certain interests automatically give rise to certain opinions is to negate human plurality.

This is why, for Arendt, I can only know what *I* would think in another location, and not what someone who resides there actually thinks. I can, of course, imagine opinions other than my own. But representing to myself other opinions is tricky, for I cannot attribute opinions to specific others without knowing—without *hearing*—that they in fact hold that opinion. That is, we cannot confuse a possible judgment from a particular perspective with a specific person's actual judgment. By ourselves, we can never really know the innumerable perspectives in the world. The unpredictability of action and speech, the ability of humans to begin and give voice to something new, means that the opinions we hear may be—or perhaps even tend to be—surprising.

It would seem, however that we can understand something about what someone's interests are. Just as opinions are always individual, interests always belong to a group (*OR* 226–227). How is this possible if (*HC* 57) no two beings or objects can share the same location? I think the appropriate image here draws on Arendt's own simile, in which the world relates and separates us as a table does the people sitting around it (*HC* 52–53). Each person has his or her own chair (and so a particular location); yet their "it seems to me" has in some ways more in common with those on their own side of the table than those sitting directly across (thus one side of the table would be a group). But in other ways, their "it seems to me" has more in common with those they face (e.g., what the table looks like where they are sitting, as opposed to at the far end). Individuals then belong to more than one "group," that is, no one group wholly defines their interest. And if it is a round table, as seems appropriate for the world, the lines between groups are blurry. But we can move around this table in a way that we cannot move into another's mind.

But moving to the other side or other end of the table is not the same as talking with the person who was already in that spot before I moved there. In Arendt's own terms, then, representative thinking of either sort can never replace attention to actual others' opinions. What lies between representative thinking on one hand,

and a kind of impossible empathy on the other, is listening. We do not simply come to the public realm with already achieved opinions; we also must reach some sort of judgment about how to act together. The formation of this kind of judgment (particularly if it is to be not partial) must be formed through actual political communication with others, and not simply through the imaginative and necessarily limited act of representative thinking.

It is not clear in Arendt's account of representative thinking how actually speaking and listening to one another work. Elsewhere Arendt is vague: "You should be instructed when you sit together with your peers around a table and exchange opinions. And then, somehow, out of this should come an instruction: not for you personally but how the group should act" (Hill 1979, 310). The opacity of this "somehow" is perhaps intentional. For Arendt it is not in the least an automatic process; there is no single right answer that practical reason properly used will provide. But this does not mean that communicative action is irrational.[21] We do not simply blurt out our opinions; we are responsible for them, expected to "give an account" of why we think what we do: "not to prove, but to be able to say how one came to an opinion and for what reasons one formed it" (*LK* 41). Arendt tells us more about this accounting, and what makes it possible, in her discussion of a faculty related to representative thinking: common sense.

It is through common sense that "our strictly private and 'subjective' five senses and their sensory data can adjust themselves to a nonsubjective and 'objective' world which we have in common and share with others" (*BPF* 221; see also *HC* 208–209, *LK* 70–72). Though here common sense seems primarily related to a world of things, the phenomenal world includes other people as fellow subjects/objects, to whom common sense is also directed. Arendt refers to this as a "community sense," meaning not a kind of knowledge that we all share, but a sense of oneself as not alone in perceiving. This Kantian *sensus communis* allows us to perceive how others see the world and how that reflects upon our own perceptions.

---

[21] Habermas is right that communicative action for Arendt is noncognitive (1977, 22–23), but he seems to have ignored the distinction between different kinds of thinking evident in earlier works (*HC, BPF*) but drawn explicitly in *LOM* I as the difference between cognition and reason (e.g., 15, 40–41). What is odder is that Beiner later does the same (1982, 136–138).

The exercise of common sense does not work automatically to persuade us of the truth or rightness of what others think. Sensing "means here 'the effect of a reflection upon the mind.' This reflection affects me as though it were a sensation, and precisely one of taste, the discriminatory, choosing sense" (*LK* 71–72). The *sensus communis* involves not merely traveling, but decision and choice. There are three maxims of the *sensus communis*; one must think for oneself, think with an enlarged mentality, and "be in agreement with oneself" (*LK* 71).[22] The exercise of common sense involves—as does all thinking—the maintenance of two interlocutors. But common sense is that "extra mental capability" (*LK* 70) that allows me not merely to see from another's location but to evaluate my own judgments through considering the judgments of others, and then to make a decision that I can live with. This is the faculty that allows me to "give an account," to provide communicable reasons for my final judgment by seeing my view in light of others, and by seeing the world (which includes my self) in light of the presence of others. The fact that I can provide a reasonable account does not mean that others will agree with me or with the significance of my reasons, for these kinds of reasons are not truths or proofs (*LK* 41). Rather, by giving these reasons one "tells one's *choices* and one chooses one's company" (*LK* 74). As Arendt so strikingly puts it, "even if all criticism of Plato is right, Plato may still be better company than his critics"; that is, he may be a better companion with which, in one's final account, to judge (*BPF* 224–226. Cf. *MDT* 7–8).[23]

It may seem surprising to invoke the lectures on Kant in attempting to think about the listening that goes on in political ac-

[22] See also *LOM* I 191: "[The self's] criterion for action will not be the usual rules, recognized by multitudes and agreed upon by society, but whether I shall be able to live with myself in peace when the time has come to think about my deeds and words."

[23] Arendt's most telling example of the worldly importance of common sense is in her discussion of one who lacked it: Adolf Eichmann. This faculty of imagining things from another's perspective in order to judge for oneself was absent in him to an extraordinary degree (e.g., regretting the failure of his SS career ambitions to his interrogator, Captain Less, a Jew). The sheer thoughtlessness that Eichmann exhibited was connected to his inability to speak in anything but clichés. His inability to imagine another's perspective not only kept him from being able to communicate, but kept him from having any unique opinions of his own. He could neither speak nor think meaningfully (*EJ*, esp. 47–55).

tion, for these lectures have been criticized for forsaking the actor's
perspective for the spectator's. Although her earlier thoughts on
judgment were explicitly political, Beiner argues, in this last incomplete work Arendt reduced judgment to "the contemplative
and disinterested dimension . . . which operates retrospectively";
that is, the judgment of the spectator, storyteller, or historian, who
judges at the end of the story (1982, 138–140). Arendt does contrast the judgment of the actor and the spectator (as far back as *HC*
184–185, 192), and it is true that Arendt's discussion in the Kant
lectures seems focused on judgment as requiring withdrawal from
the world, the closing of the eyes that allows us to remake objects
into objects for the inner sense (*LK* 68–69). Only the spectator can
be impartial, Arendt says; this makes sense because the spectator
can travel between positions—first closer, to see the actor's expression, then farther away to get a sense of the spatial dimension; now
in front of the stage, now to the side. Thus the spectator can see the
whole while the actor is bound to the stage, constrained by the audience (*LK* 55). The actor "knows only his part or, if he should
judge from the perspective of acting, only the part of the whole that
concerns him. The actor is partial by definition" (*LK* 69). But this
"if" indicates that it is not that the actor does not judge, but that his
judgments have a different purpose. The spectator is concerned
with the meaning of the story, while the actor is concerned with
what to do.

But if we look more closely at the theatrical metaphor, we realize that we have so far ignored the other relationships involved in
performance: the relationships *between* actors on the stage. Their
experience is one in which they alternate acting and watching others act, speaking and responding to others speaking. They are at
the same time both actor and spectator and must perform both
roles for the play to exist. This relationship involves a kind of working together that is performative and communicative, agonistic and
purposeful and not predictable. We perform together—we have to
attend to each other's lines and play off each other—yet we might
also be trying to upstage each other. We might be provoked by a fellow actor's insistence on what we regard as histrionic misinterpre-
tation, or we might be provoked in a quite different sense, moved
to our own best performance by the compelling performance of
another. And we may be proceeding from very different under-

standings of what the play is about, and have very different takes on what we are playing at and how it should be played.

It is this relationship, I think, that would be the model for political judging and political communication, where we are concerned with both action and meaning, with acting in a meaningful way. Arendt herself continually says that in acting, the two-in-one are "clapped together" (*LOM* I 185), that the agent and the onlooker are "contained in the self-same person" (*OR* 102), that "the actor and the spectator become united" (*LK* 75). And in this last example, it is clear that she means that the actor and the spectator are guided by the same "maxims" of judgment. Impartiality is not reserved for the spectator-historian, but is also the responsibility of the actor-spectator. The fact that citizens are actor-spectators echoes the point in *LOM* I: people are always both subjects and objects, that is, the perceiving and the perceived (*LOM* I 19–20). But "actor-traveler" might be a better way to characterize citizenship, because we are *active* in both modes.

So "common sense," a sense of oneself as not alone in perceiving, is perhaps a model for both solitary thinking and actual listening interaction, for both individual and collective opinion formation. As an actor-traveler, I think and speak for myself while listening to others. And while the group is making a decision together, all individuals are deciding what they can live with and what company they will choose, create, or reluctantly leave. To equate common sense and listening is not to say that the public realm is simply the human mind writ large, but rather that the public realm and the human mind both reflect the human mode of being in the world— an active perceptive one among many.

In Arendtian terms, then, solidarity is the principle that guides listening action; common sense (part of whose exercise is representative thinking) is the faculty that makes it possible for citizens to listen while regarding both themselves and their interlocutors as active unique beings; and respect describes the quality of the listening regard itself. It is possible that respect is developed through the exercise of solitary representative thinking. Perhaps (although Arendt does not say so) the training of our imagination in this way enables us to hear others better. The flexibility or receptivity of a mind so "trained" seems better suited to surprise: to hear the variety of opinions that may actually be voiced and to take seriously those speakers as partners in dialogue. But one criterion for the thinking dialogue is consistency or noncontradiction; one is not to be "at odds" with "the partner who comes to life when you are alert and alone" (*LOM* I 188). Can this requirement of harmony keep one from traveling too far? Seyla Benhabib has criticized Arendt's notion of harmony with oneself as contradicting plurality as a political principle. In fact, "in a world in disarray, an attitude of moral alienation may be more at home in the world than an attitude of simple harmony with oneself" (Benhabib 1988, 44–45). But Arendt was more than aware that "a world in disarray" might require the sacrifice of a certain kind of self-satisfaction. She notes that it was Lessing's "partisanship for the world" that led him to sacrifice "the claim to self-consistency" (*MDT* 7–8), and she is clearly moved by Machiavelli's "argument against morality": "Though it is true that, by resisting evil, you are likely to be involved in evil, your care for the world takes precedence in politics over your care for your self. . . . Machiavelli's 'I love my native city more than my soul' is only a variation of: I love the world and its future more than my life or my self" (*LK* 50; see also *OR* 285–286n).[24]

In addition, Arendt's notion of self-consistency has a particular meaning beyond "simple harmony." In the context of her analysis of critical thinking, to "live with myself in peace" does not mean that I am smugly self-satisfied with my words and deeds, but rather that I can "give an account" of them that makes sense to me. This accounting requires that "the two who carry on the dialogue be in good shape, that the partners be friends" (*LOM* I 187–188). This does not imply unity, for "you always need at least two tones to produce a harmonious sound" (*LOM* I 183). The point is rather to maintain the conditions that allow those tones to sound, and this means keeping both interlocutors—me and myself—glad to talk to each other. Arendt elsewhere calls this gladness to talk to one another a kind of political friendship (*MDT* 15, 24); mentally, it is perhaps a kind of self-regarding respect, in which we do not exempt ourselves from the thinking examination that we turn on the rest of the world. It does seem that the partners in the thinking dialogue

---

[24] As Martha Nussbaum points out, thinking seriously about our inability to act well in a particular situation in a sense mitigates that inability. Paradoxically, we can "achieve moral stature through this sort of finely tuned imaginative awareness of the constraints that diminish [us]." This "refining self-criticism" is "about the most, in some cases, that we can do in the direction of self-respect" (Nussbaum 1980, 427).

must be friends, for often a friend can point out to us what we are unwilling to see for ourselves. Further, it is our friends who we take seriously enough, and care about enough, to engage with in sometimes deep disagreement. It is true, however, that friendships can be permanently ruptured by such disagreement,[25] just as the dialogue of the two-in-one can be silenced by refusing to think: "Thinking in its non-cognitive, non-specialized sense as a natural need of human life . . . is not a prerogative of the few but an ever-present faculty in everybody; by the same token, inability to think is not a failing of the many who lack brain power but an ever-present possibility for everybody—scientists, scholars, and other specialists in mental exercises not excluded. Everybody may come to shun that intercourse with oneself whose feasibility and importance Socrates first discovered" (*LOM* I 191).

If not thinking is an "ever-present possibility," then with respect to political interaction, not listening is as well. It is here that the concept of friendship (political or otherwise) fails us, for there are others with whom we are not glad to talk. If the partners in the thinking dialogue need to be friends, does that mean that there are certain places we cannot imaginatively go, and certain opinions we cannot hear, without feeling so threatened that we come to "shun that intercourse"? Harmony may require two tones, but they are tones with a particular and familiar relationship to each other; can the pursuit of harmony keep us politically from hearing what might be discordant sounds?

Arendt's conception of action certainly seems more compatible with dissonance or even cacophony than with two-toned harmony. Either my analysis (and Arendt's) is wrong, and there is no connection between thinking and political listening, or there is a reason why Arendt did not see a discrepancy between her view of communicative action and her view of thinking. I suggest, of course, the latter possibility: the problem never arose for Arendt because her theoretical framework did not allow social forces to have any systematic impact on political interaction.

Neither harmony nor dissonance is a natural phenomenon; a sound counts as harmonic or dissonant with respect to a structure

---

[25] There is a very interesting example of Arendt herself choosing *not* to engage in a disagreement, precisely to preserve a friendship; see Young-Bruehl 1982, 352.

and progression of chords which is culturally and historically specific. Our own history and location in the world can influence how
we hear and are heard. Susan McClary argues that how one hears
a musical piece depends "on where one is positioned socially with
respect to the enterprise"; what sounds like noise to one person
may be perfect order to another. And whether one perceives a "ten-
tative detente" between soloist and orchestra as "rehabilitation, as
selling out, or as ironic overstatement" depends on whether one
identifies with the renegade individualist or the order-enforcing
collective (1986, 133, 147). This example may seem to be making
an Arendtian claim: we choose our company in how we listen, too.
But the political point is that social and economic power often
choose our company for us, and permit the definition and perpet-
uation of certain non-neutral standards of "harmony" and "noise."

Neither Arendt nor Aristotle investigated the forces that screen
political attention, deflecting it from some voices and opinions, focusing it on others, and in the process establishing particular ways of
hearing. Arendt herself notes that we cannot attend to everything
and everyone; if we were responsive to all "events and facts" in the
world, "we would soon be exhausted." Thoughtfulness then does
not require us to attend equally to every phenomenon, but to be in
"the habit of examining whatever happens to come to pass or to attract attention" (*LOM* I 4–5). But which communicative phenomena
attract attention does not just "come to pass." In the next chapter, I
will argue that the forces that underlie social, cultural, and economic inequality block or distort attention in ways that prevent the
kind of listening necessary for democratic politics. We begin to get a
sense of this by looking precisely at the connection between bodily-
social existence and the opinions we speak. What connects the two
is not the equation of interests with opinions that Arendt feared, but
rather the medium of political action itself: language.

Chapter 4

"THE GENUINE CONDITIONS OF OUR LIVES"

FEMINIST THEORIZING AND POLITICAL ACTION

▓ Picture the world as Arendt presents it: a world of material things between people, overgrown by and interwoven with the web of human relationships. Now, imagine that this world (and not simply the earth that it is on) has particular atmospheric conditions, a cloudlike fog surrounding and filtering through it. This thick atmosphere is uneven; it has particular patterns sustained by regular currents of wind and light, so that although the haze is everywhere, it is heavier in some areas than others. Not surprisingly, the particular atmospheric conditions in a region have some effect on the practices and habits of the people in that region. The wind currents are not random or natural phenomena, nor are they the work of some evil meteorological genius. Rather, they ripple endlessly through the present as the echoes and ramifications of past events in the world.

There are a few more characteristics to be noted about this world. First, the play of wind and light sometimes makes it difficult for people in different regions to perceive one another's presence, although (as with natural fog) people who are close together can see one another better even in areas of particularly dense haze. Further, this atmospheric condition, like any condition, never wholly conditions the human beings who live in it. And the weather patterns, like any process, can be interrupted and redirected by human action.

WHO/WHAT? PUBLIC SPEAKING AND GROUP IDENTITY

In this chapter, I contend that the picture above is an instructive representation of our world, and I address the way in which the haze of socioeconomic inequality and cultural differences mani-

fests itself in relations of attention and expression. My goal is to figure out how we can think about listening as a practice of citizenship
when listening itself has often reflected social power. Feminist
thinkers have argued that racism, sexism, class discrimination, and
heterosexism are among the forces that regulate who gets paid attention to, who/what gets heard, and how. Thus *what* we are (socially defined categories of race, class, gender, and so on) affects
who we are (our appearance in the public realm). Implicit here is
an agreement with Arendt that others' perceptions of us affect how
we can be present in the political realm. But the political problem
feminists are concerned with is that patterns of oppression and inequality result in the systematic distortion of some people's appearance and audibility.[1]

The very means by which citizens disclose *who*—speaking—can
itself communicate *what*. The content of my speech may disclose a
distinct personal identity, but my way of speaking may also point to
a specific social, cultural, racial, and gendered identity. Members of
a diverse polity may have very different languages, dialects, vocabularies, and communicative sensibilities. The world picture above is
intended to aid me in making two arguments about the social use
of language, arguments that may seem contradictory but each of
which points to real worldly phenomena.

My first argument begins by pointing out that the norms that
govern communication are not neutral, but rather highlight the

[1] My focus on the relational aspects of inequality is not intended to dismiss the
material effects of economic inequality in terms of discrepancies in politically relevant resources like time and money. See, for example, Philip Green's masterful discussion of the ways in which current economic structures distribute political
resources unevenly, and his alternative structure designed with the goal of political
equality in mind (Green 1985). But such changes in economic structures can only
be made politically; even action directed toward changing an inegalitarian system
necessarily takes place in the context of that inequality. Hence the need to examine
the possibility of democratic relations of attention in an inegalitarian context. (For
two other—very dissimilar—explorations of the relationship between economic
power and political inequality, see Gaventa 1980 and Dahl 1985.)

Many political groups have realized that organizational changes can help make
participation equally possible even in an inegalitarian context. E.g., feminist organizations often provide sliding scales for fees, child care, and transportation; the Industrial Areas Foundation recognizes the need to begin and end meetings at a
precise and predetermined time. (For detail on IAF practices, see Boyte 1989. For
an argument about the necessity of taking measures to equalize opportunities to participate, see Mansbridge 1983, 248–251.)

ways of speaking of already powerful groups. What Nancy Fraser calls the "sociocultural means of interpretation and communication" (which for her includes various idioms, vocabularies, and narrative conventions) are "stratified, organized in ways that are congruent with societal patterns of dominance and subordination" (1989, 164–165). In other words, what tends to get heard in public settings is a way of speaking associated with those who control social, political, and economic institutions.[2]

To get a sense of how this claim might play itself out, let me offer some examples of how "ways of speaking" can differ, beyond simply the matter of different languages or vocabularies. I use "ways of speaking" to refer to four particular (and interrelated) linguistic phenomena. One component of a way of speaking is *structure*, the logic and grammar of an utterance or argument. As linguist Deborah Cameron argues, what is perceived as model speaking tends to be that which resembles written speech (1985, 163–166). (Recall the admiration for Al Gore's articulateness in the 1992 presidential campaign, which seemed to center on his ability to finish complicated sentences without making grammatical mistakes or losing subject-verb agreement.) In some contexts—say, a courtroom or a public hearing—this criterion can work to the benefit of those who are highly educated, and for whom "Standard" English is their first language. It works against the less educated, immigrants, and speakers of Black English (because the latter has some grammatical principles that differ from Standard English [Jordan 1985, 127–132; Smitherman 1986]).

Second, there is the matter of *voice quality*, which includes accent and pitch. Examples of discrimination here include the negative way in which southern accents are often perceived in other regions of the country, many North Americans' discomfort with heavy foreign accents, and the evidence that lower-pitched voices are regarded as more authoritative (which works against women's generally higher-pitched voices [Cameron 1985]). A third component that distinguishes ways of speaking is the *affective disposition* that is evident. In many public settings, an objective, rational demeanor is often favorably counterposed to emotional or passionate

---

[2] Lakoff 1975 made an early and influential statement of this argument in terms of women's styles of communication. For other articulations of the point, see Jones 1987, 155 and 164–165; Cameron 1985, chap. 8; and Fraser 1992.

expression. Some theorists argue that the ability to be dispassionate is admired at the expense of women, who are socially conditioned to be compassionate (e.g., Jones 1987). A fourth component is the *framing* of an utterance, whether it is asserted straightforwardly, qualified, or phrased as a question. A more hesitant or questioning way of speaking is generally seen as a sign of deference or insecurity associated with the powerless, and particularly with women (Lakoff 1975; Rich 1979, 243–244; O'Barr and Atkins 1980).

We might point to myriad demonstrations of these points in American public life: Jimmy Carter working with a speech therapist to get rid of his southern accent, the historical predominance of men as network news anchors, the behavior of women in the classroom. But—and now we turn the corner to the second argument—we might point to numerous counterexamples as well, for what ways of speaking are taken seriously depends on the interactive context: who is speaking, who is listening, and what is being talked about. For example, someone who remains dispassionate in a situation that one's listeners think calls for an emotional response may not be trusted as much as one who displays felt emotion. This insight is at least as old as Aristotle and was much rehearsed as recently as Michael Dukakis's 1988 presidential campaign. (Patricia Schroeder, however, was criticized for crying when announcing her withdrawal from the same presidential race.) Another example is evidence that some African Americans who generally speak Standard English speak versions of Black English when they are in all-Black situations; in certain settings "Standard" English, rather than being authoritative, may make one suspect (Gumperz 1982).

We can also point to counterexamples of people *associated* with a way of speaking who do not in fact speak that way. Clearly, only some African Americans speak Black English (and only sometimes), only some immigrants have difficulty with Standard English, not all women speak in a "feminine" manner (i.e., more cooperatively or less assertively). In fact, many people use more than one way of speaking; those who regularly experience different communicative contexts become proficient at this linguistic "code-switching."

This is not to say that there is merely a diversity of communicative standards unconnected with social hierarchies, or that it is simply a matter of distinguishing public communicative norms from private ones. The view offered by my first argument describes experiences in the world (which can be confirmed by the experience of other people besides oneself, e.g., in consciousness-raising groups). But it does not make a distinction between "the public"— the common world that we all share—and the myriad of publics that exist within it. There are "subaltern" publics that are based on or arise out of certain communal experiences and shared group identities (Fraser 1992). As Sara Evans and Harry Boyte argue, it is often in these "free spaces" between personal lives and the large-scale public that we learn to speak and act publicly (1986; see also Evans 1989, esp. chaps. 3 and 4). Our experiences in these groups do not determine how we speak, although they can influence what ways of speaking best express what we want to say, for we learn how to express ourselves and communicate with others from the way people around us do, and we are not around all the same people. On the other hand, insofar as there is a wider public that we share, we are influenced by and subjected to its norms as well.

These publics and the relations within and among them take shape in a context of inequality. The norms of various subaltern publics may conflict with the norms of the dominant culture, as conveyed by the media, teachers, public officials, or other figures of authority.[3] These dominant norms create what linguists call "folk-linguistic beliefs" that affect how people are heard, and what they say. For example, there is a widespread belief that women are more uncertain speakers than most men, that they speak with more politeness and hesitation, and interrupt less. Although many theorists argue that studies of gender differences in speech are inconclusive or flawed, a woman speaking is likely to be perceived through the screen of this folklinguistic belief, even if she is consciously striving to appear otherwise (Cameron 1985, chaps. 3, 8).[4] Sara Mills points out that "strategic use of hesitation and hedging may be used by fe-

[3]E.g., antislavery activists Sarah and Angelina Grimké had been raised in the Quaker tradition in which women acted as ministers and thus had developed a public voice "schooled in biblical idiom, accustomed to inspiring women to activity by drawing on strong female figures from the scriptures." But when they exercised the skills they had learned in a public speaking tour, they violated the norms of the larger society for both how and where women should speak, and were criticized by other religious leaders (Evans 1989, 79–81).

[4]Coates 1986 and many of the essays in Coates and Cameron 1988 are critical of previous studies of gender differences in language use. See Tannen 1990a for a very popular analysis of communicative differences between women and men.

male speakers . . . to indicate that they are not intending to silence other contributions, but they may be interpreted as displaying uncertainty and low self-esteem" (1992, 9). Further, women may feel constrained to "do" gender through speech, to speak in a particular way because that is the kind of speech regarded as feminine (Cameron 1985, 155–156).

Stereotypes that are not specifically linguistic also affect our appearance in public. What we say is often filtered through the screen of our visible self; as speakers we are also white women, Black women and men, well-dressed professionals, persons with disabilities, and so on. And the way we look and sound may animate socially constructed stereotypes. For the disadvantaged, their appearance in the world has a peculiar paradoxical quality; they are at once made invisible yet "marked out by stereotypes" (Young 1990, 59). Such invisibility, Iris Young argues, can be thought of as a form of cultural imperialism, which involves "the universalization of a dominant group's experience and culture, and its establishment as the norm." Members of oppressed groups do not see their perspectives, their "interpretations of the world" expressed in the dominant culture; thus such people are made invisible in the dominant culture because they exist only as stereotypes.[5] Stereotyping is a means of avoiding another's personhood, of "denying them their variousness and complexity" (Christian 1990, 341). Patricia Hill Collins argues that "portraying African-American women as stereotypical mammies, matriarchs, welfare recipients, and hot mommas" provides the ideological support for treating Black women as objects "to be manipulated and controlled" (1991, 67, 69–70). Audre Lorde refers to this as the "constant, if unspoken, distortion of vision" that racism creates: "Black women have on one hand always been highly visible, and so, on the other hand, have been rendered invisible through the depersonalization of racism" (1984, 42).[6]

The only kind of visibility stereotypes allow, then, is visibility as an object. What makes some people invisible as citizens in the wider

[5] This stereotyping in the dominant culture can coexist with affirmation and recognition in the "subordinate" culture; following Dubois, Young calls this phenomenon "doubled consciousness" (1990, 59–60). See also Collins 1991 on the "outsider-within" perspective.

[6] See also Cliff 1990, 274; Yamada 1983, 36; and Lugones 1990b, 395–396 for more on the paradox of stereotyped visibility.

public realm is not their literal absence from the scene, but rather the imposed "masks" that present a false face and prevent what the mask covers from being visible and audible.[7] Recall that when Arendt uses "the mask" as a metaphor for a public persona, the mask (there, the legal fiction of equality) conceals politically irrelevant qualities ("what" we are) in a way that allows the individual voice ("who" we are) to sound through (*OR* 105–106). But feminist writers have used the metaphor of the mask not to solve but to describe the way "what" we are can obscure our public appearance. The problem again is not the characteristics themselves, but the kind of attention paid to them. Assumptions are made, based on how I look or speak, about who I am and what I have to say, about my opinions, concerns, interests, character (e.g., Jordan 1985, 117).

So stereotypic perception imposes a mask whose effect is to blur and muffle individuality rather than let it sound through. The "who" these masks keep hidden and inaudible is the self as citizen, as unique and opinionated human. If my membership in a group is the only lens through which I am perceived, then I cannot appear as a person with a unique story and singular opinions. The expression of human plurality is blocked by assumptions that I am simply a representation of others who look and sound like me.[8]

Politically speaking, then, it matters quite a lot how others regard us, despite the tendency of some writers to treat such concern as somehow whiny, exhibiting *ressentiment* or a compulsion toward "group self-assertion" (Brown 1993; Gitlin 1993). Many feminists would agree with Arendt here: how we are perceived affects how we can appear in public, and being perceived simply as a member of a social group obscures our distinctiveness, obscures who (in a richer sense than that captured by sociological categories) we are. The type of attention that would overcome the problem of stereotyping

---

[7] For a discussion explicitly in terms of "masks," see Anzaldúa 1990b (where she cites Yamada).

[8] In addition to stereotypes, another version of this mask is put into place through tokenism. Tokenism works through the expectation that a person with a particular identity (as a member of a group) is a proxy for all other members of that group. Viewing someone only as a representative of a group is dehumanizing in the same way that stereotyping is; that person cannot appear in public as a unique self. See Uttal 1990a, 43–44, and many of the pieces in Moraga and Anzaldúa 1983 and Anzaldúa 1990a.

might at first seem to be oriented toward perceiving others as simply, equally human and individual in a way that disregards group
identity. This is the Arendtian answer, since group identity is a characteristic we share with others (part of what rather than who we
are).[9] Group membership points to a kind of shared sameness with
some, and thus an inevitable difference from others. The Arendtian mask of the public persona is supposed to obscure this differ-
ence/sameness by creating a persona that we all share, yet which
allows our distinct voices to sound. The mask perceptually disperses
certain kinds of sameness, and equalizes certain kinds of difference; it operates as a neutralizing device.

From a feminist perspective, however, we might point out that
such a mask is inevitably constructed in particular ways, by particular hands, and with particular faces, voices, and bodies in mind. Its
earpieces might amplify certain types of voices, its eyeholes might
be composed of materials that filter perception in non-neutral
ways. To accept the mask as equalizing sidesteps the question of
whether it is possible to have a "universal" conception of citizen
identity, whether there is some discernible quality that we all share
as citizens for which the mask could be a metaphor. Feminists have
argued that men are the implicit norm of conceptions of the abstract individual; men's viewpoint and experience has been considered "universal," while women are clearly marked as a group that
does not meet universal criteria (e.g., Okin 1979, 1989; Lloyd 1984;
Young 1990). Similarly, as feminists of color and their allies point
out, many white feminists have regarded their experience as
"women's experience," rather than specifically white women's experience (e.g., hooks 1984, chap. 1).[10] In an inegalitarian society
where race, class, gender, and sexuality are relevant categories, not
being seen—or not seeing oneself—as a member of a group is a
marker of power and privilege. Just as part of oppression is being

---

[9] This is also Rawls's well-known answer to injustice; his model of just deliberation involves ignorance about precisely these aspects of our identity (1971, 12, 136).
Benhabib criticizes the moral theory underlying this model and argues for the moral
importance of particularity (1986b). Fraser makes a similar argument with respect
to politics in her critique of Habermas's conception of the "public sphere" (1992).

[10] See also Spelman's persuasive argument that we cannot even imagine a
woman without a race; "without a race" invariably turns out to mean white (1988,
52–54, chap. 5).

able to appear only as a stereotype of one's group identity, part of privilege is being able to ignore that identity.[11] This privilege is not simply a matter of a socially influenced perceptual style. Rather, as Martha Minow has effectively shown, it comes from the fact that the world is built up with particular unstated norms in mind, which make specific structures and arrangements seem "natural," although they are in fact created with particular categories of people in mind. Most contemporary workplaces and work schedules have been structured in a way that presumes a nonpregnant person without responsibilities for child care or home maintenance (and one whose Sabbath falls on Saturday or Sunday or who is not religious). The very structure of sidewalks, before mandated curb cuts, presumed an able-bodied unencumbered walker, but those using sidewalks include wheelchair users, bicyclists, and people pushing strollers (Minow 1987, 14, 38–45, 57).

Feminists might be skeptical, then, that a mask designed to cover up our qualities of "whatness" would actually serve equalizing purposes.[12] *What* we are would still affect *who* we are because the mask that facilitates political appearance is inevitably constructed with certain "whats" in mind—and in a way that makes it possible for them to ignore their particularity. But it is not just the impossibility of a genuinely equalizing mask that leads feminists to be suspicious of universal citizen identities, ones built on ignoring "what." To argue that who we are and how we attend to each other as citizens should somehow disregard social identities is to overlook the fact that the connection between what we are and who we are can be empowering. Our group identities may subject us to stereotyped attention, but they are also part of "the genuine conditions of our lives" and thus often where we "draw our strength to live and our reasons for acting" (Lorde 1984, 113, quoting de Beauvoir). Our color, ethnicity, gender, class, or religion may be a constitutive part of our public identity because they provide the contexts in which we

[11] See, for example, Lugones 1990a, Spelman 1988, Young 1990, Moraga and Anzaldúa 1983. The effect of such implicit norms, particularly with respect to Rawls's theory of justice, has been tellingly analyzed in Okin 1989 (although Okin then defends a version of Rawls's theory).

[12] In fact, Arendt's own metaphor changes, from "the mask," to notions of traveling and location; these specifically spatial metaphors are what more generally characterize her writing.

learned to speak and think the languages that both shape us and enable us to give voice to our unique selves. And it is within particular
social groups that we first are paid attention to, and learn to attend
to others—the very capacities necessary for democratic politics.

It is this particularity, this specificity, that current understandings of democratic citizenship exclude, Iris Young argues, because
they "rely on a strong opposition between the public sphere of citizenship and the private sphere of particular interest and affiliation"
(1990, 116–118). This version of citizenship stresses the commonality that brings citizens together and their ability impartially to
judge the common good for a community. But such "impartiality"
and "commonality," Young contends, generally serve to falsely universalize the perspectives of the powerful, leaving the concerns of
those not part of the dominant culture to be marked out as particular, partial, or selfish (1990, 111–116). Groups that are marked out
as groups are seen as self-interested in pursuing group-specific
claims, whereas dominant groups, precisely because they are not
marked out as groups, can speak their own claims in the language
of impartiality and "the common good."[13]

Young rejects the possibility of impartiality as traditionally
conceived, a detached "view from nowhere" that any rational citizen can adopt and thus see the same; but she also rejects the notion of politics as merely the pursuit of private, selfish interests.
Rather, in an (unacknowledged) Arendtian move, she argues that
we are drawn away from egoism and myopia, not by the existence
of a universal or impartial point of view but through "the concrete
encounter with others" (1990, 102–106).[14] Thus, "in a society differentiated by social groups, occupations, political positions, differences of privilege and oppression, regions, and so on, the
perception of anything like a common good can only be an outcome of public interaction that expresses rather than submerges
particularities" (1990, 119).

[13] See also Phillips 1993, chap. 4.

[14] Like Arendt. Young does not think that this encounter involves empathy or
taking on someone else's point of view. (See Young 1990, 105; compare, for example, Arendt, *BPF* 241. The difference is that Arendt is often talking about an imaginative journey, and Young is referring to an actual communicative encounter.) And
for a very Aristotelian formulation of the need to listen to the diversity of opinions
that exist, see Young 1990, 186.

Young proposes a specifically democratic way to connect
group identity and citizenship through a conception of a "group-
differentiated participatory public," in which the public realm,
rather than being oriented toward commonality, is understood as
a realm of group differences (1990, 95; see also Fraser 1986,
428–429). Such differences are not to be regarded as inherent in
nature, but recognized as a product of social relations; a group
arises only "in the encounter and interaction between social collectivities that experience some differences in their way of life and
forms of associations" (Young 1990, 43).[15] Young identifies two
means by which we recognize and define social groups: first, the
specific "cultural forms, practices, or way of life" that distinguishes
them from another group; second, the "affinity" members have
for one another, their "sense of identity" with the group. Young
stresses this sense of affinity as constitutive of group identity, rejecting the notion that there is a "common nature" present
among members of the same group, or inherently shared interests. Although "social groups usually share some interests," it is
not interests that make it a group; it is the shared set of practices
and the affinity that sharing creates. Group membership is, importantly, a matter of consciousness. But (although membership
must be self-conscious) it is not a matter of *joining* a group; "one
finds oneself as a member of a group, which one experiences as always already having been" (1990, 43–44, 172, 186 [on interests]
and 46 [on finding oneself]).

Examples of social groups that Young uses include Blacks,
women, gays and lesbians, and Native Americans. These examples
highlight her point that, despite our formal equality as citizens,
some groups are oppressed or disadvantaged in relation to others.
To ensure that diverse needs and interests are met and diverse perspectives included, Young argues, we need to institutionalize
mechanisms for listening to voices that might otherwise be ob-
scured. She proposes group representation as such a mechanism.
Group representation includes "self-organization of group members," "group analysis and group generation of policy proposals,"
and "group veto power regarding specific policies that affect a

[15] It is through this understanding of group difference as social and relational
that Young hopes to counter the stigma of "otherness" attached to difference
(168–172).

group directly."[16] This is not merely a return to interest group politics, for groups must engage in public deliberation, and thus must express "group needs and interests in terms that appeal to justice, that transform an 'I want' into an 'I am entitled to'" (1990, 184–185).

Young's articulation of "the politics of difference" and her concept of group representation is an inventive and intriguing attempt to combine citizenship and group identity. But there are difficulties in thinking about groups and group membership that Young does not confront, and that make institutionalizing group differences problematic. There are two problems here. One has to do with Young's definition of social groups and the consequences she draws from that definition. The other has to do with her notion that we can define a problem as exclusively a matter of concern for a particular group (see the "group veto power" clause above). It seems possible that the group's veto power would vitiate the need to persuade others of the justness of a group's claim. The proposed instances of veto power that Young mentions do at first seem just, for example, "reproductive rights policy for women, or land use policy for Indian reservations." However, to define these as matters for a particular group's veto ignores that these conflicts are to an important extent *over* who is affected (and how) by such policies. (The arguments of antiabortion activists, for example, question precisely the idea that abortion is a decision that affects only the woman seeking an abortion.) This is to say that Young, in her laudable attempt to attend to social groups as multiple publics, ignores that such groups exist in a common world.

I will return to this point later in the chapter; let me first examine the difficulties with Young's definition of groups. I begin by questioning whether in fact shared practices or "ways of life" can be identified for many of the groups Young notes. For example, what set of practices do women in the United States (of all races, classes, sexualities) share? Housekeeping and child care are two possibilities, but of course not all women engage in these activities (although it is probably fair to say that most are socialized to do so). Do African Americans across classes share the same set of cultural

---

[16]Young argues that this involvement in the policy process is likely to protect a group from the negative consequences of asserting group difference, the possibility that it will be used to justify their exclusion (185).

forms, or Native Americans across tribal differences? Or can gays
and lesbians who engage in sadomasochism, butch-femme, or drag
be said to share a set of practices or a way of life with gays and lesbians who explicitly reject such practices?

Second, even if social groups could be delineated by their practices or cultural forms, the two components Young uses to define
groups (cultural practices on one hand and affinity on the other)
do not always occur in tandem, as she assumes. Students of feminist
movements know that participating in "women's work" (or whatever activities constitute women's "set of practices") does not automatically result in an affinity for other women, or a sense of
"woman" as one's salient social identity. The politics of group membership are more complicated than this (even if, as Young suggests,
we use institutionalized consciousness raising as a politicizing strategy [1990, 153–155]). Let us consider appearance in the public
realm. Young eschews criteria like (for example) skin color to designate African Americans as a social group, for "some persons
whose skin color is fairly light . . . identify themselves as Black" (44).
True, nor do all people with dark skin necessarily feel affinity for
African Americans. In this social context, however, having a certain
shade of dark skin does generally mean that one will be perceived
as Black, and having light skin means that one can be taken for
white. Similarly, on many occasions, women are seen publicly and
legislated for as mothers or potential mothers, regardless of their
set of practices or affinities. The point is that how we are perceived
(in the sense of how we are "grouped") is not necessarily coincident
with our own sense of membership or affinity. But how we are perceived has everything to do with how we are treated—for example,
whether we are oppressed or discriminated against.

In Young's argument, it is oppression that makes group difference political; group representation is necessary specifically for
oppressed groups (1990, 187). But then the need for group representation comes from the fact that members share something like
an experience of domination that leads (in indeterminate ways) to
self-consciously shared interests, needs, or political purposes—not
necessarily a way of life or a sense of affinity. Yet this commonality is
not invoked in defining a group, as though it is somehow automatically derived from the other components of group definition. The
problem with Young's articulation of group representation in a het-

erogeneous public is that it takes group oppression and group
affinity as coincident, and thus argues that a liberatory understanding of the relationship of identity and politics relies on reclaiming and revaluing the very identity that social structures and
social perception impose upon us. This may be an important and
empowering strategy, and Young is right that many contemporary
political struggles have employed it in a desire to redefine in a positive way the identity that has been used to oppress them.[17] But
there are two related dangers in Young's approach to the relationship between social group identity and politics. It assumes that having a particular identity (being part of a particular group) leads
automatically to a particular stance, interest, or opinion. I am not
claiming that Young ignores the possibility of conflict within
groups, for she certainly does not. But for there to be a point to the
political representation of groups, there must be some *political*
commonality (why would a "sense of affinity" need political representation?). Needs, interests, and opinions are what require political representation—thus Young must be assuming that group
identity leads to some commonality of these. The second problem
is then that this argument assumes homogeneity within the group,
based on this shared identity.

Shane Phelan's study of "identity politics" in the lesbian feminist community shows us some of the antipolitical implications of
such an assumption of homogeneity (which assumption replicates
the tendency of the dominant culture to reduce members of oppressed groups to a monolithic unity). She first identifies the political value of a focus on identity: lesbian feminists used their identity
and experience as lesbians as a lens through which to articulate
new conceptions of oppression and power.[18] For example, at a time
when the liberal defense of homosexuality was based on the sanctity
of private sexual relations, lesbians challenged this separation of
public and private by arguing that their oppression was not merely
a legal phenomenon. Rather, the personal realm of (heterosexual
constructions of) family, love, and home was "riddled with power

[17] E.g., the revaluation of African American and Native American culture and
identity or the reclaiming of the label "dyke" as part of a movement toward positive
lesbian self-expression. See Young 1990, 157–162.

[18] As did the feminist movement as a whole, using the identity of "women" and
the phrase "the personal is political." See, e.g., Evans 1979; Eisenstein 1983.

relations" that were expressions of social power—that is, power as experienced and exercised outside of formal political institutions (Phelan 1989, chap. 1).

This understanding of the significance of "the personal" led lesbians to focus on creating personal relationships that did not replicate but subverted oppressive social power. The insights possible through recognizing the political significance of personal identity were soon distorted, Phelan argues, as lesbian feminists blurred any distinction between the personal and the political, between self and politics: "This collapse of politics results in the perception of one's sexuality as a matter of politics, not just at the level of *implication*—certain relations may lead one to make particular alliances, to view one's public interests in a certain way—but at that of *expression*. . . . One's body and its desires become a more reliable guide to one's loyalties than words or public deeds" (1989, 49). Thus one's political opinions were taken to be defined by one's identity, which was in turn defined by desire. Speaking was not the practice of deliberation, but rather an act of "empowered truth" by an authentic, essential lesbian self. The kind of community based on this understanding of self has no room for differences; differences of opinion cannot even be conceptualized. Not surprisingly, the presumed homogeneity of the lesbian community was challenged through an argument about different *desires*, when lesbians engaged in sadomasochistic practices began to articulate a different conception of lesbian desire and identity. Ironically, other lesbian feminists, whose politicization had involved resisting enforced definitions of lesbian identity, denied that such persons and practices could be part of lesbianism (Phelan 1989, chaps. 4–6, 8).

Phelan's conclusion is that a focus on identity led to the creation of a narrowly defined community at the expense of "politics as the art of living together," a politics concerned with "words and public deeds."[19] The solution is not to ignore identity but to relate it to politics in a somehow different way: "Identity politics does mean building our public action on who we are and how that iden-

---

[19] hooks makes a similar criticism of feminism in general when she argues that often the focus on identity "was not to radically change our relationship to self and identity, to educate for critical consciousness, to become politically engaged and committed, but to explore one's identity, to affirm and assert the primacy of the self as it already existed" (1989, 106).

tity fits into and does not fit into our society. . . . Politics that ignores our identities, that makes them 'private,' is useless, but non-negotiable identities will enslave us whether they are imposed from within or without" (1989, 170).

I am not arguing that Young's schema imposes such non-negotiable identities, but I think there is an important dynamic here to which she does not give sufficient attention. As other feminist writers analyzing race, class, and sexuality argue, internal standards of membership that presume a homogenous community (either in terms of behavior or of political stance) are themselves disempowering. The criticism of the feminist movement made by women of color is a well-known example, and there are many other such criticisms. Lorde describes the way in which lesbianism is falsely assumed not to be part of the Black experience or community, and argues that the heterosexism and homophobia that result are a dangerous waste of Black political energy (1989, 19–26). Barbara Christian analyzes the consequences of the Black Arts Movement's narrow prescription of what counted as Black language and art, and Gloria Anzaldúa points out that despite the diversity of languages and backgrounds that are present among Chicanos, "we oppress each other trying to out-Chicano each other, vying to be the 'real' Chicanas" (Anzaldúa 1987, 58; Christian 1990, 340–341). The danger of a focus on "racial purity" or other standards of membership is a political danger: as Anzaldúa says, "denying the reality of who we are destroys the basis needed from which to talk honestly and deeply about the issues between us" (1990c, 143–146).[20]

So once the public "who" is understood to include group membership, what immediately complicates things is not simply individual uniqueness, but the fact of multiple group memberships. What does it mean to, as Phelan urges, build our public actions on who we are? How (in Young's schema) does one participate as a Black lesbian, a white working-class woman, a middle-class Native American man? How does one articulate a public self given these multiple loyalties?[21] Young certainly recognizes the existence of such multiple affinities and the conflict that can result, but she does not use the fact of mul-

---

[20] See also Morales 1983 and Zook 1990, 85–96.

[21] The answer to this question makes a difference for how we are grouped politically; see Spelman's "doors" discussion (1988, 144–153).

tiplicity to question the institutionalization of groups, or to analyze the difficulties inherent in using them as a basis for a public self.[22]

At this juncture in the argument, in the face of these difficulties, contemporary feminist theory gives us two sets of analytic resources with which to proceed. The first approach would argue that these difficulties indicate the contradictions inherent in any kind of identity politics, for identity works to spawn the very deviations it prohibits. These contradictions stem from the fact that the very notion of identity exists only as a production and performance of a social-symbolic order (a power/knowledge regime, culture, discourse, the Law). It is not simply that desires do not automatically translate into a politics, as Phelan contends; rather, the argument here is that the very belief that our desires are "ours," that there is an essential self to have these desires, and that we can choose or achieve identification, is an effect of power.

I am referring, of course, to feminist work informed by poststructuralist theories. In the next section, I analyze this approach to identity and politics, focusing primarily on the work of Judith Butler. I attempt to describe the insights of this work and at the same time present an argument for turning in the second (not wholly unrelated) direction that feminist theory offers, to the work of Gloria Anzaldúa and other feminist analysts of race, class, gender, and sexuality. These latter theorists, I argue, provide a conceptual and linguistic framework for thinking about identity and politics, one that is oriented toward Young's goal of a heterogeneous participatory public and is attentive to the formation of identities in the context of power. This understanding does not rely on similar cultural forms but on the interactive agency of citizens, and expands the possibility of joining with others in political action. Before proceeding on this path, however, it is necessary to engage the challenges to both this project and to Young's own that are implicit in poststructuralist thinking.

THE "FICTION" OF IDENTITY

In this section, I describe an approach I am not sure what to call. That is, I hesitate over what term to use in the highly charged political theoretical atmosphere that surrounds such work: poststructural-

---

[22] She hypothesizes that some affinities may be more "salient" than others at different times in one's life (1990, 172–173).

ism, postmodernism, deconstruction, antifoundationalism, constructivism, and so on. I do avoid "postmodernism" because, as Butler (1992) argues, that phrase in particular seems to get used as an all-purpose antihero.[23] "Poststructuralism," although certainly open to the same problems, seems to me more useful in describing a specific trajectory of intellectual thought, one distinguished by critical engagement with Foucault, Lévi-Strauss, Lacan, and Irigaray, among others. This trajectory is characterized by its understanding of power as productive of subjectivity and its consequent focus on the radically constructed and essentially fictive nature of "the subject." The significance for politics in this reconceptualization of power is that power is not something wielded by autonomous subjects; rather, through power, subjectivity itself is created (which is to say beings are created who understand themselves to be certain kinds of subjects).

I do not focus here on poststructuralist thought in general, but on the work of feminists who argue that poststructuralist understandings of identity are useful—in fact necessary—for the pursuit of feminist and other radical political commitments.[24] I make this point explicitly in an attempt to distance myself from the frequently made criticism that poststructuralism makes politics impossible, that it does away with the subject, does away with agency, and just when oppressed peoples are gaining voices. To put it simply, I do not see how these criticisms can be made against feminist poststructuralists; I take seriously—which is to say, I read them as taking seriously—their political aims and purposes and the passion against oppression which is evident in their work. (See, for example, Judith Butler's often moving introduction to *Bodies That Matter*.)[25] Nevertheless, I am deeply critical of their implicit rejection of a positive, liberatory understanding of the relationship between identity and politics, and their lack of attention to *interaction*.

[23] Ironically, "identity politics" often suffers the same treatment; see Bickford 1994.

[24] For a sample of feminist voyagers along this trajectory, see *Feminists Theorize the Political*, edited by Judith Butler and Joan W. Scott, and Riley 1988. For an overview of feminist debates about these issues, see *Feminism/Postmodernism*, edited by Linda Nicholson, and *Destabilizing Theory*, edited by Michèle Barrett and Anne Phillips. See also Ferguson 1993, who provides an insightful analysis of various feminist configurations of subjectivity (including poststructuralist ones) and argues for holding them together in tension through an "ironic" orientation to identity and politics.

[25] For another example, see Marcus 1992, which draws on poststructuralist thinking in articulating a serious and significant feminist political analysis of rape.

My analysis focuses primarily on Judith Butler's sophisticated and influential work on gender identity, "the subject," and the materiality of bodies. This work shares a central theme, which briefly put is something like this: that which is taken to be the necessary prerequisite for politics—for example, gender identity and female bodies for feminists—is itself a political construction. Although poststructuralists are often faulted for "doing away with the subject," Butler rightly points out that "to take the subject as a political problematic is not the same as doing away with the subject" (1992, 15). And she makes a similar point with specific regard to identity: "The deconstruction of identity is not the deconstruction of politics; rather, it establishes as political the very terms through which identity is articulated" (1990, 148; see also 1993, 122–123, and Scott 1992).

For Butler, to "establish as political" means to reveal the nonnatural and discursive character of even the phenomena that we take to be prior to any articulation. For example, common feminist arguments treat gender as a culturally constructed phenomenon grafted onto naturally sexed bodies; the point is that although sexual differences exist, they do not require the attributes of gender that are attached to them. Butler argues that this is itself a discursive move that constructs "sex" as beyond or prior to discourse. Such a move does not actually place sex outside of discourse; the effect is rather that sex gets established, within discourse, as "outside," as natural—and thus "can be understood in some sense to necessitate" gender and desire (1990, 7, 129, 76–77, 22). The discursive construction of this necessity entrenches "the heterosexual matrix," the seemingly natural unity of sex, gender, and desire (e.g., female sex, feminine gender, men as the object of desire/male sex, masculine gender, women as the object of desire [1990, 6–7, 22]).

Butler insists that just as there is no essential presocial gender, neither is there a prediscursive sex, which is not to say that bodies do not exist. Her point is rather that there is no way in which we can refer to "indisputable" things about bodily sex—a clitoris, say, or some chromosomes—that is not at the same time a construction, a discursive invocation of that sex and that body (1993, 10). To say that certain things about sex are undeniable can be accomplished only through saying them; and in the saying of them, we are constituting some version of sex (in this case, inside discourse as outside). Butler does not mean that our saying is the sole and originary cause that "exhaustively composes" that sex (1993, 10–12); bodies do not fall from our mouths when we speak about them. She does mean that all utterances are performative, that what we say matters precisely because it *makes* certain bodies matter and others not matter.

In other words, it is gender, sociocultural construction, "all the way down." In rethinking gender in this more comprehensive way, Butler invokes Simone de Beauvoir: "If gender is something that one becomes . . . then gender is itself a kind of becoming or activity" (1990, 112). It is neither an inner essence nor something imposed on an inner essence; it is performative, which is to say that it is constituted by acts that are repeated over and over, acts that are designed to create the illusion that they come from within, from a coherent inner identity. Gender is then not "a stable identity or locus of agency from which various acts follow; rather, gender is . . . instituted in an exterior space through a *stylized repetition of acts*" (1990, 136–141). And, since gender goes all the way down, the very materiality of bodies is "*a process of materialization that stabilizes over time to produce the effect of boundary, fixity, and surface we call matter*" (1993, 9). That process is one Butler calls "performativity as citationality"; just as the social-symbolic order (the "Law") is produced and entrenched through continued reference to it, matter achieves being and shape through being repeatedly cited—as there, as this (1993, 12–15).

There is a serious danger in not recognizing the performativity of gender, Butler argues, for to represent something as beyond or before discourse is to preclude it from being subject to political contestation and change. For Butler, it is the very repetitiveness of the process that consolidates identities and materializes bodies that makes it possible to expose that process as a constructed ideal, to render it political (1990, 136–147; 1993, 10, 45; 1992, 13–16). Each repetition is not identical and thus opens a gap for a subversive reenactment, room for "error." What is subversive is that which throws into relief the constructed and performative nature of identity; parody, and in terms of gender identity, drag. Drag mocks gender ideals precisely by reenacting them: "In imitating gender, drag implicitly reveals the imitative structure of gender itself—as well as its contingency" (1990, 137). Drag is not necessarily and always subversive; it is so only to the extent that it "disputes heterosexuality's claim on naturalness and originality" (1993, 125).

Parody as political contestation takes into account the fact that even our resistant action is always within a field of power that constitutes us. Thus Butler rejects the notion that we can simply transcend or refuse the activities that constitute us, that we can overcome our implication in power. Gender identity is "the forcible approximation of a norm one never chooses, a norm that chooses us, but which we occupy, reverse, resignify to the extent that the norm fails to determine us completely" (1993, 127).[26] Such contestation is "a difficult labor of forging a future from resources inevitably impure" (1993, 241).

Despite the differences in theoretical language, Butler's argument is in some ways compatible with the point I made earlier, that identity is constraining *and* enabling, and with Arendt's argument that humans are both creative and conditioned beings. But note the crucial dissimilarities. Butler's point is that we are deeply determined by processes that have no specific creator, but we are capable of some kind of action nonetheless; Arendt stresses that we are distinguished by our creative capacities, yet we are also conditioned by what we create. There is a reversal in what kind of existence is taken to be primary—or perhaps what kind of power—and a marked difference in what the possibilities for action are.

We can locate these differences more specifically by looking to where Butler appears to draw the limits of politics. To "politicize" identity is for Butler to "denaturalize" it; she treats exposing the lie of the natural and normal as the primary political gesture (see esp. 1990, 142–149). This is so for deeply normative reasons; I would argue that for Butler, denaturalization is the primary political purpose because the primary danger lies in the existence of naturalized bodies/identities, because in the production of these "normal" bodies some bodies get produced that do not matter, get produced *as not mattering*, as abject rather than subject (1993, 3–4, 16).

In some ways, then, Butler ends up regarding identity itself as a political trap (e.g., 1990, 147). The only way to politicize it is to reveal its fictive and fabricated character, and though those activities

---

[26] Butler's brilliant analysis of butch/femme provides another concrete example of this resignification. We cannot escape the heterosexual matrix in which we all perform, but we unsettle its coherence by giving "erotic significance" to unexpected combinations and juxtapositions—e.g., female sex, masculine identity, women as the object of desire. "As one lesbian femme explained, she likes her boys to be girls, meaning that 'being a girl' contextualizes and resignifies 'masculinity' in a butch identity" (1990, 123, 6–7, 22).

inevitably cite the ideal again, they may also "force a radical rearticulation of what qualifies as bodies that matter, ways of living that count as 'life'" (1993, 16). But is exposing the constructedness of identity the only rearticulation possible, the only political act? Although at one point Butler suggests affirming "identities that are alternately instituted and relinquished according to the purposes at hand" (1990, 16), in general she endorses the option of rejecting and unsettling—not mobilizing—the construct of identity. As Fraser aptly puts it, "at the deepest level, [Butler] understands women's liberation as liberation *from* identity" (1991, 175). Yet mobilizing identity need not mean invoking an originary subject, before or beyond discourse, self-transparent, prior to the activities that produce it. As I will argue below, there are other ways of relating identity and politics that neither regard identity as fixed and prediscursive nor eschew identity as a trap. But before I trace out those relations, I have to confront a Butlerian question: why should we bother? Why is it important to be able to mobilize identity as a political phenomenon in this way?

To put it simply: because political purposes and aims are articulated by beings who understand themselves as human subjects with various social identities. This bald assertion does not preclude a poststructuralist analysis of subjectivation, nor does it imply that these beings are unreflective about their own subjectivity and the power relations in which it forms. It is just that political aims and purposes arise through being articulated by beings who understand themselves as various kinds of human subjects. I am not arguing that those identities are uncomplicatedly the *source* of these aims; I mean simply that these aims appear in public space through people speaking.[27] And I maintain that people generally understand themselves as both culturally constituted and capable of agency, with identities that they experience as both empowering and constraining. Of course that experience and identity are constructed for us, we are ourselves constructed as an "us" and as an "I"; contemporary feminists have known that since the earliest days of consciousness raising. Even so: *here we are*, and it is far from clear that it is politi-

---

[27] Making this point shifts even my language away from Butler's, which Fraser has criticized as "deeply anti-humanist." Such language "is far enough removed from our everyday ways of talking and thinking about ourselves to require some justification" (Fraser 1991, 172).

cally helpful to assume that constraint has ontological primacy, because it is far from clear that revealing "the lie of the natural" is the
only important political act.

Perhaps precisely because we are so deeply subjectivated, we
cannot experience the absence of identity except as extremely
painful and virtually unlivable (McGowan 1991, 245–247). Certainly, a lack of identity is constructed within our social-symbolic order *as* unlivable, but that does not mean that it can be rendered
livable any more than something constructed as livable must for
that reason be rejected. I think it is highly unlikely that the speaking "I" (the subject, women, whatever) comes from an internal
essence, or that we can reconstruct ourselves from whole untainted
cloth, outside "the Law"—although I do not see how we could ever
know for sure. But there is clearly room for theoretical and political
argument about the consequences of such an approach; indeed,
such arguments have resulted in the widespread rejection of certain early cultural feminist theories and strategies. Yet it seems
equally misguided to think that the risk of being tainted, the un-
availability of whole cloth, requires a refusal of the activities of reconstruction, although here too there is room for political and
theoretical debate. My argument is that my experienced identity
carries within it constraint and oppression *and also* offers a source
(offers *my* source) for criticism and action. The task, then, is not
simply to expose the constructions that we take as prediscursive,
but to decide what constructions might be part of better forms of
life.[28]

I think Butler may emphasize politics as parodic and denatu-
ralizing because, oddly enough, it is a safer move. Taking identity
and trying to do something with it besides exposure and parody
runs the risk of obedience to the Law; sheer transgression is less
likely to end up "reidealizing" the sexual norms it wants to subvert.
But this undefended suspicion leads to a restricted notion of politics. Simply because (to use Butler's language) a certain kind of
repetition is encouraged and enforced does not automatically

[28] As John McGowan has argued, the tendency of postmodernist texts to focus
solely on the former task bespeaks a commitment to an ideal of negative freedom
and a model of alienation, a kind of "despondent romanticism" (1991). See also his
trenchant criticism of Butler's refusal to theorize the norms that might guide political practice (1993).

mean that citing it is bad; just because a certain kind of repetition is encouraged and enforced need not preclude us from arguing about whether or not it is what we want. Political actors have to run those risks, to argue and make judgments about what actions will lead to better forms of life and more just social orders. What Butler implies but does not argue is that somehow this one transgressive act (parody) will get us there. She rejects "the grammar of the subject" (1993, 9); but she has given no argument for *why* this is the better tack to take, why parodying identity is a more efficacious political act. Talk about putting identity beyond political contestation!

Yet, in defense of Butler, one might argue that she does not in fact require a refusal of the activities of reconstruction. She and other feminists influenced by poststructuralism are simply saying that the only way to perform that reconstruction is in a parodic or ironic way—in a way that "flags" the "provisionality of categories," that provides "signposts" that continually indicate the incompleteness of those categories (Ferguson 1993, 86–91).[29] This emphasis on irony and parody chimes with those theorists who encourage the political use of the "fiction" of identity. We may realize there is no such thing as "women," but decide that "we have a political necessity for fiction and unity" (Martin 1982, 14–16). As Denise Riley argues, "It is compatible to suggest that 'women' don't exist—while maintaining a politics of 'as if they existed'—since the world behaves as if they unambiguously did" (1988, 112).[30]

I have argued elsewhere (1993) that this stance implies a rejection of a certain connection between theory and practice, a rejection I find troubling.[31] And it is not clear to me what kinds of political actions would count as ironic, what would highlight the "as if" character of the person acting (and whether people who take political action could be persuaded that it makes sense to act "as if" from a particular identity, a particular sense of self). And yet I

[29] But see also Biddy Martin's brilliant use of Butler's framework, not to proliferate or unsettle or parody identities, but to disclose the complexity of gender configurations that already exist (1992).

[30] Diana Fuss is insightful and ambivalent on this issue (1989, esp. chaps. 6 and 7).

[31] A similar discontent with this disjuncture between theory and practice has begun to appear in the realm of queer theory; see Warner 1993, Seidman 1993, and Duggan 1994.

would not distance these arguments from my own too much. The difference lies, as the reader will see, in the distinction between regarding identity as fictive, and regarding it as active and created. The latter does not require a self-distancing and ironic orientation to politics (but does not preclude it either); it leaves room for a multiplicity of modes of political action and for an enabling understanding of identity and politics. But this requires a different theoretical approach and a different vocabulary in which to think and act; I suggest that the feminist writers discussed in the next section offer such an approach and such a vocabulary.

Criticizing particular constructions of political identity does not mean that we are restricted to parody, that we have to search for a "postidentitarian" politics (Patton 1993) or suffer a rupture between theorizing in which we reject "identity" and politics in which we invoke it. My argument about identity is something like Diana Fuss's argument (1989) about essentialism: it is neither automatically liberatory nor inherently oppressive. There are good and bad versions and uses of identity, and enabling and debilitating constructions of the relationship between identity and politics. And the only way we have to decide about these versions and uses is politics. This is to say that "identity" is political not just because it is non-natural, but because it is something we can argue about. In such an argument, we take both the risk of being duped and the responsibility of trying not to be.

Despite her focus on political action as contestation, what is interestingly and problematically absent in Butler's work is an understanding of collective argument, of political contestation as a communicative performance that happens in the presence of others. For Butler, political action seems largely to be between the self and the Law, not *between selves* (even selves understood as produced by and producing that Law). This may politicize subjectivity in one way, but it virtually ignores intersubjectivity, the presence of others and the attempt to communicate with them. This absence is perhaps unavoidable because, for all her emphasis on performance, Butler deeply mistrusts the *desire* for nonparodic performance, the desire for public appearance and purposive action—that is, the desire for politics.[32]

---

[32] These last sentences rely on John McGowan's apt formulation.

The analysis in the next section takes up and mobilizes themes that Butler would not. What I have tried to do here is make an argument for theorizing in a way that allows me to pursue these themes, which have to do with how we can conceptualize democratic citizenship in a way that takes seriously group identities. I will argue for a conception of identity and politics that does not regard identity as transparent, fixed, unitary—or as a trap—or as a fiction. I draw this conception from the work of feminists who take seriously both the socially constituted nature of identity and the desire for public appearance. On this account, we might say, identity is not an *essential* characteristic, but it is an existential one. It is the mode in which we exist, a mode subject to change and critique, but which critique cannot itself be had by refusing to run the risks inherent in our existential condition. What characterizes our existential condition, for these feminists as well as for Arendt, is the presence of others. There are risks and possibilities inherent in acting together that Butler does not help us think about, but the feminists discussed below can, precisely because they analyze the active and intersubjective character of identity.

MAKING FACES: THE PARADOX OF PUBLIC APPEARANCE

My contention above was that Young's laudable attempt to create a heterogeneous participatory public in the end relied on definitions of group identity that did not do justice to the multiplicity and indeterminacy of group identity. These difficulties are not a reason for abandoning Young's project of creating a heterogeneous participatory public; rather, in continuing it I turn to the work of Anzaldúa and others, who take this multiplicity of "affinities" as the basis for articulating an alternative understanding of identity and politics.

The feminist analysts of race, class, gender, and sexuality that I discuss below are often read simply as critics of racism and class discrimination in feminist movements. Such readings overlook the fact that these writers are engaged in a theoretical endeavor to analyze what identity means for feminist political action *as interaction*.[33] Anzaldúa and the other feminist writers I draw upon propose

---

[33] See Alarcón 1990 for a discussion of various uses of *This Bridge Called My Back*, all of which ignore the volume's theoretical endeavors.

a more fluid connection between social identities and political action. I will argue that reading these theorists in response to Young, and through the lens of an Arendtian version of political action, can provide us with a conception of democratic interaction between citizens with diverse social identities.

For these writers, both "self" and "others" are socially grouped and grounded in ways that have consequences for our public identities. Although they hold that social identities influence not simply how we speak but what we have to say, they question a linkage that relies on the singularity of identity and the unity of political community, for such a conception does not do justice to the complex selves that we are. Anzaldúa writes: " 'Your allegiance is to La Raza, the Chicano movement,' say the members of my race. 'Your allegiance is to the Third World,' say my Black and Asian friends. 'Your allegiance is to your gender, to women,' say the feminists. Then there's my allegiance to the Gay movement, to the socialist revolution, to the New Age, to magic and the occult. . . . They would chop me up into little fragments and tag each piece with a label" (1983, 205).

Norma Alarcón, in her analysis of *Bridge*, notes as a common theme this recognition that the subjectivity of women of color is "multiple-voiced," its very multiplicity "lived in resistance to competing notions for one's allegiance or self-identification" (1990, 365–366). Anzaldúa's response to this fragmenting competition is not to accept the implied contradictions but rather to assert the connections: "Only your labels split me." Cherríe Moraga agrees: "What is my responsibility to my roots—both white and brown, Spanish-speaking and English? I am a woman with a foot in both worlds; and I refuse the split." And María Lugones insists, "We want to be seen unbroken, we want to break cracked mirrors that show us in many separate *unconnected* fragments" (Anzaldúa 1983, 205; Moraga 1983, 34; Lugones 1990a, 47).[34]

So the challenge that multiple identities present is not answered by a proliferation of ever more narrowly defined communities, and there is more going on here than embracing "fractured identities," as Sandra Harding would have it.[35] Yet neither is there a rejection of

[34] See also Morales 1983 and Lorde 1984, 120–121.

[35] Harding is right, of course, that such writers are challenging the unity of identity, but their challenges go further than an "exhilaration" in the "politics of hyphenization" (1986, 163–164).

identity as always restrictive and therefore suspect. There is rather an insistence on the multiplicity of identity, concomitant with a refusal of fragmentation, which provides an important alternative for thinking about the self as citizen, one that challenges neat "categories of marginality" and enables political action.[36]

This alternative first begins to take shape in the recognition that the political importance of a multiple-voiced consciousness, a plural self, is that it allows perception from a variety of perspectives (Anzaldúa 1990b, xxvii; and 1987, 79–80). An important example comes from Anzaldúa's discussion of "*la mestiza.*" *La mestiza* occupies locations that are regarded as opposed, her multiple identities do not peacefully coexist: "The clash of voices results in mental and emotional states of perplexity . . . *la mestiza* undergoes a struggle of flesh, a struggle of borders, an inner war. Like all people, we perceive the version of reality that our culture communicates. Like others having or living in more than one culture, we get multiple, often opposing messages. The coming together of two self-consistent but habitually incompatible frames of reference causes *un choque*, a cultural collision" (1987, 78).[37] Existing as a plural self is not just a matter of "celebrating" differences; it is a struggle among competing perspectives within oneself (as well as among groups competing for one's loyalties). One result of this struggle can be what Anzaldúa calls a "counterstance," simple defiance of "the dominant culture's views and beliefs." Although a counterstance can be liberating, it is limited; it is constrained by and "dependent on what it is reacting against." (This seems to me to be an argument against simply reclaiming conventionally constructed identities or constructing apparently transcendent ones.) Moving beyond that step means deciding "to act and not to react." What is created by that action is an "assembly," but not one "where separated pieces merely come together. Nor is it a balancing of opposing powers. In attempting to work out a synthesis, the self has added a third element which is greater than the sum of its severed parts. That third element is a new consciousness—a mestiza consciousness—and though it is a source of intense pain, its energy comes from contin-

---

[36] The phrase "categories of marginality" is Anzaldúa's (1990b, xvi).

[37] The three specific cultures that *la mestiza* "straddles" are white culture, Mexican culture, and indigenous culture.

ual creative motion that keeps breaking down the unitary aspect of
each new paradigm" (Anzaldúa 1987, 78–80).

La mestiza is a creative agent; the necessity of "switching modes"
is transformed into an emancipatory exercise of the capacity to
shift perspectives. As in Arendt's representative thinking, the result
is not a blending of views or a taking on of any particular view, but
the creation of a new view. "Refusing the split" means creating from
one's multiple loyalties a (nonfragmented but not complacent)
public self with a new consciousness, a new view, a new opinion.
The emphasis on struggle and work indicates that such a creation
requires courage—courage to be open to the possibilities of con-
tradiction and conflict within oneself, to hear different voices and
see from different vantage points, but to move beyond those shared
vantage points to a unique view. This "moving beyond" does not
mean making our social identities irrelevant. Our social identities
provide the fuel for the creative motion, our locatedness points us
toward the possibility of traveling and causes us to think about the
materials and activities, the desires and demands, out of which
identity is created.

An alternative reading of Anzaldúa's analysis here might argue
that the significance of the mestiza is her particular position of marginality, and not the more general capacity to shift perspectives. Anzaldúa's writing does sometimes indicate that the mestiza, from her
position in the borderlands, has a privileged vantage point.[38] Elsewhere, however, it seems that Anzaldúa thinks of mestiza consciousness as a more generally applicable kind of political thinking
that we can all learn, for it highlights a creative capacity present in
all. Multiplicity of self and the ability to shift perspectives are not
limited only to members of certain groups. This kind of thinking
involves both recognizing the specificity of one's experience (that
we are all raced, classed, and gendered in particular ways) and challenging the conventional constructions of that experience, those

---

[38] E.g., when she says (1987, 80) that the mestiza is the "officiating priestess at
the crossroads." On this reading, her claim resembles Hartsock's (1985) thinking
about "standpoints." Collins's argument about the perspectives of Black women
seems open to this dual interpretation as well; she points out that Black women's political and economic position has often made them present, yet marginalized, in a variety of communities, and she argues for the importance of the angle of vision
granted by virtue of being an "outsider-within" (1991, 11–13).

identities (Anzaldúa 1987, 83–86). For example, for a white woman
to form an opinion about racial issues would involve not merely
imagining the point of view of people of other races, but recognizing her own racial experience. She must become, in Lugones's
words, "a self-conscious critical practitioner of her culture and a
self-conscious and critical member of the racial state . . . such thinking is possible because she is a participant in both." Without such
recognition, "you do not see me because you do not see yourself
and you do not see yourself because you declare yourself outside of
culture" (Lugones 1990a, 48–51).[39]

Like Arendt's representative thinking, this shifting of perspectives seems mostly about internal opinion formation; but we have a
political need to listen to those whose vantage points we do not
share.[40] There is an implicit move in Anzaldúa's work, from subjective to intersubjective creative action. She switches from a personi-
fication—*la mestiza*—to an activity: making faces. In this later work,
identity is something created, constructed in the presence of others—and largely through words (speech and writing).

"Making faces" is Anzaldúa's "metaphor for constructing one's
identity." These faces are different from the masks "others have imposed on us," for such masks keep us fragmented: "After years of
wearing masks we may become just a series of roles, the constellated
self limping along with its broken limbs." Breaking through these
masks is not, for Anzaldúa, a matter of revealing one's true inner
nature, an essential self; rather we "*remake* anew both inner and
outer faces" (1990b, xv–xvi, my emphasis; note the distinction between private and public selves). Identity is then a matter of active
creation, of "agency." This creation happens through speech and
action: "According to the ancient *nahuas*, one was put on earth to
create one's 'face' (body) and 'heart' (soul). To them, the soul was
a speaker of words and the body a doer of deeds. Soul and body,
words and actions are embodied in Moyocoyani, one of the names
of the Creator in the Aztec framework" (1990b, xvi). Speech and ac-

[39] Note here a kind of overlap with Butler, in the argument that this "putting
outside" or "placing beyond" (culture or discourse) is a move that thwarts politics.
[40] Anzaldúa believes that the dualities of male/female, white race/colored races
artificially split qualities that we all possess; we are "spawned out of similar souls"
(1987, 80, 84–85). But this does not lead her to argue that people need only to listen
to or discover internal voices, as her writings on coalition make clear (1990d).

tion here are entwined with embodiedness and embeddedness, with one's physical and social self, not simply as a constraint or a necessary condition, but as the material with which we create. Anzaldúa stresses the conscious making of identity, but such consciousness is not separate from the physical and social substance of our lives. This understanding gives rise to the possibility of a public identity that is more than just a string of labels, yet does not ignore the relevance to our lives of the groups those labels name.

This depiction of identity is suggestive not simply because of its stress on active construction, but also because of what is being constructed. A face is an outward appearance—"the world knows us by our faces" (Anzaldúa 1990b, xv)—we cannot see our own face, except in a mirror. A face is oriented toward others. Identity is not then a merely internal affair; it takes shape partly in appearing to others. The "face" metaphor is instructive because it both admits of a conscious expressiveness (I can to some extent compose my face to reflect or conceal what I want) but also an inescapable concreteness (my face is physically my face, its color, shape, its moles and markings and features undeniably mine).[41] "Face" is a particularly apt metaphor that stresses intersubjectivity and brings together—rather than regards as contradictory—our embeddedness in the socially constructed givens of our existence, and our capacity to present ourselves self-consciously in a way that engages but does not simply reflect those givens. This conception of identity—as actively created through being present in public—takes seriously the political significance of the connection between "what" and "who" we are; it obscures neither our distinctiveness nor our location in the world. As a political actor, I do not require a mask that conceals these givens; I require from others an attentiveness to what I do with them, a listening and a looking flexible enough to perceive my activity.

Agency and constraint meet here in the understanding that the self can appear in public only through the regard or attention of others, and that awareness of the attention of others can affect the creation/presentation of self (what Anzaldúa calls the "politics of address"). While "voice" is often used as a metaphor for identity,

---

[41] Unless I undergo plastic surgery, of course. For an interesting set of reflections on the connection between identity and face from the perspective of one undergoing reconstructive surgery, see Grealy 1993.

here it is also the actual means by which we create identity. And speaking is no less a matter of effortful construction than is "making faces," for there is an equivalent to the masking that screens our faces from others: "We cross or fall or are shoved into abysses whether we speak or remain silent. And when we do speak from the cracked spaces, it is *con voz del fondo del abismo*, a voice drowned out by white noise, distance, and the distancing by others who don't want to hear" (Anzaldúa 1990b, xxii). Yet there is not necessarily one inner natural voice that could sound through clearly and simply if it were not for distance and distancing. Our multiplicity means that there may be more than one voice which is "ours": "We sometimes have to choose with which voice (the voice of the dyke, the Chicana, the professor, the master), in which voice (first person, third, vernacular, formal) or in which language (Black English, Tex-Mex, Spanish, academese) to speak and write in" (Anzaldúa 1990b, xxiii).[42]

Given that speech is central to citizenship for many democratic theorists, how could citizenship ever have been thought to involve transcending particularity? My speech itself can reflect the particularities of my life, the groups of which I am a part, yet I use it self-consciously to express myself as a unique who. Language is the material that enables political action, the words, concepts, and expressive capacities that we put together to try to communicate something (and in the process, communicating ourselves). This may involve combining different "voices" or languages, in order to "refuse the split," to express our nonfragmented self (e.g., see Lugones 1990a, 46 and passim). How can either the content or the form of what we say not have anything to do with our social experiences in the world, especially since we make sense of those experiences through language?[43] Languages of course are not static; we

[42]See also Anzaldúa 1987, 58–59, where she argues that there is no one "authentic" Chicano language. Although it is true that Anzaldúa sometimes uses the language of "finding" or "discovering" a voice, I think her analysis of voice largely stresses choice and creation, although both are influenced by what materials we find most comfortable or most useful (that is, it is not a wholly unconstrained choice).

[43]For Arendt as well, identity and language were connected; "Germany for me means my mother tongue," she wrote Jaspers. "What remains is the language, and how important that is one learns only when, more nolens than volens, one speaks and writes other languages" (*AJ* 16, 70). Arendt learned English very well, and continued to write in German; but she could not, she said, work in both at the same time.

shape them as they shape us. The conditions of our lives (the groups of which we are a part, the "voices" in which we can speak) are part of what we draw from in political thinking. (Recall how Arendt's representative thinking is a dialogue between the "conditioned," located me and the thinking me.) The metaphor of "making" indicates that I start with certain living "materials" which I can gather up, reject, transform; but I can also travel elsewhere and find other materials. Neither my way of speaking nor the content of my opinions is determined by my social conditions, but neither do they simply sound out of thin air above or beyond the world.

Although she does not explicitly use the language of "citizenship," Anzaldúa's discussion of identity and communicative interaction in a sense integrates Aristotle and Arendt, for she directs us toward the kind of regard that takes into account both social conditions and human plurality. And feminist discussions of masking and not-hearing point out that the character of the distance between us is significant. There is not simply inevitable worldly distance (as Arendt would have it), but also "cracked spaces," the distancing and distorting haze.

Recognizing the effects of this haze means, as Anzaldúa indicates, making choices about how we speak. How we make those choices might depend on who we are talking with, in what context, and how we want to be heard. It depends, then—as Aristotle taught us—on who we are and on who our listeners are. A striking illustration of the "politics of address," and the difficulties of constructing a public identity in an inegalitarian context, comes from June Jordan's essay "Nobody Mean More to Me Than You and the Future Life of Willie Jordan." During a semester when Jordan was teaching a course on the art of Black English, the brother of a Black student in the class was killed by the police under questionable circumstances (he was shot in the back eight times while unarmed). Among the actions the class decided to take was to write individual letters of protest in Black English to the police and to the media, which letters would be "prefaced by an explanatory paragraph composed by the entire group." Now, Jordan writes, "the tactical question was this: Should the opening, group paragraph be written in Black English or Standard English?" I quote Jordan at length as she describes "one of the longest, most difficult hours of my own life":

> That one question contained several others, each of them extraordinarily painful to even contemplate. . . . Should we use the language of the killers—Standard English—in order to make our ideas acceptable to those controlling the killers? But wouldn't what we had to say be rejected, summarily, if we said it in our own language, the language of the victim, Reggie Jordan? But if we sought to express ourselves by abandoning our language wouldn't that mean our suicide on top of Reggie's murder? But if we expressed ourselves in our own language wouldn't that be suicidal to the wish to communicate with those, who, evidently, did not give a damn about us/Reggie/police violence in the Black community? (1985, 135)

In the end the class voted unanimously to use Black English in the opening paragraph. They decided it was the only way to express themselves with integrity, to "be who we been." Yet they felt certain that the decision had "doomed" their message (136). In this case, they felt, there was no voice in which they could speak that would both communicate themselves, and communicate to the others they wanted to address.

This example points to the difficulty of politics as a matter of communication among citizens with a variety of voices and languages in a context in which some are taken more seriously than others. Those who want their speech to be taken more seriously are not only concerned with getting *what* they have to say heard; they want to be able to be heard themselves, to engage in the practice of citizenship. It is precisely this difficulty which underscores that communicating politically is not just a matter of speaking in the "right" voice so that we will be heard (that voice may not express who we publicly are trying to be). This desire for recognition is not just a nebulous psychological want, less important somehow than real material needs and concrete obstacles. We can address those needs and obstacles politically only through acting together, and we can act together only if we pay attention to one another. To say that politics is not possible without this mutual recognition is to say that people who are not paid attention to do not get to participate equally in public argument *about* those real material needs and obstacles.

There is here an implicit agreement with Arendt, that appearing in the world through speech and action is a central human experience, and that the quality of the attention paid is central to that appearance. Just as speakers must reflect on how to speak (and what to say), listeners must be self-conscious about how they listen (and what they hear). Taking responsibility for listening, as an active and creative process, might serve to undermine certain hierarchies of language and voice. If feminist theorists are right that "silence and silencing begins with the dominating enforcement of linguistic conventions" (Alarcón 1990, 363)—that is, if oppression happens partly through not hearing certain kinds of expressions from certain kinds of people—then perhaps the reverse is true as well: a particular kind of listening can serve to break up linguistic conventions and create a public realm where a plurality of voices, faces, and languages can be heard and seen and spoken.[44] The goal here is not that each person will be heard in some sort of authentic pristine clarity, but that no person will have less control than anyone else, no one more liable to being distorted than any other.

This may seem an oddly negative way to phrase a question of equality. The public realm is an arena of equality, but also an arena of struggle. With Anzaldúa and others, we can recast Arendt's agonal struggle for distinction as a struggle for public identity, understood as a work of the self in the presence of others. But there is a crucial Arendtian corollary to this understanding, which is often not explicitly discussed in feminist work. The very need to challenge unjust ways of seeing can lead to frustration with the opacity and distance that are not necessarily the results of oppression but rather the inevitable accompaniments of plurality. It is tempting to see the struggle against being erased and distorted as a struggle to appear in some pure, unmediated sense, a struggle to appear as

[44] See also Anderson 1986, 76. The suggestion that listening makes a difference may seem naive in the context of the above example of conflict between the police and a Black community. The increasing popularity of the idea of "community policing" may indicate otherwise. In community policing, an officer regularly walks the streets of a particular neighborhood and communicates with its inhabitants (rather than simply cruising through). Community policing is intended not merely to reduce crime, but to ease community-police tensions. The assumption is that an officer who regularly hears, sees, and knows the people in the neighborhood would not automatically see a young black man on a corner as a possible threat; he or she would see that it is "Mrs. Johnson's son on his way to work" or "that guy who always goes by at this time of day." Similarly, the people in that community might come to perceive the officer not only as a representative of an oppressive social system, but as someone who hears their concern for the neighborhood.

who I think I am, to be heard as who I want to be. (Arendt might say that this is the danger of metaphors of work and making; there is an implicit desire for mastery.) But our listeners are, paradoxically, like us—unique and active. It is the inevitable role that reception plays that makes the public action of citizenship a genuinely collective endeavor, one in which no individual can simply impose her or his will on another and insist on being heard in a particular way. The "who" that is formed by the story of my public actions and judgments is not necessarily the heroine of the story I would write, precisely because others' reactions to me are themselves *actions*, unpredictable and novel. This is the paradox of public appearance: our very appearance as an active unique "who" relies on the attention of active others whose perceptions we do not control. If we acknowledge those with whom we are acting as capable of judgment—and I cannot conceive of a feminism or a democracy that does not—we cannot simply demand to be a particular public who, to be heard in a particular way. Arendt's crucial reminder is that communicating with each other in the realm of citizenship is still struggle, is still action, and as such it is as unpredictable and uncontrollable as the other citizens with whom we necessarily engage.[45]

There is a difference between being regarded as an object or being otherwise not-heard (a kind of attention that is antipolitical) and being heard differently than we want to be. *The latter is an unavoidable political possibility.* But there are no neat ways to mark the difference, or to easily identify what lies between distortion on one hand and an impossible empathetic transparency on the other. And this is why political interaction can be so difficult, so frustrating, so demanding, particularly in a context of inequality. This may be a difficult realization for those of us who are members of oppressed groups to have to confront, but it is crucial to a democratic understanding of the unique dynamic between speaking and listening. I am both attending and being attended to whether I am speaking or listening. Both speaker and listener are at the same time perceiver and perceived, and democratic politi-

---

[45] Another way to say this is that the risks inherent in acting together stem from the fact that every performance is also a communication to those attending, and creativity is present on both ends; both performing and attending are modes of *action*, which is inevitably interaction.

cal communication requires that in neither of these roles is one regarded (or self-regarded) as a stereotyped object, but as a conscious, active subject.

Let us return to the above example from June Jordan. The students' choice to initiate communication bespeaks their partial willingness—despite the history of troubled relations between the police and the Black community—to see their addressees as potential listeners. Yet they regarded those listeners as determined by "what" they were, as whites, as cops. One might argue that the students played a role in "dooming" this communication by regarding their addressees as "those controlling the killers" rather than as, say, fellow citizens. The latter kind of regard does not require that the students ignore their own history or that they turn a saintly eye on those who as a group seem enemies. It does require their recognizing that cops and cop-controllers are *like themselves* more than their "conditions," are capable of action, of the unexpected, and that it is possible that we can act as "co-builders of a common world" (*OT* 458) and not simply be locked in a speechless and unhearing battle. As Amos Oz points out with respect to the Israeli-Palestinian conflict, "the opposite of war is not love; the opposite of war is peace." And the possibility of peace rather than war came when "each now realized that the other side is real and, in fact, is here to stay" (1993, 14–16).

This mutual recognition is impossible unless we conceive of others as capable of recognizing us. Such recognition does not require that we regard the differences between us as irrelevant; in fact, it requires taking them seriously, but also taking seriously our capacity to act together. An example of a different approach to the "politics of address" can be discerned in an essay of Lugones's in which she writes in "Ingles and several varieties of Spanish." She argues that it is through this mix of languages that she speaks as an unbroken, multidimensional "I." This multidimensionality "is here to be appreciated or missed and both the appreciation and the missing are significant . . . I want to exercise my multidimensionality even if you do not appreciate it" (1990a, 46). This may sound like an implicit demand for sheer accommodation, but can that really be her point? Surely Lugones cannot be implying that everyone in the public realm must speak Spanish (and thus also Hmong, Italian, Korean, Dakota)? And in fact it is evident that she is not making such a demand. Her mixing of languages, her creation of "voice," is (like all political action) a performance expressly designed to be communicative, a way both to disclose herself and to communicate to others. Using multiple "tongues" in a context where one's interlocutors do not speak all those tongues is a way of throwing into relief the differences between people, of pointing to the distance between us. Even if I do not make any effort to understand the Spanish, I am forced to realize I am missing something. And it is a way of insisting on mutuality of effort from others, of placing responsibility "*actively* on your and not just my shoulders" (Lugones 1990a, 50). If I do not read Spanish, I may find a translator or a dictionary, or I may be able to figure out some of the words but not all. But the meaning of Lugones's performance is not an insistence on pure self-expression; the point is the possibility of joining together. "For 'our' sake, for the sheer possibility *de un 'nosotras,'* I will swallow my tongue '*a medias*,' half-way" (1990a, 50).

Lugones then rejects the choice between speaking in her own language and not being listened to, or wholly accommodating her speech to dominant norms. Contentiously, agonistically, she pursues the possibility of an "us" that is created by mutual effort. This is not a parody, nor is it a performance characterized by irony—it is earnest and angry. Yet this approach leaves room for a variety of orientations and performances (none of which require humorlessness or rigidity): room for anger and purpose; for pleasure, for teasing, for confusion; for intensity and seriousness and frustration. This mobilization of identity indeed politicizes subjectivity—and politicizes intersubjectivity as well. Lugones's strategy points toward a kind of attention that results in neither transparency nor masking, and toward a space of appearance that allows something between an impossible "purity" and an oppressive falseness. This kind of attention preserves the tension between "I" and "us," rather than erasing it in favor of one or the other.

It was when the attentiveness that lets human plurality appear was not forthcoming that Arendt herself was willing to pay attention to social identities; indeed, under certain conditions she insisted on it. Such attention can be justified on Arendtian grounds by noting that the forces that create and give particular meaning to different social groups have real worldly effects.[46] Arendt herself felt the reality of her Jewishness: "For many years I considered the only adequate reply to the question, Who are you? to be: a Jew." If attacked as a Jew, Arendt argued, one must respond in that identity, as a Jew; not to do so would be "nothing but a grotesque and dangerous evasion of reality." By "a Jew" she did not mean "a special kind of human being" but was rather indicating a "political fact" (*MDT* 17–23; see also *JP* 121). And responding "in terms of the identity that is under attack" means challenging interpretations of that fact, not denying its worldly reality. "In the case of a friendship between a German and a Jew under the conditions of the Third Reich it would scarcely have been a sign of humanness for the friends to have said: Are we not both human beings? It would have been mere evasion of reality and of the world common to both at that time: they would not have been resisting the world as it was. A law that prohibited the intercourse of Jews and Germans could be evaded but could not be defied by people who denied the reality of the distinction. . . . They would have had to say to each other: A German and Jew, and friends" (*MDT* 23).

Although she defended a conception of the world in which there were firm distinctions between what should be private and what public, Arendt recognized that worldly conditions may require actions that are perverse in those terms; the political importance of social identities may vary with the conditions under which one lives. Speaking as "a Jew" was a necessity brought about by the existence of totalitarian regimes that used social identities to determine not only who could be citizens, but who could live as humans on the earth. Under such conditions, Arendt could only resist "in terms of the identity under attack." And not surprisingly, then, she could only regard the necessity of such resistance with something like regret.

[46] Groups are artificial, that is, socially constructed; but "the human condition consists in man's being a conditioned being for whom everything, given or man-made, immediately becomes a condition of his further existence" (*HC* 147). The forces that create and give particular meaning to different social groups may be intangible in the sense that they are not objects, but (as Arendt says about the web of human relationships) "for all its intangibility, this in-between is no less real than the world of things we visibly have in common" (*HC* 183). These forces are real because they appear to others; we can talk about them and know that we are talking about the same phenomena.

There are, as Arendt herself would note, "important differences in degree" in worldly conditions (*JP* 249); she herself obviously felt differently about her Jewishness later.[47] But one need not argue that the United States is a "racial state" to the same extent that Nazi Germany was in order to argue that, on Arendt's own terms, who we are as citizens draws from our social identities because we live in a world that has made those identities, those groupings, matter (and in a way that is often a matter of law; see Minow 1987; Halley 1993). And like anything else in the world, the forces that create and give meaning to these groupings can both separate *and* relate us. Although we perceive them from different locations, we can recognize these groupings as a feature of our common world that has consequences for how we live, how we live together, and how we can appear in the world.

To change those consequences, to challenge the meaning of those identities, requires a place in that world. With respect to "the Jewish question," Arendt argued that the crucial project was "building up" a world of Jewish culture, as Jews were doing before Israeli statehood with the kibbutzim (collective settlements) and the Hebrew University. But this "building up" did not mean the establishment of a Jewish state; on the contrary, she contended that establishing a Jewish state on already inhabited lands surrounded by hostile neighbors was a dangerous example of ignoring the world, discounting "the concrete factors of the situation." Attention to actual worldly conditions meant for Arendt that a binational federated structure, one that rested on "Jewish-Arab community councils," was necessary to counter "the mutual refusal to take each other seriously" (*JP* Part II, esp. 131–136, 184–192, 198–201, 212–215).

---

[47] I am referring to the exchange between Scholem and Arendt over *Eichmann and Jerusalem* (*JP* 240–250). It is hard to know exactly how to interpret this exchange. Arendt certainly seems to be claiming (as Honig 1992 persuasively argues) that her Jewish identity is a factual matter of private identity. It seems significant, however, that she does not simply ignore Scholem's statements about her Jewishness. She chooses to argue publicly that that factual identity does not automatically result in certain opinions or political stances. But precisely what makes facts political is the existence of differing interpretations and opinions about them (*BPF* 238, 249). So in an odd way, Arendt is allowing that there can be political disagreement (as there is between her and Scholem) about whether and how private identities can have political meaning, even though her own argument is that they do not.

There are two models of worldly togetherness here, and both are expressed in the writings of Anzaldúa, Lorde, Lugones, and others. Groups based on identity have in recent decades been building up a place in the world by creating bookstores, presses, coffeehouses, record labels, cultural centers, shelters, newspapers, and cooperative businesses and residences. These places, and the political groups that are rooted in them, can provide a context in which we feel we can appear as most ourselves, groups that are our political "home," to use Bernice Johnson Reagon's terminology. These autonomous institutions have important and empowering roles; however, Reagon points out, the hominess of such groups often turns out to be based on exclusion, or a false sense of sameness. As Anzaldúa notes, our multiplicity and distinctiveness as individuals mean that there are differences even within groups that are seen, from within or without, as homogeneous (Reagon 1983, 357–360; Anzaldúa 1990c and 1990d, 220). The hominess of these groups in the end is not so different from that of the world, which is to say that they are characterized by plurality as well. If we are capable of perception that can encompass the paradox of plurality on the level of the human species, I suggest that this paradoxical perception is possible on the level of social groups as well. Appearing as a member of a social group need not mean that I or my interlocutors reduce myself and others in the group to the same stance, opinion, or experiences—any more than we do everyone else in the human species.

And this recognition of multiplicity within groups is often the impetus or the reminder to turn outward and acknowledge that we live in a common world with others—to develop, as feminists have begun to do, the second model of togetherness.[48] Established social groups do not exhaust the possibilities of human togetherness; it is not simply individual identities that are created, rather than given, but political groups as well. Moraga says, "I would grow despairing if I believed . . . we were unilaterally defined by color and class." Anzaldúa agrees: we cannot let "color class and gender separate us

[48] Interestingly, Arendt says that "the only larger groups who ever actively promoted and preached Jewish-Arab friendship came from [the] collective settlement movement" (*JP* 214). So in this case, the unitary togetherness of the kibbutzim led to the possibility of talking with one's adversaries. See also Evans and Boyte 1986, esp. 157–158, 187–202.

from those who would be kindred spirits" (Moraga 1983, xiv; Anzaldúa 1983, 205–206). The issues we care about are shaped by our past experiences, and we may feel a connection with those who share our culture, our rituals, our oppressions. But if our group membership does not automatically produce a particular political opinion or commitment, then our politics need not be defined by lines that we had no hand in drawing. Rosario Morales insists,

> We know different things   some very much more unpleasant things if we've been women poor black or lesbian or all of those we know different things depending on what sex   what color what lives we live   where we grew up   what schooling   what beatings   with or without shoes   steak or beans   but what politics each of us is going to be and do is anybody's guess. (1983, 93)

Political collectivities are created, and created in ways that do not necessarily accord with already existent groups or with fully shared experiences. This insight has led to critiques of "sisterhood" as a model for feminist solidarity, and an increasing emphasis in feminist theory and practice on alliances and coalitions.[49] These specifically political groups are created through a conscious decision to ally with others with whom we share political commitments or interests, or simply through the recognition that we share a common world. And our capacity to make these decisions stresses the indeterminacy of the relationship between given identities and politics.

This recalls Arendt's understanding of the generativity of action—but here not only are individual identities created through political action, but new group identities as well. The creation of these alliances contests the lines of difference and sameness that would sort us only in established ways. This conception of action allows us both to claim and transfigure given identities—to resist in terms of the identity that is under attack, and to challenge those terms by creating new political confederations. Coalitions might be a model for that particular kind of political togetherness, one that is not based on established group identity, but not dismissive of it either.

[49] Dill 1983; hooks 1984; Ackelsberg 1983; on coalition/alliances, see Reagon 1983, Albrecht and Brewer 1990, and the relevant sections of Moraga and Anzaldúa 1983, and Anzaldúa 1990a.

The possibility of these alliances is a source of exuberance and hope in feminist writing, yet all who stress their importance attest to the difficulty and pain involved. As Reagon points out in her much-cited essay, a coalition is not necessarily safe, comfortable, or nurturing; it can be threatening to our sense of self and community. Papusa Molina talks of *el miedo*, the constant fear "of exploring, of exposing ourselves, of daring to be vulnerable and risk looking at each other" (Reagon 1983; Molina 1990, 328 and passim). Lorde argues that the source of the fear is not sheer difference; something that is wholly different from us is not necessarily threatening, we do not have to listen because we could not possibly understand. The fear comes from seeing someone as the same in some ways yet different in others, as we try "to see whole people in their actual complexities" (1984, 117–118). Fear might also come from the possibility Nancy Fraser has raised: that in the end our interests and opinions may deeply conflict with those of the very people with whom we want to make common cause (1991, 175).

Some feminist writers suggest that the motivation for overcoming this fear must come from love for one another.[50] But as Lorde insists: "What about interracial cooperation between feminists who don't love each other?" (1984, 113). We may share political commitments, interests, or opinions without loving one another or feeling a deep sense of community. As does Arendt, Lorde recognizes that being ourselves and being with others—subjectivity and intersubjectivity—are in tension and in utter mutual reliance: we both fear and need "the visibility without which we cannot truly live" (1984, 42). And like Arendt, Lorde argues that the tension is not resolved by love but addressed by courage: "We can learn to work and speak when we are afraid in the same way we have learned to work and speak when we are tired." Working and speaking together do not require unitary conceptions of community and identity, and

---

[50] Lugones 1990b, 401; Molina 1990, 329; Anzaldúa 1990c, 228–229. This is why I do not draw on Lugones's conception of "world-travelling," despite its suggestiveness (and some commonalities with Arendt). Such activity relies on a kind of lovingness that enables us to see with another's eyes (Lugones 1990b, 394). Lugones also suggests that the effort of mutual recognition discussed above may require "the devotion of friendship" (1990a, 47). (See also Spivak's [1992] stress on friendship and intimacy as necessary accompaniments of translation.) Obviously, given my analysis of Aristotle and Arendt in the preceding chapters, I do not agree that love and friendship are required for the mutual recognition that politics involves.

cannot wait for "the final luxury of fearlessness" (44): "You do not have to be me in order for us to fight alongside each other. I do not have to be you to recognize that our wars are the same. What we must do is commit ourselves to some future that can include each other and to work toward that future with the particular strengths of our individual identities. . . . Only within that interdependency of different strengths, acknowledged and equal, can the power to seek new ways of being in the world generate, as well as the courage and sustenance to act where there are no charters" (1984, 142, 111).[51]

But even members of a coalition are not simply arguing and acting with one another, but with and against those outside the coalition. I submit that the difficult "joining with" of an alliance characterizes political action in general, which action does not necessarily issue from shared substantive commitments. Even conflicting interests are *inter-est*, between us, relating and separating us. For Arendt, the courage and attention that make politics possible do not spring from our feelings for each other so much as from a kind of care for the world. It is the world that we share, that relates and separates us—the human artifice that is built up on earth and populated by us humans: the houses, the office buildings, the vacant lots, the parks; the hospitals, factories, restaurants; the schools, the shelters, the streets. We do live in this common world together, and we cannot evade that togetherness if we want to preserve a world with space for the exercise of distinctively human capacities and the perhaps distant possibility of a just politics. We must regard even those we are struggling against as fellow political actors, as human citizens, because (as Reagon asserts and as Oz says the Israelis and Palestinians realized), no one is voluntarily going to go away (Reagon 1983, 365). Sharing a commitment to living in the world together may sound like a pretty minimal basis for political interaction, since it does not involve love, compassion, or even civic friendship. But it is of great significance in a world where there continue to be so many attempts to determine by violence who will live on this earth and who will not.

To regard you as a fellow citizen does not require that I simply acquiesce in your view of me, or that I defer to my listeners' evalua-

---

[51] Like Arendt, Lorde tends to use the language of war and warriors, but when she is indicating precisely the possibility of politics and not war, power and not simply violence.

tion of my opinion, of who we are and what we are doing. Even when I approach political action with the recognition of the agency of others, my own lack of mastery, and the unpredictability of action, I am still acting purposefully; I am trying to do something (and be someone). The listening attention crucial for citizen interaction does not resolve the effort that is central to political action, which involves both thinking collectively with others and judging for one's self. In other words, political action always engages the tension between subjectivity and intersubjectivity; somehow, recognizing the agency of others has to coexist with our own striving. Figuring out what is behind that "somehow" requires an exploration of how we can discern a difference between distorted listening and simply active listening—that is, between treating each other as objects and taking each other seriously. In the next chapter, I examine in more detail what democratic political listening might look like—and sound like.

Chapter 5

LISTENING AND ACTION

RECONSTITUTING THE
INTERSUBJECTIVE WORLD

We do not have to choose between the pour soi *and the*
pour autrui, *between thought according to us and according
to others. . . . If I wanted to deny myself for their benefit, I
would deny them too as "Selves." They are worth exactly
what I am worth, and all the powers I give them I give simultaneously to myself.*
—MERLEAU-PONTY, *Signs*

*I have to cast my lot with those
who age after age, perversely,*

*with no extraordinary power,
reconstitute the world.*
—ADRIENNE RICH, *"Natural Resources"*

In this chapter, I probe what listening involves as a practice of
democratic citizenship in a diverse, unequal social order. My analysis has three main parts. I begin by examining what listening requires from the point of view of the listening subject, in light of the
conception of citizen action I have been developing. I then turn
from the *subject* to the *world*, and investigate how listening can appear as a political phenomenon. Finally, I use Arendt and Merleau-
Ponty to argue for a particular understanding of political interaction
between subjects in a *common* world. Such interaction does not necessarily take its meaning from, or its purpose to be, consensus. I suggest instead a different normative goal that can better guide political
action in an inegalitarian pluralistic social order.

THE INNER SIDE OF LISTENING

Listening is often invoked as a sympathetic orientation that provides an alternative to the dominating quality of "the gaze" and the despotic quality of speech. Let me briefly address these claims, in order to place listening in the context of other perceptual activities. Some have argued that seeing, unlike hearing, does not bind us up in a situation of responsiveness; rather it leaves us free, unconstrained. (And only the viewer is active; "being seen," after all, is not an activity). This lack of involvement was once celebrated as "the nobility of sight" (Jonas 1966), but more skeptical commentators argue that this lack of engagement becomes troubling when the "object" of attention is another person. "The gaze" distances the viewer from others and leaves him or her unmoved. The viewed become dehumanized objects, fixed in a visual field (see Sartre 1956, 340–365; Levin 1989, 30–31). In addition, Foucault's analyses of the practices of surveillance and their effect on subjectivity have helped us understand the workings of the "disciplinary" gaze: "an inspecting gaze, a gaze which each individual under its weight will end by interiorising to the point that he is his own overseer, each individual thus exercising this surveillance over, and against, himself" (Foucault 1980, 155; and 1977 passim).[1] And a multitude of specifically feminist criticisms have been made of both the objectifying and the disciplinary qualities of the gaze (examples here range from the work of Luce Irigaray to Naomi Wolf's *The Beauty Myth*).[2]

"Appearing in public" is not just empowering, then; these analyses point to more sinister possibilities. But these dangers stem from the lack of mutuality in the perceptual activity, not from an inherent quality in the activity itself (as some feminists have already argued with respect to looking; e.g., Kaplan 1983; Disch and Kane 1996). The activity of visual perception often happens simultaneously with other perceptual activities. Merleau-Ponty points out that it is only the silent human gaze that discomfits us and feels objectifying (a dog's gaze does not disturb us in the same way); among hu-

---

[1] Listening is not immune here; when practices of eavesdropping and bugging are institutionalized, they can produce the same kind of disciplinary self-censorship.

[2] For an encyclopedic account of both the centrality of vision in the history of Western philosophy and the equally stubborn antiocularcentrism in twentieth-century thought, see Jay 1993.

mans, "the other's gaze is felt as unbearable only because it takes the place of possible communication" (*PP* 361). But with the first spoken word, the relation with the other changes; and thus some writers argue that listening is, quite unlike seeing, a drawing together.[3] But I think it is a mistake to contrast too sharply the two modes of perception, because they often work together. "Being seen" may not be an activity, but viewing people is not the same as viewing statues—we can see another's *movement.* Seeing can provide an interpretive context that enriches listening, for example, through body language or facial expression. (And the distinction between seeing and hearing simply dissolves in languages like ASL.) What we see may either confirm our sense of what we are hearing or clash with it; the exercise of seeing can remind us that the other *is* other, that their voices are not simply in our own heads. So this distancing quality of seeing need not be oppressive, particularly if (as Merleau-Ponty suggests) it is combined with hearing.[4]

In a similar way, speaking is also inescapably intertwined with listening. The relationship between speaking and listening is characterized by a mutual sensitivity that is not simply interpretive but bodily as well. In the most basic physical sense, sound has its origin in movement, the movement that disturbs air molecules and sends sound toward us. Hearing is always the hearing of an action.[5] The

[3] See Levin 1989, 182; Ihde 1976, 15; Corradi Fiumara 1990, 16–17. What this drawing together involves is different for each theorist. Corradi Fiumara argues that the distance created by indifference makes listening impossible, but notes, as would Arendt, that listening must preserve distance too. Attempting to merge into one another (through perceived sameness or desire for intimacy) erases the conditions necessary for communication, for it erases the possibility of a separate other telling us something new. It is thus not the distance itself but the character of the distance between us that is important (Corradi Fiumara 1990, 100–103, 112). I find this much more persuasive than Levin's stress on overcoming separateness and "resonating" deeply with one another (1989, 182), at least from the perspective of political interaction.

[4] I can find no analyses of the specific forms listening takes for blind people. It seems possible that certain qualities of sound (e.g., directionality, voice timbre) could play similar roles in preserving distance and providing interpretive cues.

[5] But hearing itself also involves movement; cells inside the ear move in order to process sound (Jonas 1966, 137; Ackerman 1990, 177). Hearing experts have developed a device that allows them to hear this movement of cells inside the ear—which allows them, in other words, to listen to hearing (Minneapolis *Star Tribune*, February 25, 1993, 1E).

movement through which humans make meaningful sounds is speech, and we attend to that speech through listening. The receptive quality of listening is indeed unique by virtue of always being *a movement toward another's activity*, an active involvement in a joint project. Speaking and listening are active *responses* to each other, and they connect us in a way that no other sensory interaction does. In taking listening seriously, we need not elevate listening over speaking as the primary political or social activity, but rather understand their interdependency, the dynamic between them, and the necessity for engagement in both modes.[6]

Both listening and speaking require attention to others. Both are inseparable from particular physical processes, yet these processes do not simply determine the content of what is said or heard. Listening, like speaking, is a creative act, one that involves conscious effort.[7] What kind of effort are we making when we try to listen to one another in public? We know from previous chapters that we are trying to perceive one another as unique, and yet not unsituated. What does this sort of auditory perception require from us?

Simone Weil's concept of attention might seem useful here because it rests on valuing the concrete person, understood as neither merely a physical body nor simply an inner consciousness or "personality." Weil argues that one should value, not something "in" or "about" a person, but simply the person himself: "the whole of him.

[6] Thus I think Corradi Fiumara is mistaken when, in bringing forward the neglected possibilities of listening, she stresses the negative qualities of speech. Speech is "a form of domination and control," a means of "despotic doings"; we are "an assertive culture intoxicated by the effectiveness of its own 'saying' and increasingly incapable of paying 'heed' " (1990, 2, 52, 8; see also Levin 1989, 20–21). As I argued earlier, oppression does work in part by taking seriously only certain kinds of speech and by undervaluing listening; but this is not the same as arguing that speech by its very nature is oppressive. Corradi Fiumara often seems to be making the latter argument; when she does mention the mutual reliance of speaking and listening, it is difficult to see how she conceives of their relationship given her frequent contrasts between the virtues of listening and the vices of speaking (1990, 154, 161).

[7] We do not necessarily experience the physical and the creative as separate moments in the act of hearing; thus I do not contrast "mere" hearing to listening as, e.g., Forester does (1989, 108–110). Both the physical process and the creative act are present whether we are listening to someone's voice, "listening" to sign language, or lip-reading, although the processes are different in each case. For a detailed discussion of signing and speech-reading as physical and intellectual processes, see Benderly 1980.

The arms, the eyes, the thoughts, everything" (1962, 9). Genuinely to attend to that person is to "read" him or her justly. In reading other people, I must be careful not to impose my own preconceptions on them; I must be ready to perceive the unexpected, to see them as who they are in themselves, not as I want them to be (1979, 188–189).

For Weil, that attention requires a profound stilling of the self. Attention "should be a looking and not an attachment," as I put aside my own desires and will (1979, 169–174). "To listen to someone is to put oneself in his place while he is speaking" (1962, 28). To do so in a way that does not impose our reading on him requires a kind of self-annihilation. To be genuinely open to another, "all that I call 'I' has to be passive" (1979, 171; also 1962, 27–28).[8]

Although Weil's is a particularly stark formulation, this understanding of listening as a self-annulling openness is not uncommon. For David Levin, listening requires a "yielding" and "neutralization" of our "attractions and aversions." This does not preclude making critical judgments; but those judgments must come from the "neutral space" of genuine listening in which judgment has been suspended (1989, 224–225, 233, 228, and 256–257). Corradi Fiumara speaks of a "fundamental openness" in listening, in which we allow ourselves to be "overwhelmed." This self-effacement is necessary (as in Weil) in order not to impose our own interpretations onto the subject or object of attention. We have to be open to the possibility of "helplessness and disorientation," for if we genuinely listen, differences, "anomalies," and contradictions appear (Corradi Fiumara 1990, 73, 77, 39, 43, and 50–51).

We might question whether this state of hyperreceptivity is even possible (except perhaps in a mystical or meditative experience, as Weil's "waiting on God").[9] Can I really leave behind my

[8] The point of this attentiveness is not to allow another "I" to appear, but to pass over into the "impersonal" (Weil 1962, 14–17). Dietz argues that this emphasis on passivity does not mean that Weil's thought is not valuable politically; we can also read in Weil's "attention" an alternative form of justice, one that does not rely on a public morality of rights. But what remains politically problematic is that "instead of pursuing the question of who the 'attentive' self is, she calls for annihilation of the 'I' " (Dietz 1988, 125–140, esp. 138).

[9] Weil herself notes that such attention is about as probable as "a stag advancing voluntarily to offer itself to the teeth of a pack of hounds"; it is possible only "supernaturally" (1962, 23).

own frameworks, thoughts, and orientations, and suppress my sense of self in this way? Can I really detach my eyes and ears from the being who sees and hears the world through them? I am doubt-ful about the general possibility of this kind of listening; but in any case, this profound and self-abnegating openness cannot be char-àcteristic of listening in a political sense, if we recall what Aristotle and Arendt taught us about what characterizes political interaction. Given the uncertain nature of political questions and the conflict-ing perspectives of political actors, being able to hear differences is certainly central to political listening, and disorientation is defi-nitely possible. But political listening cannot be grounded in pas-sivity or an absence of self, for politics itself requires precisely the opposite. In politics, as Merleau-Ponty says, "there is a relationship of consultation and exchange with others which is not the death but the very act of the self" (S 215). It is the *interaction* of our efforts that results in a decision, a joint action; if I somehow absent myself when you speak, in order to "hear" you, and you do the same for me, in what sense are we really together as peers? Politics requires self-involvement with others in action, where we do not "draw back" but actively engage with one another with directions(s) and pur-pose(s).[10]

However, when I reflect on the actual practice of listening, I cannot escape the concept of openness. I cannot describe what I am doing when I am listening without coming back to some version of "being open to," just as "closedness" seems the invariable char-acteristic of not-listening. How then might we characterize the openness involved in specifically political listening?

In a sense, Merleau-Ponty's phenomenology of perception (see Chapter 1) has already helped us to address this question. In lis-tening, I construct an "auditory gestalt" in which I make myself the ground, the horizon, against which the other becomes the focused-on figure. This action does not involve self-abnegation or absence, but a perceptual taking up of the world in which meaning relies on our both being present and perceived as present—me as ground

---

[10] "Draw back" is Weil's phrase (1979, 170–171). There is a sense in which some form of drawing back may come in, for politics occasionally requires making judg-ments about what we should be closed to as well. Such a decision must obviously be carefully considered. Judicially we have the example of the Supreme Court, whose refusal to hear cases is a deliberative decision not to deliberate particular claims.

and you as figure. The openness involved in listening is, as I said earlier, an active willingness to construct certain relations of attention, relations in which neither of us has meaning without the other. This kind of listening and speaking together engages both agency and situatedness: I cannot hear you except against the ground of who I am, and you are speaking, not in the abstract, but to me—to who you think your listeners are.

There must of course be an equality in terms of the role one plays. All must engage in shifting back and forth between perspectives, speaking and listening in turn. In this listening and speaking, "what is sought is not a fictitious coincidence of myself and others" (*PP* 337). I try to experience the world as you construct it for me, but this is not the same as experiencing it as you do; it is still, always, *for me*. Merleau-Ponty uses the example of talking with a patient who is hallucinating to describe how communication can happen with someone who perceives quite differently than I do: "I misunderstood another person because I see him from my own point of view, but then I hear him expostulate, and finally come round to the idea of the other person as a centre of perspectives . . . it is not a question either of taking him at his word or of reducing his experiences to mine, or coinciding with him, or sticking to my own point of view, but of making explicit my experience, and also his experience as it is conveyed to me in my own . . . and to understand one through the other." What I come to understand is not simply the other's perspective, but my perspective in light of his, and his in light of mine—"I learn to know both myself and others" (*PP* 337–338).[11]

This knowledge is not absolute, for neither my nor my interlocutors' perceptions are beyond criticism or amendment. I can understand the patient's belief to be hallucinatory in a way that mine is not; I do so by reference to an "intersubjective world." No one else perceives the sounds the hallucinating patient does: the "hal-

---

[11] It should be clear that Merleau-Ponty's understanding which I am using here is different from the foreground/background structure that Marilyn Frye argues is characteristic of "phallocratic reality." Such a reality (where the lives and experiences of men are the foreground and those of women the background) is possible only because those in the foreground do not regard the others as "authoritative perceivers" (or, in Merleau-Ponty's words, a "centre of perspectives"). As a result, phallocratic reality is not characterized by the kind of shifting and reconstructing that is central to Merleau-Ponty's approach. See Frye 1983, 166–169.

lucinatory phenomenon is not part of the world, that is to say, it is not *accessible,* there is no definite path leading from it to the experience of the sane" (*PP* 339). Such a judgment could be made only through the effort of understanding described above, and the goal of such effort is to try to create a path, a passage to another's experience. This metaphor of "the path" characterizes Merleau-Ponty's understanding of communication between embodied subjects (e.g., *S* 63, 3). Thinking about listening as creating a passage brings together Arendt's idea of traveling and Anzaldúa's conception of creating bridges (1990d). It is an activity that seems particularly appropriate to listening. We do not simply float over to another's position in our heads; we create together a concrete worldly means of getting at each others' perspectives. Or, rather, of getting as close as we can get; we cannot inhabit others' perspectives or hold their opinions as they do, we are still travelers coming from somewhere else. (The road from Athens to Thebes is not the same as the road from Thebes to Athens, and each also *seems* different to an Athenian than to a Theban, although they might travel either together.) The distinction between representative thinking and this actual interaction is that we cannot do the latter alone—we cannot go anywhere, we do not know what direction to head, without a joint effort.

That effort—of creating the path as we travel—may take many different shapes. We need not simply, flatly delineate our point of view—we may tell stories, ask questions, burst out with emotion, communicate in the myriad ways humans can. We may painstakingly, sentence by sentence, build up or carve out a path; we may with one blastingly communicative performance open a way; we may steer ourselves waveringly toward a point of tangent, overlap, and veer away again.

This pathbuilding requires from us a joint effort of persistence, and of courage. I have argued in earlier chapters that courage is necessary for citizenship, for politics is an inherently risky and uncertain enterprise in which our actions can have unpredictable consequences and our words can be misunderstood. Courage and citizenship were connected long ago by the Greeks, who regarded courage as virility or manliness, particularly as demonstrated in battle. But the risks of battle are different than the risks of deliberation; this is perhaps why Aristotle says that battle courage only "resembles" genuine courage (*NE* Book 3, chap. 8). Salkever argues that Aristotle's questioning of virility as a virtue is connected to a more general critique of Athenian participatory politics. The life of a committed citizen, which involved battle courage and the pursuit of glory, is not necessarily the best (i.e., rationally governed) human life. Still, developing the "deliberative capacity" that is the central trait of humans requires a kind of courage (as Aristotle must have decided, since he preserves courage as a virtue). The courage I describe here is perhaps a version of the Socratic courage to follow arguments "wherever they lead."[12] What more precisely are the risks in following arguments—in speaking and listening—and what kind of courage is required?

The riskiness of listening comes partly from the possibility that what we hear will require change from us. A deliberative decision may mean real material change for the participants. But speaking and listening together may also engender a change in consciousness. As Lorde says, "change means growth, and growth can be painful"; but "we sharpen self-definition by exposing the self in work and struggle" (1984, 123). This exposure, the possibility of this sharpening, can be scary. In a sense, we fear being wrong, or being in the wrong. The opinions I have—views I have come to after imaginative work and struggle, perhaps—may be threatened by what you have to say. Or maybe I have lived my entire life in accordance with my inherited beliefs. Suddenly what you have to say throws a harsh light on those views, I no longer recognize them, my world teeters. Most of us have views whose loss would make us question who we are and what world we live in (as Arendt must have realized in arguing that opinion is central to identity). The same risk is present in speaking. Once I reveal my (perhaps hard-earned, perhaps long-cherished) opinion, I myself may be persuaded that it is deserving of scorn or neglect. Or I may remained convinced of its value, but suffer the pain of being attacked, ridiculed, or of not being listened to (e.g., Mansbridge 1983, 60–65). In political interaction between diverse beings, as Romand Coles has so compellingly put it, "many of the perspectives and practices that we take to be essentially constitutive and unquestionable aspects of our identity are challenged by others, who explicitly or tacitly suggest that what we

[12] Salkever 1990, chap. 4. The discussion of Socrates' version of courage is at 187.

hold dear is in fact trivial, illusory, oppressive, obnoxious, slave-like, unhealthy, and on and on" (1996, 377).

Concern about these possibilities lead J. Donald Moon to argue that a participatory politics based on "unconstrained self-revelation" seriously underestimates the value of privacy.[13] But it is not our intimate or private selves that we are revealing in public; understanding the political self as a constructed self, or as Boyte argues, understanding politics as a craft, can perhaps mitigate feelings of risk (Boyte 1989, 92–93).[14] We may bolster our courage by reminding ourselves that criticisms are not of our most intimate selves, but of how we have performed, how we are acting in public.

But performance itself can be scary; even Arendt, for all her appreciation of the importance of appearing in public, suffered stage fright (see Young-Bruehl 1982, 251, 301, 463). There is, she noted, a kind of courage involved in simply "leaving one's private hiding place and showing who one is" (*HC* 186). Arendt does not specify exactly what the risk is here, but it must have something to do with the possibility that we may not want to be the person we end up showing. It is not only that we cannot control how others perceive us; there is also the possibility that we may perform badly in front of our peers. In the words of one of Mansbridge's informants in Selby: "it does take a little bit of courage. 'Specially if you get up and make a boo-boo. I mean you make a mistake and say something, then people would never get up and say anything again. They feel themselves inferior" (1983, 60).

The fears of being wrong, in the wrong, and performing badly are not necessarily countered simply by having "the courage of one's convictions." Corradi Fiumara cites Nietzsche to the effect that such steadfastness is easy; questioning one's conviction is what is hard (1990, 80). As Aristotle might remind us, however, it de-

---

[13] Moon is here criticizing Benhabib in particular, although in a way that I think exaggerates the "unconstrained revelation" of self necessary for Benhabib's model of transformative discourse. He argues further that her emphasis on a discourse of needs "coerces" traditional or religious groups that believe in a language of duty. He admits that his own solution—understanding public life in a way that abstracts from our individual identities—also disadvantages some, but it is not clear why the disadvantages of his approach are less burdensome than Benhabib's (1991, 219–227).

[14] Mansbridge 1982 discusses concrete ways to structure interaction to lessen fear of conflict.

pends. "The same things are not fearful to all people," Aristotle points out, and "terrors which are humanly bearable differ in magnitude and degree, and so do the circumstances which inspire confidence" (*NE* 1115b). For Aristotle, courage does not mean the absence of fear. It is appropriate in scary situations to feel fear, and one who does not is reckless, an unpraiseworthy extreme. A courageous man for Aristotle feels fear about the right things for the right reasons, but what further distinguishes him is how he behaves. Genuine courage involves a choice about how to act in the face of fear (*NE* Book 3, chap. 7, esp. 1115b; see also 1117a).

What counts as a courageous action depends on the person (for we fear different things in different ways) and on the situation or "circumstances" (for there may be variances in danger—of kind or of degree—for those involved).[15] So the choice to act courageously might lead to very different actions. For example, testifying at a public hearing about police brutality might make a black man vulnerable to reprisals from the police; that man has chosen to act courageously by speaking. For the police commissioner at that same public hearing, acting courageously might require a special effort to listen, given the possible harm to the police force. Again, this does not mean that neither feels fear or reluctance, but that they act courageously, consciously, in spite of that fear.

Fear may in fact be what allows us to question our convictions. Fear of being "wrong" (of having an opinion that is incomplete or mistaken in some way) can contribute to our ability to listen, if it is a mean between the lack of fear and excessive fear. Someone who never feels the possibility of incompleteness will have difficulty genuinely hearing someone else, but someone who is overly frightened by it will be silent when she should speak. Aristotle describes this intermediate feeling as "shame," in Salkever's apt words, "the habitual disposition to worry that one's initial response to a situation might be wrong." The development of this "sense of carefulness or hesitancy" is crucial to being able to deliberate (Salkever 1990, 192–194). Yet shame can be an illegitimate instrument of control as well, because the standards for "decent" acts are not neutral; it is not

---

[15] See *Rhet.* II.5 for Aristotle's examples of situations in which people rightly fear, and ones that should inspire confidence. The two are here distinguished by the possible danger involved, which varies depending on who you are and what your circumstances are.

so long ago since it was shameful for a woman to speak in public. For many, the development of a sense of shame is less necessary than the development of a sense of self-respect (although the latter could be seen as reconstituting what counts as shameful).[16] For some (or for different people in different contexts), the tendency is not toward the extreme of shamelessness, but its opposite; the fear to overcome is the fear of saying what we think, of acting as though our opinion deserves serious attention. Salkever (and Aristotle, of course) recognize that shame must be a mean between shamelessness and "hopeless dread." But finding that mean is complicated by the fact that certain constructions of decency have more to do with perpetuating inequality than with living a thoughtful human life.

For these reasons, although I am making generally the same point here as Salkever,[17] I have tried to recast the notion of public courage, rather than using the concept of shame. The virtue of shame for Aristotle is that it prevents action (action that would cause me to feel shame *if* I did it [*NE* 1128b]). But courage helps me act in the face of that fear of being wrong. And that fear itself can play a role in helping me choose how to act at a given moment. As I argue in the next section, everyone has the responsibility of both speaking and listening. But we might be guided on an individual level, as Aristotle would suggest, by an awareness of the extreme to which we tend. If I recognize that I speak easily and frequently, I might try tending toward listening more—in so doing, as Aristotle says, I would probably find the mean. Since our communicative tendencies come from both our individual character and our social/cultural background, recognizing my tendencies means locating myself in the world, and choosing actions I judge appropriate to the context.

The unpredictability of politics generates other fears and involves other risks besides that of being wrong and performing badly. By leaving our private places, we are not simply revealing ourselves; we are also assuming responsibility for the world. We are interrupting and redirecting existing action processes and creating new ones.

---

[16] See Nussbaum 1980 for an argument that connects shame and self-respect.

[17] Salkever's larger point—that the qualities that permit a thoughtful human life are supported as much by family life and personal friendship as by political action—does seem to me crucial for thinking about politics and society, and provides an important counterinterpretation of Aristotle.

When we act, we have an effect on the world that we live in, and it is one that we cannot control but that we have chosen. Merleau-Ponty speaks of "the folly of action, which assumes responsibility for the course of events . . . by action, I make myself responsible for everything" (*S* 72). In collective action, this is a shared responsibility. But this does not necessarily mitigate fear, because our involvement with one another, our "essential equality," means that we are responsible also "for all deeds and misdeeds committed by people different from ourselves" (*OT* 438 [1951 edition]). We are responsible and yet not in charge; we cannot control the situation, but we are accountable. This kind of fear can lead to not-listening as well, the reluctance to admit another as a "co-builder of a common world." But as Lorde says and Arendt would agree, it is precisely because the world is at stake that we cannot wait for "the final luxury of fearlessness" (Lorde 1984, 44, 41). Concern for the world (as well as the possibilities of forgiveness and promising [*HC* 236–247]) may help us deal with this unpredictability, and bolster courage.

Courageous listening in the face of fear means avoiding two extremes: one in which I simply, defensively, do not hear, and one in which I simply exchange my opinion for yours. Both extremes avoid the effort and danger involved in creating a passageway between us. What gives the paths we create worldly reality? We know that for Arendt the quality of realness comes from multiple perspectives on what appears; if listening is to be understood as a political rather than a private phenomenon, then it must somehow *appear* in the world. The physical and imaginative processes of speaking appear, of course, as spoken words. But how can listening itself be made visible or audible? How can it appear in public?

THE OTHER SIDE OF LISTENING

I think the difficulty of answering this question of how listening reveals itself is partly responsible for the theoretical neglect of listening in political theory, even in the work of theorists for whom it clearly plays a role (e.g., Aristotle, Arendt). Writers in other fields, although they do not pose the political question, suggest some possible answers. *Silence* is frequently mentioned as one of the conditions for, or inevitable correlates of, genuine listening. As Don Ihde muses, "If there is an ethics of listening, then respect for silence must play a part in that ethics." It is silence that creates, in Corradi Fiumara's words, "a co-existential space which permits dialogue to come along;" thus "authentic dialogue needs to have *time* for the silence of listening." Levin says that silence simply is "our listening openness" (Ihde 1976, 184; Corradi Fiumara 1990, 99, 96–97; Levin 1989, 232).

Silence properly understood is not merely a lack of sound, nor is it an absence. It is connected to sound as part of meaning, as rests in music or pauses in speech. That is, it is given form by the occurrence of sound—silence only has presence as silence because it points to something beyond itself which throws the silence into relief. Silence and speech too are mutually reliant on each other for meaning (Ihde 1976, 111–113; Sontag 1983, 187, 192–194).[18]

The "ecology" of speech and silence, argues Corradi Fiumara, is subject to "environmental degradation," an imbalance that results in "the excess of something and the extinction of something else." Our auditory space is crowded with excess verbiage as we chatter constantly to fill up the space between us and keep from actually hearing our distance from one another. It is only creative silence that lets us "be with" someone while preserving the listening space necessary to hear that person. Thus, Corradi Fiumara suggests, "a sufficient 'degree' of silence could be regarded as a medium suited to enhance the linguistic life of the symbolic animal and to avert irreversible deteriorations" (1990, 98–104).[19]

Silence, then, can be seen as an intentional act, an "effort to give space to the inexpressible" (Corradi Fiumara 1990, 98)—or an effort to make room for a variety of expressions which may surprise and challenge. But silence has multiple meanings, for it can also indicate suppression, an intentional silencing. Silence can also be a form of communication which is not indicative of listening; it may reveal an unwillingness to engage in debate, a reluctance to take up another's words. This reluctance may come from fear of conflict or fear of retribution (as in Selby's town meeting, where both fears worked to keep some people silent).[20] Or it may come from a desire

---

[18] See also Adrienne Rich's "Cartographies of Silence": "[silence] is a presence / it has a history a form / Do not confuse it / with any kind of absence" (1978, 17).

[19] See also Levin 1989, 79, on the use of meaningless noise to avoid silence.

[20] See Mansbridge 1983, 47–71. Uttal also discusses the way silence masks conflict (1990b, 317–319). See Tannen 1990b for an analysis of literary and dramatic uses of silence to stress, manage, or diffuse conflict.

to manipulate. Thomas Kochman (1981) describes the dynamics of a racially mixed classroom in which the silence of the white students was not perceived as respectful listening but as unfair withholding of their views. Silence can be a way of finding out about others while I remain shielded, protected.

In these examples, silence appears as a way to avoid conflict. But it can also be used to highlight conflict. "Willful silence" can be a form of protest against the way language is being used, a principled resistance to a certain kind of, or context for, communication. Anne Norton (discussing an essay of Ivan Illich's) maintains that unlike speech, silence has no hierarchies of competence; as a means of protest, silence is "radically democratic" because it is equally open to all (1988, 91–92).[21] This silent rejection of language, Norton says, signals an "abandonment" of politics. But we might also think of such silence as a particular kind of political (or metapolitical?) act, one whose point is precisely to throw into question the meaning of political speech. The refusal to take up another's words and participate together is an exercise of power which can, paradoxically, block the creation of power. Words that continually fall into dead silence can have no worldly reality and lead to no joint action. This silent refusal, as deliberate not-listening, is clearly a drastic political act. As such, it cannot be an end in itself but must point to the possibility of communication beyond silence. It may be best thought of as a kind of civil disobedience, or the equivalent of a worker's strike. Just as the effort of a strike is a refusal of work for the sake of work (that is, for better conditions of work), silence can communicate a refusal of political communication for the sake of better political communication.

However, Norton's contention that silence is a means of protest equally accessible to all is questionable. Some people may have more at stake and may feel that silence is too risky (as sometimes a strike is judged to be). Conversely, in a society where the political and economic arrangements consistently benefit particular groups, those groups may be silent without fear that their interests will not be taken into account (Green 1985, 15).

[21] The phrase "radically democratic" is Illich's. See also Trinh 1990, 372–373, and Ihde 1976, 184 on "the silent refusal."

More powerful groups in society are often, deliberately or unintentionally, the ones who do not listen or who silence others. Theorists like Sharon Welch and David Levin thus stress the need to listen to the voices of the oppressed (Levin 1989, 85; Welch 1990, 133). They do not, however, talk about the oppressed as listeners. It is difficult to do so at a time when many oppressed groups are "finding their voice"; calling for increased listening in general might be seen as an oblique attempt to resilence those groups. But in stressing the interdependence of speaking and listening, this project attempts precisely the opposite: to theorize a public space in which all voices are heard. That does not mean that those who are members of oppressed groups do not need to, or should not have to, listen. Such an exemption is neither democratic nor necessary; the disempowered have always had to listen, and will continue to need to, in order to know what is at stake for those in power. Political listening is certainly strategic in this sense, and all citizens must listen to determine the source and extent of conflict and the possibilities of taking various actions together.[22] Exempting some from listening (either implicitly or explicitly) can stifle the vitality of political interaction, and could also result in a kind of patronizing hierarchy of citizenship: certain citizens cannot be expected to exercise certain responsibilities and thus are somehow lacking, not wholly mature citizens. This would be a modern version, perhaps, of the French revolutionaries' mistake (see *OR* 81–89). If I regard you as exempted from listening because of your oppression, I certainly am not regarding you as a partner in political action. It is as though I am doing something *for* you, rather than our acting together—or, on a collective level, as though *we* are letting *them* into *our* public, rather than creating one together through speaking and listening.

The mutuality of speaking and listening is highlighted by the practice of *question-posing*, another activity that some scholars argue reveals listening. Through requests for clarification and other kinds of "interpretive digging" (Forester), participants show their willingness to take seriously what each other has to say. Questions show me as the speaker that listeners are "working with me to under-

---

[22] Listening has precisely this meaning in the practices of the Industrial Areas Foundation; see Boyte 1989, 148–151. See also Griffin (1978, 202): "Sound only a milder form of the shock waves made by explosions, by blasts . . . we survive by hearing."

stand" (Uttal 1990b, 319; Forester 1989, 111). That work, like po-litical action in general, is risky, for it may reveal conflict and deep differences that cannot be neatly reconciled. But even in disagree-ing, you are still working with me, and our disagreement still influ-ences the outcome of deliberation. With the kind of responsive effort that questioning is an example of, a speaker can still be part of the collective work even if everyone else ends up disagreeing with her or him.

As Forester notes, however, questioning can equally demon-strate a lack of engaged listening: "At times we may demand exces-sive clarity, precision, or definition from others and avoid our own responsibility to draw out implications and think, pay attention to meaning" (1989, 115). Questioning can in fact reveal the limits of one's willingness to listen, for a question is always directive, it puts forth the terms of discussion in some specific way. Thus "the way in which a question is posed limits and conditions the quality, and level, of any answer that can be possibly worked out" (Corradi Fiu-mara 1990, 34). Just as we can imagine a questioning response that probes, extends, or gives new meaning to a speaker's remarks, we can imagine a question designed primarily to evade or obscure those remarks. This indeterminacy in the meaning of questioning extends to *argument* as well. Argumentative responses are central to collective figuring out, and they act much like question-posing; they may show a desire to engage with a speaker, or a defensive reluc-tance to shift perspectives even temporarily.

So no one of these communicative phenomena—silence, ques-tion-posing, or arguing—can be pointed to as unequivocal worldly signs of listening. Yet we can often discern listening and its lack. I sus-pect most of us can recall times when we genuinely felt heard and sit-uations in which we knew we were not being listened to. "Being listened to" *is* an experience we have in the world, whether or not we can point to an unambiguous indication of listening. The lack of such an indication need not prevent us from theorizing or commu-nicating about listening, because there is, after all, no such guarantee with respect to speech. Although we can literally know when words have come from a speaker's mouth, or signs from her hands and body, we have no definite way to show that speakers *mean* their words, that they are sincere, that the opinions expressed are really their own. Speakers may be lying, filibustering, or saying something they do not believe out of anger or a desire to derail decision-making. As Habermas has argued, there are no transcendent grounds by which to prove the claims to truth, sincerity, and appropriateness that are implicit in speech. Such claims can only be "redeemed"—or challenged—through more speech, by talking about the problematic claim.[23] One need not agree with Habermas's formal model of speech to conclude that challenges to listening can be addressed similarly. Judgments about (and challenges to) the activity of listeners happen, and can happen, despite the absence of infallible concrete measurement. We can move from speaking and listening about a problem to speaking about communicative phenomena themselves—the level of attention, or why we feel unheard. Our experience is not the final or unquestioned criterion here. Rather, in such a discussion, we are offering our experience to the perspective of others, and some may and some may not confirm our sense of what is going on.

The terms of such challenges and judgments depend on what we understand ourselves to be listening for, that is, what we are doing or trying to do together. How is the effort of pathbuilding related to the purposes of deliberation? What—to return to the question opened many pages ago with Aristotle—does collective figuring out involve, and what does that tell us about the kind of attention we must pay to one another? Merleau-Ponty's answer involves a notion of "understanding" which is much like Arendt's account of "judging," for both are rooted in the possibility of intersubjectivity. But what does it mean to understand and make judgments intersubjectively? Does "intersubjective" imply "intersubjective agreement"? And on what? If speaking and listening are the means by which we make these intersubjective judgments, for what are we listening? In other words: what is it exactly that is between or among subjects in "intersubjectivity"?

In the next section, I explore these questions by using Arendt's and Merleau-Ponty's understanding of relations between subjects in the world. Both Arendt and Merleau-Ponty see human existence as conditioned by both bodily and social processes on one hand, and creative subjectivity on the other. But the two have opposite reac-

---

[23] This argument of Habermas's has appeared in many different forms; see 1990, 57–62; 1987, 121–122; 1984, 306–310; 1979, 1–5, 63–65.

tions to this situation; Arendt stresses the importance of a conceptual (or perceptual) separation between these two aspects of human existence, while Merleau-Ponty contends that we can understand them only as inextricably intertwined. ("If for example we wanted to isolate mind and body by relating them to different principles, we would hide what is to be understood—'the monster,' the 'miracle,' man" [S, 202]). Despite this disagreement, their accounts of relations between subjects in the world end up looking very much alike. This suggests that we can perhaps preserve Arendt's valuable conception of plurality and action without necessarily severing it from social and bodily existence.

Let me note that what Merleau-Ponty does not probe is precisely what Arendt and Anzaldúa do: the political significance of the fact that despite our existence as "situated subjects," we can perceive ourselves as solely one or the other (as Merleau-Ponty's own critiques of "empiricism" and "intellectualism" make apparent). Arendt is concerned with the dangers of reducing human existence to its "bodily" and social side, whereas Anzaldúa confronts the oppressive nature of a politics that assumes we are "disembodied," or unsituated, and examines the significant but indeterminate connection between social identity and political action. Merleau-Ponty's account gives phenomenological ballast to Anzaldúa's argument by examining how perceptual experiences influence our being in the world with others.

LISTENING IN THE INTERSUBJECTIVE WORLD

For Arendt and Merleau-Ponty, it is "the world" itself that is between subjects. Arendt says that "the common world is what we enter when we are born and what we leave behind when we die"; this world rests on the literal earth but is given its character through being a home for objects and other people.[24] Arendt most often talks of the common world as the public realm, as distinct from "our privately owned space" in the world (e.g., HC 52); she does not focus on the public significance of "intermediate" worlds of culture or community that exist together in the common world.

---

[24] Other people are unavoidably part of my world, even if I choose solitude or solipsism, for those choices have meaning only in reference to a world of other humans. See Arendt, HC 22, on solitude and Merleau-Ponty, PP 360, on solipsism.

But Merleau-Ponty conceptualizes worldliness differently. There are multiple, overlapping fields of existence. The "primary" world serves as the ultimate horizon of meaning for us all, but we have also acquired various secondary worlds—worlds of thought, of relationships, of particular locations (*PP* 293, 130, 430). The concatenation of these worlds provides a subject's "intentional arc": "the life of the consciousness . . . is subtended by an 'intentional arc' which projects round about us our past, our future, our human setting, our physical, ideological and moral situation, or rather which results in our being situated in all these respects" (*PP* 136). Our intentional arcs situate us in time, among things, and among other people. They provide secondary horizons against which we understand ourselves, others, and the primary, common world.

The common world remains crucial because it is the field in which our experience of all other worlds happens; Merleau-Ponty calls it "the primordial unity of all our experiences" (*PP* 430). For Arendt, it is between us in a sense that both "relates and separates" us (*HC* 52–53). The shared quality of the common world—its reality—"relies on the simultaneous presence of innumerable perspectives and aspects in which the common world presents itself." That is, it requires the presence of others who have these varying perspectives, which are directed toward the same object. The common world is where "things can be seen by many in a variety of aspects without changing their identity, so that those who are gathered around them know they see sameness in utter diversity" (*HC* 57–58). But what is the difference between seeing "sameness in utter diversity," and seeing the world "under only one aspect" (an apolitical kind of perception characteristic of mass societies and tyrannies [*HC* 57–58])? To put it another way, what kind of "sameness" is indicative of "utter diversity"?

Merleau-Ponty's understanding of the character of worldly perception can help us grasp this difference. "It is my involvement in a point of view which makes possible both the finiteness of my perception and its opening out upon the complete world as a horizon of every perception" (*PP* 304). To return to the example discussed in Chapter 1: when I am looking at a lamp, I know it exists in a perceptual field that my perspective does not exhaust, and that other people can see the aspects of the objects that to me are hidden. My perspective "comes up against" the perspective of others "through the intermediary of time and language" (*PP* 68–69). Merleau-Ponty and Arendt agree that in normal (or nontyrannical) perception an object cannot even be seen under only one aspect; such an object would be a flatness or transparency that admits of no other sides. Conversely, an object seen by everyone from different perspectives has "fullness": "the house itself" is not the house seen from my point of view, nor from "nowhere," but "the house seen from everywhere" (*PP* 69).

This fullness is achieved for Arendt through the workings of common sense, the sense whereby we are aware of others' perspectives and try to fit our own in with them (*HC* 208–209; *LK* 70–72; *BPF* 221, and see Chapter 3 above). For Merleau-Ponty, a similar operation is called, simply, rationality: "To say that there exists rationality is to say that perspectives blend, perceptions confirm each other, a meaning emerges" (*PP* xix). The world is "the native abode of all rationality" (*PP* 430); we can share a common world through this sense, whose existence thus means that the fact of our different perspectives does not isolate us from one another. When "Paul and I" are looking together at a landscape, Merleau-Ponty argues, we do not feel "incarcerated in our separate perspectives": "Paul's finger, which is pointing out the church tower, is not a finger-for-me that I think of as orientated towards a church-tower-for-me, it is Paul's finger which itself shows me the church tower. . . . When I think of Paul, I do not think of a flow of private sensations indirectly related to mine through the medium of interposed signs, but of someone who has a living experience of the same world as mine, as well as the same history, and with whom I am in communication through that world and that history" (*PP* 404–405).

This is not to say that Paul sees the world just as I do. To extend Merleau-Ponty's example, I may see far in the distance part of a pointed roof that seems too small to be a house. Paul, much taller than I or perhaps standing on higher ground, says that it is a small shed with no windows. This fits in with my perceptions; that object takes on a kind of fullness for both of us. This fullness is not an "ideal unity" but an open one (*PP* 406). Paul and I might see the object differently if we moved closer, or we might see that it has windows on the other side if we moved around it. It does not become a different object for us as we move (*PP* 329); rather, our perspectives (old and new, Paul's and mine) merge to reveal an object seen from as close as we can get to "everywhere."

Politically speaking, of course, it is not just seeing and pointing that bring our perspectives together. The visual fullness of an object seen from "everywhere" has its auditory parallel; this fitting in or merging happens through speaking and listening. Speaking and listening between subjects highlight the indeterminacy not only of the world but of subjectivity itself, an indeterminacy that is given shape by togetherness: "In the experience of dialogue, there is constituted between the other person and myself a common ground . . . my words and those of my interlocutor are called forth by the state of the discussion and they are inserted into a shared operation of which neither of us is the creator" (*PP* 354). Just as for Arendt, no one is the "author" or "producer" of the story in which she or he plays a part (see *HC* 184). Speaking and listening, like all political action, have a spontaneous quality. They do not just re-present already established views; rather, "the objection which my interlocutor raises to what I say draws from me thoughts I had no idea I possessed" *(PP* 354). For "words have power to arouse thoughts . . . they put responses on our lips we did not know we were capable of" (*S* 17). This spontaneity reveals a speaker's capacity to "outrun" previous thoughts, "to find in his own words more than the thought he was putting into them" *(PP* 388–389; also *PP* 178–179, *S* 18–19). In this sense, Merleau-Ponty says, "there is in all expression a spontaneity which will not tolerate any commands, not even those which I would like to give to myself" (*S* 75). It is this spontaneity that allows genuine thinking together, that makes collective action possible. We have the capacity to hear something about the world differently through the sounding of another's perspective; we are able to be surprised by others and by our own selves. Speech is spontaneous, action is unpredictable; the "fitting in" and "merging" is not a matter of snapping together separable solid views or of mere addition. Rather, the field of meaning is itself expanded, recast.[25]

How does this spontaneity coincide with the "sense of carefulness or hesitancy" discussed above? It at first sounds odd, given the connotations of "deliberate," to think of deliberation as involving spontaneity or surprise. Something done deliberately is something done "on purpose," and carefully, rather than being impromptu.

[25] It is this kind of gestalt switch that is Habermas's model of understanding: see Habermas 1987, 121–122. But politically there are other possibilities, as I discuss below.

But it is in fact only this context of purposefulness and intention that gives meaning to the idea of unexpectedness. As Merleau-Ponty points out, "no matter what surprises the event may bring, we can no more rid ourselves of expectations and of consciousness than we can of our body" (*S* 218; see also *PP* 452–456). Political attention that is capable of being surprised is not radically, perfectly open; in the context of such openness, the concept of surprise itself would have no meaning (just as spontaneity would have none without the contrast of preplanned aims). But neither is such attention "closed," as with stereotyping. Because perception is directed toward embodied beings who look and sound a particular way, we cannot see and hear them simply as pure consciousnesses. We can regard them as—like us—embedded and unique, and we can be surprised about what that means, as we can surprise ourselves. It is precisely because we each have our own expectations, intentions, and purposes that surprise and spontaneity can come from interacting with others, and have meaning as part of collective deliberation.

So far, this account of political perception and communication is not incompatible with an account of politics which sees participation as deeply transformative. The merging of our perspectives might be seen as the transformation of private views into a concern with the public good, as theorists like Tocqueville and Barber suggest. Or it might reveal our ability to connect across difference: one of Studs Terkel's interlocutors in *Race* is a former Klansman who tells a compelling story of transformation caused by working with a Black civil rights activist on a local schools project (1992, 270–283).

But—as stirring as examples like Terkel's are—our inherence in a common world is not enough to ensure or even make probable that we can merge, or fit together. In Sonia Kruks's telling commentary on the Paul-and-the-landscape passage, she reminds us that perceptions are organized by "different and even opposed *practical* goals."

> [If] Paul is a tenant farmer and I am his landlord . . . we may well stand side by side, looking, but Paul will look with the eye of a cultivator and a tenant. He will perhaps notice the degree of slope as suggesting the danger of soil erosion; the presence of shade-giving trees along one edge as cutting out necessary sunlight; both signify that the land will not yield as much for his labour. . . . For me the

land perhaps signifies family continuity, the inheritance that I will
pass on to my children (who will also stand here and appreciate the
magnificence of the very same row of trees); or perhaps above all
it signifies my economic security, my ability to derive a steady income from its rent. (1990, 135–136)

In fact, the more we see and communicate about what Arendt
would call the "worldly character" of a thing (its location, function,
length of stay), the more our perspectives may diverge. Although
we may literally see the same object—touch the same tree, hear the
same wind in the same leaves—when it comes to doing something,
to taking action, that object may have very different meanings. If
Paul as the tenant farmer wants to cut down those trees and I as the
landlord want to preserve them, this disagreement comes from the
different meanings the trees take when viewed against our separate
backgrounds, despite their presence in our common perceptual
world.

Of course, it would be unusual for a tenant and a landlord to
be deliberating about what action to take. But suppose that I am an
enlightened landlord who includes my tenants equally in making
decisions about managing the land. It may be that Paul and I will
never be able to hear each others' perspectives well enough to decide together on taking an action. This of course benefits the status
quo—if no decision is made, the trees will remain standing. My perspective (and not Paul's) wins out by default.[26] But there is a third
possibility between merging and not being able to hear each other,
one that our ability to consciously direct perception makes possible.

We are oriented, Merleau-Ponty says, to perceive the world in a
particular way. "If someone is lying on a bed, and I look at him from
the head of the bed, the face is for a moment normal"; it looks simply like a face, despite the fact that it is actually upside down. But if
I look long enough, or if someone points out to me features in a
particular way, I see it very differently: "In front of me I have a
pointed, hairless head with a red, teeth-filled orifice in the forehead and, where the mouth ought to be, two moving orbs edged
with glistening hairs and underlined with stiff brushes" *(PP* 252).

[26] This is a problem because the status quo is not necessarily neutral or freely
chosen (Minow 1987, 54–55); thus deadlock can work to the benefit of those who
prefer the status quo. See Mansbridge 1983, 169, for another example of such deadlock and its nonpolitical resolution.

Merleau-Ponty is using this example literally, to show that humans in general are oriented to the world in a particular way, but let us say that my "intentional arc" leads me to be oriented to right-side-up faces, while yours leads you to be oriented the other way. If I concentrate while you are pointing out to me the "red teeth-filled orifice in the forehead," I may experience a "gestalt switch" and see it your way—learning something about both your intentional arc and the world. But if I blink or look away, my habitual frame of reference returns, the face is righted, unchanged by my encounter with your perspective. So the world will not necessarily shift for me. By an effort of refocusing, I can again see it "your" way, but that way does not seem "as real" for me.

So another possible result of communicative interaction is the realization that two or more perspectives exist in the world but in a way that will not merge. Meaning is still recast by our communicating; what is disclosed is the coexistence of our disjoint perspectives. The hallucinating patient does not stop hearing voices after the dialogue described above; he does not agree with me that they are not real. But he can come to understand his own experience in the light of others: "Then I must be the only one who hears them" *(PP* 339). It is this kind of understanding that he and I share. This does not mean that he must stop hearing those voices, be "normalized," before we can act together. In this case, listening accomplishes neither the resolution nor the transformation of conflict, but rather clarifies its nature and meaning. I may still struggle to persuade others that it is better to see it my way rather than your way. But we are not doomed to inaction if we cannot agree on the meaning of our perception, for the very fact that our perspectives will not merge may call for a particular action. That is, we may decide what to do *because* of that revealed conflict.

The perspective of Amos Oz (the Israeli novelist and peace activist) on the Israeli-Palestinian conflict provides an example of this kind of understanding:

> Time and again I receive invitations from well-meaning European and North American institutions to come and spend a few days in idyllic retreat with Palestinian artists and intellectuals in order that we might get to know and like one another. . . . These people seem to believe only in "misunderstandings" that may somehow be settled through group therapy or marriage counseling, in quiet,

pleasant surroundings. Well, I've got some news: there are no basic misunderstandings between Israelis and Palestinians, and there is a very real conflict: they want the land because they think it belongs to them; we want it because we think it belongs to us. This conflict can be resolved through compromise, through a partition, but not by simply having a nice cup of coffee with the enemy. Rivers of coffee cannot extinguish the tragedy of two peoples loving the same homeland. (1993, 15–16)

In effect, Oz says, we do not need, nor can we expect, a warm embrace between these old rivals in this tragic conflict. But what we have is a politically very significant change in the terms of the dispute: "not 'who is going to go away altogether?' but 'who is going to get what?' " (1993, 14, 17).

Let me offer another, smaller-scale example that seems particularly timely in the context of current public debates about speech and "political correctness." A column in the *New York Times* a few years ago tells the story of an interaction between Nora Weinerth, "an advocate for the mentally ill," and Doug Marlette, a syndicated newspaper cartoonist.[27] Weinerth is one of the founders of the National Stigma Clearinghouse, which investigates and protests media and advertising treatments that stereotype or trivialize mental illness. Marlette is the creator of the strip "Kudzu," in which he satirizes readers of the imaginary *Modern Depression* magazine and its advice column written by "Mr. Goodvibes." The strips that Weinerth objected to and regarded as dangerous included jokes about suicide and people who take antidepressant medication. Marlette, who received many letters in protest, insisted that he was only making fun of the "feel-good gurus" who exploit the mentally ill. Weinerth's skeptical response: "I know his position . . . that's the same old position."

Weinerth had been successful in persuading many companies—including Nike, John Deere, and Planters—to discontinue advertisements that mocked or caricatured mental illness. When *Modern Depression* strips continued to appear, she called Marlette. This phone conversation, and their reactions to it, provide a valuable illustration of the difficult, open-ended work of listening. "I

---

[27] Although I describe it in detail here, this remarkable column is worth the trouble of looking up. See Michael Winerip, "Humor to One, Pain to Another," *New York Times,* June 6, 1993, p. 21. All quotes below are from this source.

was in a siege mentality," Marlette said, worried about cancellation of the strip, irritated by the implied constraints that humor should operate under. On the phone, he was quiet at first; he said later that he expected Weinerth to be like other advocates, "pious, lots of long angry silences . . . [but] she was interested in talking, not squelching."

Weinerth: "He seemed more knowledgeable than others who casually make jokes. I said you seem to know about depression. I was taking a chance personalizing it." And indeed Marlette did know about depression; as he told her, his mother struggled with mental illness and repeated suicide attempts. As the conversation continued, Weinerth urged him to make clearer whom he was making fun of; otherwise people "will see these comics and call people on medication morons." Marlette protested that humor can't be so literal or polemical; "if it's too clear, it's not satire."

The discussion ended with nothing resolved (Marlette said he intended to continue using the theme). But perhaps each of them (and certainly Weinerth) had experienced that temporary gestalt switch, which enabled them to see and hear from the other's perspective and realize that these disjoint perspectives coexist in the world. This exchange did not take place in some paradise of peacefulness, but rather in the context of contemporary social and economic tensions and gender dynamics (it is perhaps not incidental that Weinerth was the one who initiated both the communication itself and the form it took). And it has no happy ending, indeed it has no ending at all:

> After the two hung up, [Weinerth] said: "The intellectual side of me found the idea of talking about satire with Doug Marlette very seductive. And the part of me that is a sister to someone with a heartbreaking mental illness said, "my God, I want to embrace this man, to feel his pain."
>
> But the part of me that's an advocate thought, "My God, what have I done? Did I end up shaking hands with the Devil?"
>
> As for the Stigma Busters' next step in the Kudzu campaign? "I don't know," said the advocate.

Weinerth was able to construct an auditory gestalt in a way that allowed her to hear Marlette against the ground of her multiple identities; yet this produced no easy answer. At the time the column was written she had not yet figured out what to do in the face of this complex reality (in which, you will notice, an ironic and an earnest political orientation came face to face—or ear to ear). And perhaps she would not figure out what to do by herself, but in deliberations with other advocates for the mentally ill.

Taken together, these examples support both Merleau-Ponty's and Arendt's contention that agreeing on either a direction for action or a perceptual field is not automatic, although neither is it prevented, by virtue of our different perspectives. Thus intersubjectivity does not, for either theorist, mean tapping into a kind of "collective consciousness"; it is rather, in Merleau-Ponty's words, a "living relationship and tension among individuals" *(SNS* 90).[28] Political listening requires an attitude somewhere between sheer defiance and sheer docility, one that allows us neither to ignore others nor to privilege them: "We do not have to choose between the *pour soi* and the *pour autrui*, between thought according to us and according to others. . . . If I wanted to deny myself for their benefit, I would deny them too as 'Selves.' They are worth exactly what I am worth, and all the powers I give them I give simultaneously to myself" *(S* 73; see also 214–218). So the possibility of making sense—of taking meaningful action together—rests on the "discordant functioning" of intersubjectivity *(SNS* 97), on the struggle between peers. We have nothing by which to judge our perceptions except other perceptions: "My own opinions, which remain capable of error no matter how rigorously I examine them, are still my only equipment for judging. It remains just as hard for me to reach agreement with myself and with others, and for all my belief that it is in principle always attainable, I have no other reason to affirm this principle than my experience of certain concordances" *(SNS* 95).[29]

[28] See also Lisa Disch's inspired discussion of the "paradoxical quality" of Arendtian public space, which is like "cubist paintings of ordinary things that are nearly unrecognizable by virtue of being represented, in a single composition, from a multiplicity of discontinuous perspectives. Cubism achieves visually what Arendt is trying to do conceptually, to challenge the unitary assumption that sameness is necessarily coterminous with identity" (Disch, forthcoming).

[29] Similarly, as discussed above, it is my experience of being listened to that lets me know it is possible, despite the lack of any unequivocal standard by which to judge its presence. Again, this is not to say that experience is somehow the ground for truth, but rather that it provides (disputable) evidence for certain possibilities.

By the same token, we also have experiences of a lack of concordance. What makes the "mysterious affinity" of intersubjectivity mysterious is that it is often absent and cannot be willfully called upon or imposed. The possibility of meaning is real, but so is the possibility of absurdity and chaos and not-hearing. Every undertaking, Merleau-Ponty tells us, "is something of an adventure, since it is never guaranteed by any *absolutely* rational structure" *(SNS* 166). If there were a guarantee of either *sens* or *non-sens*, both Arendt and Merleau-Ponty agree, there would be no need for action at all. Either life would proceed according to its rational plan despite what we do, or nothing we do would matter because everything is absurd *(SNS* 168). What we do when we act is attempt to make sense together, in a world in which "sense" is an "order which is not given" *(SNS* 166).

To make this sense, we must be able to "read" the world in a way that "recognizes chaos and non-sense where they exist, but which does not refuse to discern a direction and an idea in events where they appear" *(SNS* 169). But (although Merleau-Ponty does not explicitly say so) even the recognition of non-sense is giving a kind of meaning to a situation; that recognition refers back to meaning by pointing out its lack, just as silence points to sound and solitude to the world of other humans. Even in the recognition of non-sense, as is implicit in Merleau-Ponty's discussion of occupied France, we can act meaningfully. But we may be limited in terms of who we can act with, and our actions must take into account the chaotic character of their background (see *SNS,* chap. 10).

"Non-sense" does not refer to the same condition that is our lack of individual control over our collective sense-making. Kruks does argue that for Merleau-Ponty politics is a realm "where individual projects lose their meaning in the encounter with other projects and with institutions," a realm where "*sens* so easily gives birth to *non-sens*" (1990, 139). But this cannot be quite right, because for Merleau-Ponty as for Arendt, others and institutions are always part of our world. There is no realm of "pure" projects where intentions would proceed undisturbed and uninterpreted. "All of our actions have several meanings, especially as seen from the outside by others, and all these meanings are assumed in our actions because others are the permanent coordinates of our lives" *(SNS* 37). There is only the world in which to make of ourselves a project, and any meaning that project has takes place in the world—which is to say, with both theorists, that "freedom exists in contact with the world, not outside it" *(SNS* 148; for Arendt, see *OR* 30–31, 124). A "pure" subject (or a "constituting consciousness," to use Edmund Husserl's term) is not just an unrealistic dream but is literally unreal, for it does not appear in the world—which is the only place that phenomena can appear to us. "We are involved in the world and with others in an inextricable tangle" *(PP* 454).

The tangled nature of our existence means that our multiple "worlds" are enmeshed in a common world. So when we give meaning to something, we do not wholly or finally constitute it. Rather, "it is taken up by us, reconstituted and experienced by us insofar as it is bound up with a world" *(PP* 326)—a world that always has multiple possible meanings, but whose ambiguity is not equivalent to nonsense. As Arendt says, "It is because of this already existing web of human relationships, with its innumerable, conflicting wills and intentions, that action almost never achieves its purpose" *(HC* 184). Yet it does produce a meaningful story—as long as there are listeners who perceive and become speakers in turn.

There are, then, at least three possible results of the "discordant functioning" of intersubjective communication: a perceptual merging of perspectives on the world, a recognition of coexisting and discrepant perspectives, and an inability to make sense together at all (which inability may be due to the context, to lack of communicative effort, or to some mixture of these). The sense (or rationality) characteristic of the public realm thus is not one of instrumental control, nor is it one that requires substantive consensus on the meaning of phenomena and events (proposed or actual). If this is so, is there any common purpose that underlies our individual purposes, any aim that might serve as a normative or evaluative standard? I think there is, for both theorists, and it is neither consensus nor control, but something like continuation. As we undertake specific actions, we might have in mind the underlying guide of keeping the field of action open, to act in a way so that future action is possible, so the field of freedom is maintained or expanded. "The very notion of freedom demands that our decision should plunge into the future . . . if freedom is doing, it is necessary that what it does should not be immediately undone by a new freedom" *(PP* 437). In Kruks's apt example: "For Sartre, collaborating during the Occupation was just as free a choice as resisting. But Merleau-Ponty wants to be able to distinguish between the two: one was a choice which diminished the realm of freedom, whereas the other implied an act of good faith in the possibility of sustaining freedom" (1990, 141). Arendt would call this preserving the public realm, or perhaps caring for the common world. But we can understand that now not as preserving the boundaries of the public realm from being encroached upon by the social, but as maintaining and possibly expanding the realm and reach of the practice of freedom.[30] Whether our perspectives merge, or we disagree but must act, we might be guided by what would make it possible to act together in the future, or to expand the reach of our deliberations to include still others. The reverse can be a guideline, too, as Arendt indicates in citing Kant's proposition in *Perpetual Peace* that "no state shall, during war, permit such acts of hostility which would make mutual confidence in the subsequent peace impossible." Arendt calls this proposal "the most important and also the most original": do not act in such a way that makes future action together impossible (*LK* 74–75).

The world itself is what is in-between, what relates and separates us as subjects. Through speaking and listening to one another, we give that in-between particular meaning: we figure out how it relates and separates and how we might change and reconstitute the character of those relations and that distance. The goal here is not to erase the distance, but to be able to speak, listen, and act together across it. It is not our agreement that defines our intersubjectivity in this sense but our effort. Action is judged by "the attempt . . . the undertaking . . . the *work*" (*S* 72). This does not mean that the actual consequences of political effort do not matter; it is just that those consequences can be dealt with only through human action. So the consequences of an action for continued action matter, and action has these second kinds of consequences because our efforts themselves make something real in the world. They provide an example of what is possible, of what has, through our attempt,

---

[30] A similar standard is part of Welch's "ethic of risk" (1990), which she draws from the "heritage of persistence" in African American women's novels. In contrast to an "ethic of control" (in which one acts only when a particular outcome is guaranteed), an ethic of risk leads us to act in the face of uncertainty in order to keep open a "matrix of resistance" which makes future action possible.

become part of the story people can tell. "The meaning of an action does not exhaust itself in the situation which has occasioned it, or in some vague judgment of value; the action remains as an exemplary type and will survive in other situations in another form. It opens a field" *(S* 72).[31]

Let me conclude this chapter by telling the story of a particular exemplary action that happened several years ago when, in the midst of feminism's "sex wars," I attended a protest on the campus where I was a graduate student. A feminist group at this public university had originally designed the action to protest the student union's sale of pornographic magazines like *Playboy*. News of this protest spawned a simultaneous counterdemonstration by feminists supportive of anticensorship principles and alternative sexualities. So there we were, lines of feminists, both sides chanting and holding signs, one side with a bullhorn, the other without. I was not involved in organizing either protest, and frankly I do not remember being very thoughtful about my own participation; I had not done much representative thinking, let us say. That failure was made clear to me by the gutsy act of a woman on "the other side," who came over and spoke with several of us. I cannot remember her exact words, but what she said was something like "I want to hear what you have to say, I don't want us to just yell at each other. Tell me what you want, why you're doing what you're doing." It was not a loving or peaceful act. Her face was tight and pinched, her compadres were chanting in the background, and what she was doing was clearly difficult for her, perhaps more so because she was the only one, on either side, who made that effort. She must have felt acutely vulnerable, "appearing" in that particular way and place—not as someone who floated above the conflict, not as someone who stayed "at home," but as someone who, quite literally, traveled: from her group to ours and back.

In retrospect, the effort of that one woman highlighted the effort that the rest of us had failed to make: to come together to communicate, however angrily, about our differences. This interaction

---

[31] See also Arendt on the value of exemplars, *LK* 76–77. The desire to be a particular kind of exemplar need not come from a personal desire for immortality, but may be motivated by concern for others, a desire to encourage their action by showing its possibilities, or by leaving a particular legacy (e.g., the heritage of persistence that Welch 1990 discusses).

could have happened before the protest, but it could have happened there, in that space as well, if more of us had thought to turn our attention to each other. But one group's attention was directed toward the union and its administration, and thus the other group's attention was directed at their backs and at passersby. If we had turned to face each other, it would not necessarily have precluded facing the union or other power structures, and we certainly may not have been able to agree on an action we might take as a group. But we would have done some of the difficult hard work of politics that many of us were unthinkingly avoiding, and thus we would have been in the end different actors, setting into motion a different, and what I now think might have been a more fruitful, chain of actions and reactions. I do not want to sound too tragic about lost opportunities, though; my point is more that the *example* of this lone woman's travels, even if it did not change the outcome of that particular political action, still opened up a set of possibilities that continue to reverberate in the world.

This world is an inescapably material one, as the examples cited thus far indicate: a world of stores and schools and people of different races, of borders and land and media artifacts. It is a world characterized precisely by the inseparability of creative action and elemental materiality. We reconstitute this in-between world through the joint attempt to make sense, by creating auditory paths that allow the possibility of meaningful action together. As Aristotle argues, such effort makes it possible to live a thoughtful human life, a life in accordance with the human *telos*. It might also make it possible to live in accordance with democratic ideals. If we are ever to move from our inegalitarian social order to a diverse, egalitarian, and democratic one, we must speak and listen in a way that sustains and extends the possibility of actively making sense together.

EPILOGUE

*What is certain is that if there is some universal Reason we
are not in on its secrets, and are in any case required to
guide our lives according to our own lights. . . . Who would
dare reproach us for making use of this life and world
which constitute our horizon?*

*Public life . . . associates us with those we have not chosen,
and with many blockheads.*

There is no true freedom without risk.
                                        —MERLEAU-PONTY, *Signs*

▣ Thinking about the relationship between social identities and
citizenship troubles many in a world that includes such dark examples of "identity politics" as Nazi Germany and present-day Bosnia.
But universalist conceptions of citizenship have been no less compatible with the attempted destruction of those outside the "group"
of humanity (as historical examples like the genocide of Native
Americans and the institution of slavery demonstrate). No conception of citizenship, whether universalist or identity-connected, can
provide an insurmountable bulwark against evil, or against antipolitical attitudes. But we exist as political beings in a world which (to
paraphrase Martha Minow) has made social identities matter. Our
sense of ourselves as citizens must do justice to the fact that we are
"part and parcel of a world" (*JP* 174), that is, must recognize how we
exist in the world, not resignedly, but to change that world and our
place in it. My sense of who I am comes from my individual, group,

and linguistic experiences. These experiences are given to me, and yet are what make it possible for me to move beyond givenness, to communicate with others and thus act into the world. As Merleau-Ponty stresses, "we exist in both ways *at once*" *(PP* 453): "I am a psychological and historical structure, and have received, with existence, a manner of existing. . . . The fact remains that I am free, not in spite of, or on the hither side of, these motivations, but by means of them. For this significant life . . . does not limit my access to the world, but on the contrary is my means of entering into communication with it" *(PP* 455). How might we, from the context of these significant lives, sustain and extend the possibility of meaningful communicative action together?

POLITICS PRESENT AND FUTURE: PRACTICES AND INSTITUTIONS

We can begin by giving some political and institutional specificity to the "space of appearances." It is important to recognize the many contexts in which this speaking and listening already take place, because the quality of our regard affects what counts as reality. Citizens are often constructed in public discourse these days as alienated, disaffected, and nonparticipatory. (As my students often insist, it is just not *realistic* to expect ordinary people to take political action.) To counter that widespread and incomplete perception, let me spend a few paragraphs detailing some interactive contexts in which citizens do engage in the contemporary United States.

Theorists of participatory democracy commonly invoke neighborhood and block organizations, school- and church-related groups, jury duty, town meetings, YMCAs and YWCAs (e.g, Barber 1984). There are also an extraordinary variety of grassroots groups of different sizes and purposes, who understand themselves in various ways: some self-consciously identity-based, some solely problem-driven, some coalitions of interests, and many that blur these lines.[1] Numerous political groups focus on a particular issue or set of issues: religious issues, racial and gender equality, cultural or linguistic rights, housing and homelessness, abortion, rape, welfare and

---

[1] For obvious reasons, I do not here include as "political" groups that advocate violence.

poverty, gun-control and anti-gun-control, breast cancer, literacy, AIDS, euthanasia, violence, drugs, gay-bashing, joblessness, peace— not to mention, as Sheldon Wolin points out, groups focused on "rent control, utility rates and service, environmental concerns, health care, education, nuclear power, legal aid, workers' ownerships of plants, and much more" (1992, 252).

To be even more specific: in the medium-sized midwestern city where I lived for many years, I can recall a number of active groups, including Up and Out of Poverty; Women, Work, and Welfare; Mothers Against Drunk Driving; Friends for a Non-Violent World; Minnesota Concerned Citizens for Life; the American Indian Movement; the Rape and Sexual Violence Center; the Adhoc Committee Against Police Brutality; Tornado Warning (a group concerned with women's health issues); the Center for Peace and Justice (an umbrella organization for several peace and justice groups); United We Stand (Ross Perot's organization); the Committee in Solidarity with the People of El Salvador and other groups focused on Central American issues; the Southside Anti-Prostitution Project; Youth Against Military Madness; the Minnesota Women's Press; the Abortion Rights Coalition; the Urban Coalition; Feminists for Life; the New Party; the Melpomene Institute (women's health research and advocacy); the Coalition for Women in Athletic Leadership; numerous food co-ops; not to mention strong neighborhood associations, local and national electoral caucuses, political theaters, active community centers, and a profusion of school and university-related groups (including the Graduate Student Union, whose drive to unionize graduate students eventually failed).[2]

[2] This listing is not intended to be perfectly representative of all political views; my own commitments certainly directed my attention in particular directions. In any case, attempts at representativeness are complicated by the multiple commitments citizens have, because this multiplicity makes it difficult clearly to designate members of a particular group as "progressive" or "conservative." Members of Mothers Against Drunk Driving may disagree strongly on abortion rights, members of Feminists for Life may have very different opinions on the welfare system. For this reason, I would object to the criticism that these groups do not count as adversarial communicative contexts. Sharing a concern on one issue does not a unitary political context make, nor does it eliminate the need for deliberation about what to do. (And recall the difficulties and inequities that can arise from unitary *assumptions*; see esp. Reagon 1983 and Young 1990.)

A few of the above organizations are nationwide or exist in multiple localities; such organizations also provide opportunities for citizen engagement and interaction. In many places, people are active in their local National Organization for Women; Habitat for Humanity; Sierra Club (particularly active, in my former home, in a dispute about citing a hazardous waste facility, which dispute also spawned grassroots groups on both sides of the issue); Christian Coalition; Amnesty International; Sister Cities project; ACORN; ACT UP; Planned Parenthood; Women's International League for Peace and Freedom; Queer Nation; Common Ground; League of Women Voters.

Other visible and audible groups include workers' groups like Mujeres Unidas y Activas (self-organized Latina domestic workers) and labor unions, Focus on the Family and other groups of the religious right, Men Against Violence Against Women, groups organized through the Industrial Areas Foundation, libertarian groups like the National Organization to Repeal Marijuana Laws, self-governing homeless shelters, groups that run soup kitchens and adult literacy programs, tenants' associations, tax-reform groups, drug use prevention groups, the Coalition for Immigrant and Refugee Rights and Services and other transnational grass-roots groups,[3] preservation societies, the Gay and Lesbian Health Project, the Coalition for Affordable Housing, and on and on.

This lengthy, awkward, and noncomprehensive accounting is not intended as a rhetorical sledgehammer to crush any suggestion that citizens do not participate. Indeed, my sense is that a central problem in the U.S. context is that many citizens *want* to participate (and in a way that goes beyond giving money to organizations) but do not know how to "get involved" meaningfully. We simply do not have enough accessible and robust forums for interactive political participation. However, the recitation above is intended to point out that supposed truisms like "citizens don't participate" and "at least not in face-to-face situations" do not describe our political context very well. Rather, the situation seems to be that many people are politically active and many are not. If we want to preserve and increase the space for political action, it is peculiarly counterpro-

[3] See Smith 1994 for an astute identification and analysis of transnational grassroots groups and the way they refigure political space.

ductive to ignore this diversity and discursively to construct "citizens" in a way that obscures the actual occurrence of precisely the activities central to citizenship.[4]

So anyone who wants to study closely actual instances of democratic speaking and listening should not have much trouble finding enough cases! But my claim is not that all is well in the polity. For these interactive activities are only one kind of force in the constitution of public space, which is to say that there are multiple venues or institutions in which we perform as citizens and as listeners. And some of these institutions run the risk of undermining or overwhelming crucial capacities of citizenship, and blocking the possibility of reciprocal speaking and listening. The deliberative, communicative contexts listed above are embedded in a broader cultural context, one that is forcefully shaped by the mass media and by what Sheldon Wolin has called the "megastate."

Other analysts have joined Wolin in criticizing the form that state power takes in the contemporary American context, particularly the intermingling of governmental and private institutions and elites. This web of relationships "has the net effect of unifying governmental and private power to produce a wider and deeper effect than if either had operated singly" (Wolin 1989, 186). The expansion of power made possible through scientific discoveries and technological developments, along with the dynamics of imperialism and capitalism, have produced a system of power in which political problems can be "depoliticized"—that is, prevented from appearing in the public realm and addressed largely through elite debate which disregards or manipulates formal political processes. The ends of "economic health" or "national security" become justifications for undemocratic action—in the name of democracy (Wolin 1989, chaps. 10 and 11; Greider 1992).

[4] This occurs even with a practice as minimal as voting. Voting turnout statistics for presidential elections could be cited not to prove the lack of civic-mindedness among Americans, but rather as an almost astonishing phenomenon: millions and millions of busy Americans take the time to vote—in a context in which they are constantly told that they are disaffected and powerless, that their vote does not matter, that all their fellow citizens think politics is totally corrupt anyway. Constructing the situation in a way that highlights this unexpectedness then opens the door to asking why voting is worth it for millions of people, which could provide insight on how to raise turnout (which I agree is crucial).

As Wolin tells us, "Political identity is shaped by the ways a society chooses to generate power and to exercise it." This form of state power requires a certain version of citizen identity, one in which citizens "identify [their] own well-being . . . with the expansion of American power" and accept an "attenuated" relationship with that power. The collectivity becomes defined by a certain economic structure and a certain kind of potency in international affairs; the identity of citizen is reduced to that of consumer and patriot (1981, 10, 15, 18; 1989, 189).

Just as the megastate disposes us toward certain kinds of citizenship, the media shapes us as certain kinds of listeners. Social critics are raising a variety of pressing concerns about mass media. Many are troubled by the increasing concentration of the ownership of media into a few corporate conglomerates which control a majority of newspapers, magazines, publishing companies, movie studios, radio stations, TV networks, and cable TV channels. And the impact of online communications technology—electronic mail, the World Wide Web, and other components of the "information highway"—remains to be seen. (Some argue that it is a profoundly democratic and decentralized space that provides for thoughtful interchange as well as widespread distribution of information, while critics warn of its atomizing and elitist potential.) These increasingly widespread concerns about who owns communications systems, what standards regulate them, and what the effect of new technologies will be, bear directly on thinking about citizenship. As media scholars tell us, the form of communication constrains what can be said in and through that form, which also constitutes audiences with particular characteristics (Postman 1985; Angus 1994). What kinds of attention do various media foster, what kind of citizens do they work to construct, what forms of power do they produce or prevent? Let us consider the example of what is arguably the most powerful and problematic medium: television.

Postman argues that television has changed the way that we think by imposing certain forms of speaking, listening, and watching. Television "is our culture's principal mode of knowing about itself . . . how television stages the world becomes the model for how the world is properly to be staged." The styles and sensibilities that television has spawned thus infuse other social realms—religion, politics, business (1985, 92; see also Greider 1992, chap. 14). Worse yet, the television commercial—the selling of a product through a brief, entertaining set of images—has become "the fundamental metaphor for political discourse." In fact, what passes for political dialogue are the various kinds of events and advertisements that focus on creating memorable images and "sound bites" (Postman 1985, 126; Phelan 1991; Gitlin 1991).

Television presents information—news and politics—in a shallow, fast, and radically decontextualized way, and thus undermines the capacity of its watchers to think deeply, confront contradictions, work through problems. The guiding principle seems to be, in Postman's words, "no prerequisites . . . no perplexity" (1985, 126; also Wolin 1989, Greider 1992). Television affects not only how we think but who we are; it constructs particular social relations and possibilities. The form of relations that television materializes is "the one-to-many relation of a centralized source broadcasting to a plurality of isolated receivers" (Angus 1994, 248–249). This is true whether we watch television with others or alone; we are the recipients of a cultural production that is designed to be consumed by people who have no other connection with each other, whose only connection is through that centralized source. What characterizes this relationship is unidirectionality: "the inability of listeners to transform themselves into speakers." This is not a lack of capacity on the part of individual listeners, but rather a feature of mass communication systems themselves. These systems preclude "reciprocal communication" in which "what is newsworthy and what is political" emerge from interaction between speaker and listener (Angus 1994, 233–234).

Yet even if television becomes more widely interactive, allowing for responses from viewer-listeners (see the discussion in Barber 1984), it is still a peculiarly truncated form of interaction. As Angus points out, even if listeners have an equal chance to respond on television, it is still a one-to-many relationship in which the central broadcasting source is not oriented to particularity, and in which the many are separated and not in mutual communication (1994, 248–249). Receivers of this kind of communication may be able to express immediate preferences, but they cannot engage in deliberation.

Television, the megastate, and other systems of communication and patterns of power will undoubtedly continue to coexist with more reciprocal and democratic forms of political action. Yet there are means by which we might begin to turn the former to the service of the latter. Angus suggests that, in addition to ensuring the right to respond on television, democracy requires that television audiences "may be compensated, as it were, for being an audience by the right to initiate and reply in . . . a forum of equal social significance." Since there are no forums as socially significant as television, what would be necessary is formal support for other media "such as public meetings, art shows, guerrilla video, and so on" (1994, 249–250). Further, even if television does not permit genuine deliberation between initiator and audience, it can broadcast deliberations themselves. James Fishkin's program for a National Issues Convention would involve a representative group of some six hundred citizens meeting over several days with presidential candidates in deliberative settings; Fishkin proposes televising these deliberations (Fishkin 1991). There is a profound difference, politically speaking, in one's opinion being formed by being told what the results of a deliberation were, and one's opinion being formed by watching and listening to the process of deliberation for oneself.[5]

In fact, the media could play a role in addressing some of the problems of citizenship lurking in the shadow of the megastate. I think Wolin is right that at the national level, one of the crucial tasks for citizens is to disrupt the dynamic of secrecy, "to prevent important political matters from being depoliticized and turned into in-house discussions" (1989, 191). The mass media can play a democratic role in this reclamation of political deliberation, particularly if they follow the lead of the "public journalism" move-

[5]Despite Postman's pessimistic claim that showing people in the act of thinking is "as disconcerting and boring on television as it is on the Las Vegas stage," I see no reason for believing this is always true. I would in fact offer anecdotal evidence, which other teachers might be able to confirm, that even the sleepiest class shows a marked increase in attention when I signal that I am in the act of thinking myself (as opposed to the equally important activities of questioning, facilitating, explaining, arguing). Interestingly, Postman does hold out hope for the role of schools in changing how we watch television. And I confess that I find tempting his idea of banning political television commercials, or at least requiring them "to be preceded by a short statement to the effect that common sense has determined that watching political commercials is hazardous to the intellectual health of the community" (1985, 90, 155–163).

ment by eschewing detachment, relating context and consequences, and institutionalizing means for citizens to frame the issues to be pursued.[6]

As these remarks indicate, democratic political action is sustained by some social forces and subdued by others. Plurality, Arendt reminds us, is fragile. And as one discerning commentator on Arendt has put it, "There is no safeguard against tyranny, violence, and totalitarianism except relatedness, the embodiment of plurality in as many political, institutional settings as possible" (McGowan, forthcoming). We have the capacity to "fashion new institutions," to invent and reinvent new forms of political life (Wolin 1992, 249). What kinds of practices might generate political listening? What forms of political life do justice to the multiple, embedded, and creative character of citizen identity?

One example emerges from the work of Lani Guinier. Guinier has criticized the electoral institution of single-member districts, arguing that districting assumes that geography (or in the case of race-conscious districting, race) is a proxy for interests. This system thwarts the deliberative formulation of interests and opinions across racial or geographic lines, and the winner-take-all result discourages ongoing participation by voters who are in a consistent minority. Guinier suggests that her model of proportional representation would encourage the formation of "voluntary interest constituencies"; interests, and thus groups, would be self-defined. (In other words, what would matter is one's *opinion* about interests and identity.) This mechanism takes into account the need for group representation in contexts of inequality, for voters *may* mobilize on the basis of interests connected with racial identity and would gain some representation, even if they are a numerical minority. But because it does not institutionalize a predefined group identity, Guinier's "interest representation" model invites deliberative group formation across racial lines and other social cleavages (1994, esp. chaps. 4 and 5). Such an institution could connect representative electoral politics with deliberative politics, foster the cre-

---

[6] See Merritt 1995; Greider 1992. In one political campaign, the *Charlotte Observer* constituted a panel of five hundred citizens who guided coverage and determined what questions reporters would ask at press conferences. I thank Bob Leweke for bringing this example to my attention.

ation of coalitions, and permit citizens to act as the complex and
creative political selves that we have the capacity to be.

THE TENSIONS OF CITIZENSHIP

The exigencies of living together in the same material world can
rouse the commitment to political interaction with even disliked
and dissimilar others. Thus we need to identify tendencies which
obscure that literal togetherness, and be cautious of ways of building up the world that raise seemingly impenetrable barriers. I am
not referring to places like girls' schools, or African American cultural centers; these rooms of one's own play an important role in
providing sustenance and strength for living in the unavoidable
wider world. Rather, I am thinking of tendencies toward "gated
communities," high-density public housing, and even shopping
malls where security guards make sure that certain people (e.g.,
Black teenagers) feel unwelcome. Whom we "happen" to see regularly as we move through the world has an influence on whom we
think of as citizens, and whom we think to engage with as citizens.
We endanger the possibility of democratic politics when we create
such enclosures, particularly when we become so accustomed to
their walls that we forget they are there, for then we begin to imagine that "the world" consists of those inside our gates. What we lose
in building up the worldly artifice in this way is not just democracy
but a fully human reality, which depends on the presence of a multiplicity of perceiving and perceived others. The ability to live with
an attenuated sense of reality is part of what must be combated; as
Kim Curtis (forthcoming) has so beautifully argued, our primary
challenges involve "how to take in and remain provoked by the
real."

Yet as I intimated in Chapter 4, there may be drastic situations
when we choose not to "take in" and decide not to interact. As
Arendt would insist, the conditions of human plurality are preserved through thoughtfulness and judgment, not the loyal following of rules (*LOM* I 177). Thus the normative guide of keeping the
conditions for action open, or a bias toward listening, is not an absolute that can be unfailingly relied on. The possession of such a
guide is not one that exempts us from judgment, like sheer toler-
ance; we may in fact decide not to listen, not to interact. But this decision itself must be made deliberatively, that is, it requires listening

in the first place. (I mentioned the Supreme Court before as an example of the deliberative decision not to deliberate certain questions, which is to say not to listen to certain arguments). And such a decision must be made in a way that permits the possibility of starting anew, of reopening the question of who we will listen to, of listening to a promise of change or a new account of another's actions. To cite again Arendt's striking translation of the New Testament's counsel: "And if he trespass against thee . . . and . . . turn again to thee, saying, *I changed my mind*; thou shalt *release* him" (*HC* 240n).

This "releasing" itself is a human power, a matter of initiating new action (*HC* 239–241), and as such is obviously not without risks. What can make these risks bearable is the fact that releasing others from the past is not incompatible with binding them with promises for the future. Let us look at an actual example of such "releasing," which occurs in Mansbridge's Helpline discussion. Members of the Shelter (a department of Helpline that provided temporary shelter for juvenile runaways) had a policy of excluding from the shelter members of the Scorpions, a "local street gang." New workers at the Shelter began to question this policy. As one explained: "People who hadn't been around long—and I was one of them—felt that the Scorpions were telling us they had changed, they weren't the Scorpions anymore, and that their ways of crime and violence sort of thing, they weren't into that anymore, that they were peaceful people. And from our experience that was the case. We heard histories of them invading the Shelter, using physical force, and causing all kinds of trouble. But that was from way back, considerably before we got there. And there just wasn't any evidence of it" (Mansbridge 1983, 166).

The first discussion about the possibility of changing the policy ended in a "formally consensual" decision to keep the old policy. In this case, the consensus masked serious disagreement, and "some of the four dissenters found it difficult to implement a policy in which they did not believe." The Shelter gathered to "thrash the problem out again," the result of which was a policy permitting the Scorpions to use the shelter. But "this new policy of allowing contact was a disaster. The Scorpions terrorized the kids in the Shelter. The newcomers then asked for a return to the old policy, and the Shelter reinstated it, this time with unanimous, heartfelt consensus" (1983, 167).

Members of the Shelter found it possible—not without disagreement—to "release" the Scorpions from their past actions *and* to hold them to particular promises. Helpline is, of course, toward the unitary end of Mansbridge's spectrum, and the members of the Shelter were not recognizing the Scorpions as fellow citizens or partners in decision-making, but as young people equally in need of the Shelter as other young people. However, this example does have its parallel in more adversary political contexts, for example, the recent movement of "Gangs for Peace" and the convening of gang "summits" in various cities. These summits invariably cause political conflict in the cities where they are held, as residents disagree about the gangs' commitment to peace, the proper role of political officials and community leaders, and other issues. It is precisely a controversy about how seriously these two publics can take each other as co-builders of a common world, whether gangs and other city residents can regard one another as fellow citizens in order to take joint action about problems of violence and poverty. A bias toward listening would argue for releasing the gangs from their criminal past for the sake of exercising together responsibility for our common world. But this argument would be only just that—an argument, made in the process of deliberation, subject to challenges from others.

In other words, the conception of citizenship that I have developed here is characterized by a tension between openness and commitment, a tension that is never finally or fully resolved. Such resolution would in fact mean the end of citizenship, for citizenship is the practice of living with that tension. Our attitude toward that lack of finality need not be celebratory; I certainly do not think that politics requires a joyous acceptance of indeterminacy. Not surprisingly, members of the Shelter were deeply exasperated with the need to remake decisions over and over again (Mansbridge 1983, 167). And as Merleau-Ponty observes unhappily, "in politics one has the oppressive sensation of blazing a trail which must be endlessly reopened" (*S* 3).

No one can be actively engaged in the tension of citizenship all the time, or even most of the time, and politics is not the whole of human existence. Yet neither is it just an endlessly repetitive labor. I have focused here on the difficult side of political action, on fear, courage, and conflict. I have done so to explicate the character of

communicative participation in adversarial contexts, and to develop
a democratic conception of listening adequate to contemporary politics. But caring for the world and caring about making our presence
felt in the world has another side as well, which the theorists I discuss recognize in various ways. For Aristotle, sharing speech about
the just and unjust, advantageous and disadvantageous, is part of human happiness and flourishing, and it appeals to the pleasure of
learning something new and strange. Arendt is always eloquent on
the "joy and gratification that arise out of being in company with our
peers, out of acting together and appearing in public" (*BPF* 263; also
OR 119–131, *MDT* 15). This has its parallel in Mansbridge's identification of the "exhilaration" and "reciprocity" that comes from
"working with equals" (1983, 29). And Lorde emphasizes the sustenance that comes from examining together "the words to fit a
world" (1984, 41).

This intertwining of exhilaration and exasperation is the specific experience of a democratic politics that stresses speaking and
listening together. The significance of such a conception lies in its
potential to shape a particular kind of polity, one in which citizens
recognize each other as "builders of worlds or co-builders of a
common world" (*OT* 458). This "effective recognition" (*S* 222) requires communication with one another and joint effort. It provides a crucial complement to the unidirectional communication
that often characterizes what we think of as political action, communication directed less at those with whom one disagrees and
more at institutions with the power to determine public policy (the
courts, Congress). I do not argue that this kind of communication
is unnecessary; law and legislation are also central to democratic
politics, and participating in these practices shapes the world as
well. But a reorientation of our attention toward one another as
fellow citizens is equally essential. I end, appropriately, with
Arendt's words: "Only when we come to feel ourselves part and
parcel of a world in which we, like everybody else, are engaged in
a struggle against great and sometimes overwhelming odds, and
yet with a chance of victory, however small, and with allies, however few . . . only then will we be able to rid the world of its nightmarish quality" (*JP* 174).

REFERENCES

Ackelsberg, Martha A. 1983. "Sisters or Comrades? The Politics of Friends and Families." In *Families, Politics, and Public Policy*, ed. Irene Diamond. London: Longman.

Ackerman, Diane. 1990. *A Natural History of the Senses.* New York: Random House.

Ackrill, J. L. 1980. "Aristotle on Action." In *Essays on Aristotle's Ethics*, ed. Amelie O. Rorty. Berkeley: University of California Press.

Alarcón, Norma. 1990. "The Theoretical Subject(s) of *This Bridge Called My Back* and Anglo-American Feminism." In *Making Face, Making Soul/Haciendo Caras*, ed. Gloria Anzaldúa. San Francisco: Aunt Lute Foundation.

Albrecht, Lisa, and Rose M. Brewer, eds. 1990. *Bridges of Power: Women's Multicultural Alliances.* Philadelphia: New Society Publishers.

Anderson, Linda. 1986. "Hearing You in My Own Voice: Woman as Listener and Reader." In *The Art of Listening*, ed. Graham McGregor and R. S. White. London: Croom Helm.

Angus, Ian. 1994. "Democracy and the Constitution of Audiences." In *Viewing, Reading, Listening*, ed. Jon Cruz and Justin Lewis. Boulder, Colo.: Westview Press.

Anzaldúa, Gloria, ed. 1990a. *Making Face, Making Soul/Haciendo Caras.* San Francisco: Aunt Lute Foundation.

———. 1990b. "Haciendo Caras, una entrada/an Introduction." In *Making Face, Making Soul/Haciendo Caras*, ed. Gloria Anzaldúa. San Francisco: Aunt Lute Foundation.

———. 1990c. "En Rapport, In Opposition: Cobrando cuentas a las nuestras." In *Making Face, Making Soul/Haciendo Caras*, ed. Gloria Anzaldúa. San Francisco: Aunt Lute Foundation.

——. 1990d. "Bridge, Drawbridge, Sandbar, or Island: Lesbians-of-Color Hacienda Alianzas." In *Bridges of Power*, ed. Lisa Albrecht and Rose M. Brewer. Philadelphia: New Society Publishers.

——. 1987. *Borderlands/La Frontera*. San Francisco: Spinsters/Aunt Lute Press.

——. 1983. "La Prieta." In *This Bridge Called My Back*, ed. Cherríe Moraga and Gloria Anzaldúa. New York: Kitchen Table: Women of Color Press.

Arendt, Hannah. 1992. *Hannah Arendt Karl Jaspers: Correspondence, 1926–1969*, ed. Lotte Kohler and Hans Saner, trans. Robert Kimber and Rita Kimber. New York: Harcourt Brace Jovanovich.

——. 1982. *Lectures on Kant's Political Philosophy*, ed. Ronald Beiner. Chicago: University of Chicago Press.

——. 1981. *The Life of the Mind*. One-volume ed. New York: Harcourt Brace Jovanovich.

——. 1978. *The Jew as Pariah*, ed. Ron H. Feldman. New York: Grove Press.

——. 1973. *The Origins of Totalitarianism*. New ed. New York: Harcourt Brace Jovanovich.

——. 1972. *Crises of the Republic*. New York: Harcourt Brace Jovanovich.

——. 1968a. *Between Past and Future*. Enlarged ed. New York: Penguin Books.

——. 1968b. *Men in Dark Times*. New York: Harcourt Brace and World.

——. 1965a. *On Revolution*. New York: Penguin Books.

——. 1965b. *Eichmann in Jerusalem*. Rev. ed. New York: Penguin Books.

——. 1958. *The Human Condition*. Chicago: University of Chicago Press.

Aristotle. 1991. *On Rhetoric*, trans. George A. Kennedy. New York: Oxford University Press.

——. 1988. *Politics*, ed. Stephen Everson. Cambridge: Cambridge University Press.

——. 1965. *Nicomachean Ethics*, trans. Martin Ostwald. Indianapolis: Bobbs-Merrill.

Arnhart, Larry. 1981. *Aristotle on Political Reasoning*. DeKalb: Northern Illinois University Press.

Austin, M. M., and P. Vidal-Naquet. 1977. *Economic and Social History of Ancient Greece*. Berkeley: University of California Press.

Ball, Terence. 1979. "Interest-Explanations." *Polity* 12 (Winter): 187–201.

Barber, Benjamin. 1984. *Strong Democracy: Participatory Politics for a New Age*. Berkeley: University of California Press.

Barker, Ernest. 1959. *The Political Thought of Plato and Aristotle*. New York: Dover.

Barrett, Michèle, and Anne Phillips, eds. 1992. *Destabilizing Theory: Contemporary Feminist Debates*. Stanford: Stanford University Press.

Beiner, Ronald. 1983. *Political Judgment.* Chicago: University of Chicago Press.

———. 1982. "Hannah Arendt on Judging." In *Lectures on Kant's Political Philosophy.* Chicago: University of Chicago Press.

Benderly, Beryl Lieff. 1980. *Dancing without Music: Deafness in America.* Washington, D.C.: Gallaudet University Press.

Benhabib, Seyla. 1992. "Models of Public Space: Hannah Arendt, the Liberal Tradition, and Jurgen Habermas." In *Habermas and the Public Sphere*, ed. Craig Calhoun. Cambridge: MIT Press.

———. 1988. "Judgment and the Moral Foundations of Politics in Arendt's Thought." *Political Theory* 16(1): 29–51.

———. 1986a. *Critique, Norm, and Utopia: A Study of the Foundations of Critical Theory.* New York: Columbia University Press.

———. 1986b. "The Generalized and the Concrete Other: The Kohlberg-Gilligan Controversy and Feminist Theory." *Praxis International* 5(4): 402–424.

Bickford, Susan. 1994. "Anti-Anti-Identity-Politics: Feminism, Democracy, and the Complexities of Citizenship." Presented at the Southern Political Science Association Meeting, Atlanta, November 1994.

———. 1993. "Why We Listen to Lunatics: Antifoundational Theories and Feminist Politics." *Hypatia* 8(2): 104–123.

Bowles, Samuel, and Herbert Gintis. 1986. *Democracy and Capitalism.* New York: Basic Books.

Boyte, Harry C. 1989. *Commonwealth: A Return to Citizen Politics.* New York: Free Press.

Brown, Wendy. 1993. "Wounded Attachments." *Political Theory* 21(3): 390–410.

Butler, Judith. 1993. *Bodies That Matter.* New York: Routledge.

———. 1992. "Contingent Foundations: Feminism and the Question of 'Postmodernism.' " In *Feminists Theorize the Political*, ed. Judith Butler and Joan W. Scott. New York: Routledge.

———. 1990. *Gender Trouble.* New York: Routledge.

Butler, Judith, and Joan W. Scott, eds. 1992. *Feminists Theorize the Political.* New York: Routledge.

Calhoun, Craig, ed. 1992. *Habermas and the Public Sphere.* Cambridge: MIT Press.

Cameron, Deborah. 1985. *Feminism and Linguistic Theory.* New York: St. Martin's Press.

Canovan, Margaret. 1983. "A Case of Distorted Communication: A Note on Habermas and Arendt." *Political Theory* 11(1): 105–116.

Christian, Barbara. 1990. "The Race for Theory." In *Making Face, Making Soul/Haciendo Caras*, ed. Gloria Anzaldúa. San Francisco: Aunt Lute Foundation.

Cliff, Michelle. 1990. "Object into Subject: Some Thoughts on the Work of Black Women Artists." In *Making Face, Making Soul/Haciendo Caras*, ed. Gloria Anzaldúa. San Francisco: Aunt Lute Foundation.

Coates, Jennifer. 1986. *Women, Men and Language*. London: Longman.

Coates, Jennifer, and Deborah Cameron. 1988. *Women in Their Speech Communities*. London: Longman.

Cohen, Joshua, and Joel Rogers. 1983. *On Democracy*. New York: Penguin Books.

Coles, Romand. 1996. "Liberty, Equality, Receptive Generosity: Neo-Nietzschean Reflections on the Ethics and Politics of Coalition." *American Political Science Review* 90(2): 375–388.

Collins, Patricia Hill. 1991. *Black Feminist Thought*. New York: Routledge.

Cooper, John M. 1980. "Aristotle on Friendship." In *Essays on Aristotle's Ethics*, ed. Amelie Oksenberg Rorty. Berkeley: University of California Press.

———. 1977. "Aristotle on the Forms of Friendship." *Review of Metaphysics* 30(4): 619–648.

Corradi Fiumara, Gemma. 1990. *The Other Side of Language: A Philosophy of Listening*. New York: Routledge.

Curtis, Kimberley. Forthcoming. "Aesthetic Foundations of Democratic Politics in the Work of Hannah Arendt." In *Hannah Arendt and the Meaning of Politics*, ed. Craig Calhoun and John McGowan. Minneapolis: University of Minnesota Press.

Dahl, Robert A. 1985. *A Preface to Economic Democracy*. Berkeley: University of California Press.

Dewey, John. 1929. *The Quest for Certainty*. New York: Minton, Balch.

———. 1927. *The Public and Its Problems*. Athens: Ohio University Press.

Dietz, Mary G. 1995. "Feminist Receptions of Hannah Arendt." In *Feminist Interpretations of Hannah Arendt*, ed. Bonnie Honig. University Park: Pennsylvania State University Press.

———. 1991. "Hannah Arendt and Feminist Politics." In *Feminist Interpretations and Political Theory*, ed. Mary Lyndon Shanley and Carole Pateman. University Park: Pennsylvania State University Press.

———. 1988. *Between the Human and the Divine*. Totowa, N.J.: Rowman and Littlefield.

Dill, Bonnie Thornton. 1983. "Race, Class, and Gender: Prospects for an All-Inclusive Sisterhood." *Feminist Studies* 9(1): 131–150.

Disch, Lisa. Forthcoming. " 'Please Sit Down, but Don't Make Yourself at Home': Arendtian Visiting and the Prefigurative Politics of Consciousness-Raising." In *Hannah Arendt and the Meaning of Politics*, ed. Craig Calhoun and John McGowan. Minneapolis: University of Minnesota Press.

———. 1994. *Hannah Arendt and the Limits of Philosophy*. Ithaca: Cornell University Press.

Disch, Lisa, and Mary Jo Kane. 1996. "When a Looker Is Really a Bitch: Lisa Olson, Sport, and the Heterosexual Matrix." *Signs* 21(2): 278–308.

Duggan, Lisa. 1994. "Queering the State." *Social Text* 39 (Summer): 1–14.

Eisenstein, Hester. 1983. *Contemporary Feminist Thought*. Boston: G. K. Hall.

Elkin, Stephen L. 1987. *City and Regime in the American Republic*. Chicago: University of Chicago Press.

Evans, Sara M. 1989. *Born for Liberty: A History of Women in America*. New York: Free Press.

———. 1979. *Personal Politics*. New York: Random House.

Evans, Sara M., and Harry C. Boyte. 1986. *Free Spaces*. New York: Harper & Row.

Ferguson, Kathy E. 1993. *The Man Question: Visions of Subjectivity in Feminist Theory*. Berkeley: University of California Press.

Finley, M. I. 1983. *Politics in the Ancient World*. Cambridge: Cambridge University Press.

Fishkin, James. 1991. *Democracy and Deliberation*. Princeton: Princeton University Press.

Forester, John. 1989. *Planning in the Face of Power*. Berkeley: University of California Press.

Foucault, Michel. 1980. *Power/Knowledge*. New York: Pantheon Books.

———. 1977. *Discipline and Punish*. New York: Pantheon Books.

Fraser, Nancy. 1992. "Rethinking the Public Sphere." In *Habermas and the Public Sphere*, ed. Craig Calhoun. Cambridge: MIT Press.

———. 1991. "False Antitheses: A Response to Seyla Benhabib and Judith Butler." *Praxis International* 11(2): 166–177.

———. 1989. *Unruly Practices: Power, Discourse, and Gender in Contemporary Social Theory*. Minneapolis: University of Minnesota Press.

———. 1986. "Toward a Discourse Ethic of Solidarity." *Praxis International* 5(4): 425–429.

Frye, Marilyn. 1983. *The Politics of Reality*. Freedom, Calif.: Crossing Press.

Fuss, Diana. 1989. *Essentially Speaking*. New York: Routledge.

Gaventa, John. 1980. *Power and Powerlessness: Quiescence and Rebellion in an Appalachian Valley*. Urbana: University of Illinois Press.

Gitlin, Todd. 1993. "The Rise of 'Identity Politics': An Examination and Critique." *Dissent* 40(2): 172–177.

———. 1991. "Bites and Blips: Chunk News, Savvy Talk and the Bifurcation of American Politics." In *Communication and Citizenship*, ed. Peter Dahlgren and Colin Sparks. New York: Routledge.

Grealy, Lucy. 1993. "Mirrorings: To Gaze upon My Reconstructed Face." *Harper's* 286 (February): 66–74.

Green, Philip. 1985. *Retrieving Democracy: In Search of Civic Equality.* Totowa, N.J.: Rowman and Allanheld.

Greider, William. 1992. *Who Will Tell the People?* New York: Touchstone, Simon and Schuster.

Griffin, Susan. 1978. *Woman and Nature: The Roaring inside Her.* New York: Harper Colophon Books.

Guinier, Lani. 1994. *The Tyranny of the Majority.* New York: Free Press.

Gumperz, John J. 1982. *Discourse Strategies.* Cambridge: Cambridge University Press.

Gutmann, Amy. 1985. "Communitarian Critics of Liberalism." *Philosophy and Public Affairs* 14(3): 308–322.

Habermas, Jürgen. 1990. *Moral Consciousness and Communicative Action.* Cambridge: MIT Press.

———. 1987. *The Theory of Communicative Action.* Vol. 2, trans. Thomas McCarthy. Boston: Beacon Press.

———. 1984. *The Theory of Communicative Action.* Vol. 1, trans. Thomas McCarthy. Boston: Beacon Press.

———. 1979. *Communication and the Evolution of Society*, trans. Thomas McCarthy. Boston: Beacon Press.

———. 1977. "Hannah Arendt's Communications Concept of Power." *Social Research* 44: 3–24.

———. 1970a. "On Systematically Distorted Communication." *Inquiry* 13: 360–218.

———. 1970b. "Towards a Theory of Communicative Competence." *Inquiry* 13: 360–375.

Halley, Janet E. 1993. "The Construction of Heterosexuality." In *Fear of a Queer Planet*, ed. Michael Warner. Minneapolis: University of Minnesota Press.

Harding, Sandra. 1986. *The Science Question in Feminism.* Ithaca: Cornell University Press.

Hartsock, Nancy C. M. 1985. *Money, Sex, and Power: Toward a Feminist Historical Materialism.* Boston: Northeastern University Press.

Hill, Melvyn A., ed. 1979. *Hannah Arendt: The Recovery of the Public World.* New York: St. Martin's Press.

Honig, Bonnie. 1992. "Toward an Agonistic Feminism: Hannah Arendt and the Politics of Identity." In *Feminists Theorize the Political*, ed. Judith Butler and Joan W. Scott. New York: Routledge.

hooks, bell. 1989. *Talking Back.* Boston: South End Press.

———. 1984. *Feminist Theory: From Margin to Center.* Boston: South End Press.

Ihde, Don. 1976. *Listening and Voice: A Phenomenology of Sound.* Athens: Ohio University Press.

Irwin, Terence, trans. 1985. Aristotle, *Nicomachean Ethics*. Indianapolis: Hackett.

Isaac, Jeffrey C. 1993. "Situating Hannah Arendt on Action and Politics." *Political Theory* 21(3): 534–540.

Jay, Martin. 1993. *Downcast Eyes: The Denigration of Vision in Twentieth-Century French Thought*. Berkeley: University of California Press.

Jonas, Hans. 1966. *The Phenomenon of Life*. New York: Harper & Row.

Jones, Kathleen B. 1987. "On Authority: Or, Why Women Are Not Entitled to Speak." In *Nomos XXIX: Authority Revisited*, ed. J. Roland Pennock and John W. Chapman. New York: New York University Press.

Jordan, June. 1985. *On Call*. Boston: South End Press.

Kaplan, E. Ann. 1983. "Is the Gaze Male?" In *Powers of Desire*, ed. Ann Snitow, Christine Stansell, and Sharon Thompson. New York: Monthly Review Press.

Kochman, Thomas. 1981. *Black and White Styles in Conflict*. Chicago: University of Chicago Press.

Kruks, Sonia. 1990. *Situation and Human Existence*. London: Unwin Hyman.

Lakoff, Robin. 1975. *Language and Women's Place*. New York: Harper & Row.

Lasch, Christopher. 1990. "The Lost Art of Political Argument." *Harper's* 281 (September), 17–22.

Levin, David Michael. 1989. *The Listening Self*. London: Routledge.

Lloyd, Genevieve. 1984. *The Man of Reason*. Minneapolis: University of Minnesota Press.

Lord, Carnes. 1981. "The Intention of Aristotle's 'Rhetoric.' " *Hermes* 109: 326–339.

Lorde, Audre. 1988. *A Burst of Light*. Ithaca, N.Y.: Firebrand Books.

———. 1984. *Sister Outsider*. Trumansburg, N.Y.: Crossing Press.

Lugones, María. 1990a. "Hablando cara a cara/Speaking Face to Face." In *Making Face, Making Soul/Haciendo Caras*, ed. Gloria Anzaldúa. San Francisco: Aunt Lute Foundation.

———. 1990b. "Playfulness, 'World'-travelling, and Loving Perception." In *Making Face, Making Soul/Haciendo Caras*, ed. Gloria Anzaldúa. San Francisco: Aunt Lute Foundation.

MacIntyre, Alasdair. 1981. *After Virtue*. Notre Dame: Notre Dame University Press.

Mansbridge, Jane J., ed. 1990. *Beyond Self-Interest*. Chicago: University of Chicago Press.

———. 1983. *Beyond Adversary Democracy*. Chicago: University of Chicago Press.

———. 1982. "Fears of Conflict in Face-to-Face Democracies." In *Workplace Democracy and Social Change*, ed. Frank Lindenfeld and Joyce Rothschild-Whitt. Boston: Porter Sargent.

Marcus, Sharon. 1992. "Fighting Bodies, Fighting Words: A Theory and Politics of Rape Prevention." In *Feminists Theorize the Political*, ed. Judith Butler and Joan W. Scott. New York: Routledge.

Martin, Biddy. 1992. "Sexual Practice and Changing Lesbian Identities." In *Destabilizing Theory*, ed. Michèle Barrett and Anne Phillips. Stanford: Stanford University Press.

———. 1982. "Feminism, Criticism, and Foucault." *New German Critique* 27: 3–30.

McCarthy, T. A. 1978. *The Critical Theory of Jürgen Habermas*. Cambridge: MIT Press.

———. 1973. "A Theory of Communicative Competence." *Philosophy of Social Sciences* 3: 135–156.

McClary, Susan. 1986. "A Musical Dialectic from the Enlightenment: Mozart's *Piano Concerto in G Major, K.453*, Movement 2." *Cultural Critique* 4: 129–170.

McGowan, John. Forthcoming. "Must Politics Be Violent?: Arendt's Utopian Vision." In *Hannah Arendt and the Meaning of Politics*, ed. Craig Calhoun and John McGowan. Minneapolis: University of Minnesota Press.

———. 1993. "Thinking about Violence: Feminism, Cultural Politics, and Norms." *Centennial Review* 37(3): 445–469.

———. 1991. *Postmodernism and Its Critics*. Ithaca: Cornell University Press.

Merleau-Ponty, Maurice. 1964a. *Sense and Non-Sense*. Evanston: Northwestern University Press.

———. 1964b. *Signs*. Evanston: Northwestern University Press.

———. 1964c. *The Primacy of Perception*. Evanston: Northwestern University Press.

———. 1962. *Phenomenology of Perception*. London: Routledge & Kegan Paul.

Merritt, Davis. 1995. *Public Journalism and Public Life*. Hillsdale, N.J.: Lawrence Erlbaum Associates.

Mills, Sara. 1992. "Discourse Competence: Or How to Theorize Strong Women Speakers." *Hypatia* 7(2): 4–16.

Minow, Martha. 1987. "Justice Engendered." *Harvard Law Review* 101: 10–95.

Molina, Papusa. 1990. "Recognizing, Accepting and Celebrating Our Differences." In *Making Face, Making Soul/Haciendo Caras*, ed. Gloria Anzaldúa. San Francisco: Aunt Lute Foundation.

Moon, J. Donald. 1991. "Constrained Discourse and Public Life." *Political Theory* 19(2): 202–229.

Moraga, Cherríe. 1983. "Preface." In *This Bridge Called My Back*, ed. Cherríe Moraga and Gloria Anzaldúa. New York: Kitchen Table: Women of Color Press.

Moraga, Cherríe, and Gloria Anzaldúa, eds. 1983. *This Bridge Called My Back.* New York: Kitchen Table: Women of Color Press.

Morales, Rosario. 1983. "We're All in the Same Boat." In *This Bridge Called My Back*, ed. Cherríe Moraga and Gloria Anzaldúa. New York: Kitchen Table: Women of Color Press.

Nichols, Mary P. 1992. *Citizens and Statesmen.* Lanham, Md.: Rowman and Littlefield.

———. 1987. "Aristotle's Defense of Rhetoric." *Journal of Politics* 49: 657–677.

Nicholson, Linda J., ed. 1990. *Feminism/Postmodernism.* New York: Routledge.

Norton, Anne. 1988. *Reflections on Political Identity.* Baltimore: Johns Hopkins University Press.

Nussbaum, Martha. 1990. *Love's Knowledge: Essays on Philosophy and Literature.* Oxford: Oxford University Press.

———. 1980. "Shame, Separateness, and Political Unity: Aristotle's Critique of Plato." In *Essays on Aristotle's Ethics*, ed. Amelie O. Rorty. Berkeley: University of California Press.

O'Barr, William M., and Bowman K. Atkins. 1980. " 'Women's Language' or 'Powerless Language'?" In *Women and Language in Literature and Society*, ed. Sally McConnell-Ginet, Ruth Borker, and Nelly Furman. New York: Praeger.

Ober, Josiah. 1989. *Mass and Elite in Democratic Athens.* Princeton: Princeton University Press.

Okin, Susan Moller. 1989. *Justice, Gender, and the Family.* New York: Basic Books.

———. 1979. *Women in Western Political Thought.* Princeton: Princeton University Press.

Ostwald, Martin, trans. 1965. Aristotle, *Nicomachean Ethics.* Indianapolis: Bobbs-Merrill.

Oz, Amos. 1993. "An Unsentimental Mideast Peace." Excerpt from the Tanner Lecture, *Harper's* 287 (October): 14–17.

Pateman, Carole. 1970. *Participation and Democratic Theory.* Cambridge: Cambridge University Press.

Patton, Cindy. 1993. "Tremble, Hetero Swine!" In *Fear of a Queer Planet*, ed. Michael Warner. Minneapolis: University of Minnesota Press.

Peterson, Sandra. 1992. "Apparent Circularity in Aristotle's Account of Right Action in the *Nicomachean Ethics*." *Apeiron* 25 (2): 83–107.

Phelan, John M. 1991. "Selling Consent: The Public Sphere as a Televisual Market-place." In *Communication and Citizenship*, ed. Peter Dahlgren and Colin Sparks. New York: Routledge.

Phelan, Shane. 1989. *Identity Politics.* Philadelphia: Temple University Press.

Phillips, Anne. 1993. *Democracy and Difference.* University Park: Pennsylvania State University Press.

Pitkin, Hanna Fenichel. 1981. "Justice: On Relating Public and Private." *Political Theory* 9(30): 327–352.

——. 1973. "The Roots of Conservation: Oakeshott and the Denial of Politics." *Dissent* 20: 496–525.

Postman, Neil. 1985. *Amusing Ourselves to Death.* New York: Elisabeth Sifton Books/Viking.

Rawls, John. 1993. *Political Liberalism.* New York: Columbia University Press.

——. 1985. "Justice as Fairness: Political not Metaphysical." *Philosophy and Public Affairs* 14(3): 223–251.

——. 1971. *A Theory of Justice.* Cambridge: Harvard University Press.

Reagon, Bernice Johnson. 1983. "Coalition Politics: Turning the Century." In *Home Girls,* ed. Barbara Smith. New York: Kitchen Table: Women of Color Press.

Rich, Adrienne. 1979. *On Lies, Secrets, and Silence.* New York: Norton.

——. 1978. *The Dream of a Common Language.* New York: Norton.

Riley, Denise. 1988. *"Am I That Name?" Feminism and the Category of 'Women' in History.* Minneapolis: University of Minnesota Press.

Ring, Jennifer. 1991. "The Pariah as Hero: Hannah Arendt's Political Actor." *Political Theory* 19(3): 433–452.

Salkever, Stephen G. 1990. *Finding the Mean: Theory and Practice in Aristotelian Political Philosophy.* Princeton: Princeton University Press.

Sandel, Michael. 1982. *Liberalism and the Limits of Justice.* New York: Cambridge University Press.

Sartre, Jean-Paul. 1956. *Being and Nothingness.* New York: Washington Square Press/Simon and Schuster.

Schofield, Malcolm. 1986. *"Euboulia* in the *Iliad." Classical Quarterly* 36(1): 6–31.

Scott, Joan W. 1992. "Experience." In *Feminists Theorize the Political,* ed. Judith Butler and Joan W. Scott. New York: Routledge.

Seidman, Steven. 1993. "Identity and Politics in a 'Postmodern' Gay Culture." In *Fear of a Queer Planet,* ed. Michael Warner. Minneapolis: University of Minnesota Press.

Sherman, Nancy. 1989. *The Fabric of Character: Aristotle's Theory of Virtue.* Oxford: Oxford University Press.

Smith, Michael Peter. 1994. "Can You Imagine? Transnational Migration and the Globalization of Grassroots Politics." *Social Text* 39 (Summer): 15–33.

Smitherman, Geneva. 1986. *Talkin and Testifyin: The Language of Black America.* Detroit: Wayne State University Press.

Sontag, Susan. 1983. "The Aesthetics of Silence." In *A Susan Sontag Reader.* New York: Vintage Books.

Spelman, Elizabeth V. 1988. *Inessential Woman.* Boston: Beacon Press.

Spivak, Gayatri Chakravorty. 1992. "The Politics of Translation." In *Destabilizing Theory*, ed. Michèle Barrett and Anne Phillips. Stanford: Stanford University Press.

Tannen, Deborah. 1990a. *You Just Don't Understand: Women and Men in Conversation*. New York: Morrow.

———. 1990b. "Silence as Conflict Management in Fiction and Drama." In *Conflict Talk*, ed. Allen D. Grimshaw. Cambridge: Cambridge University Press.

Terkel, Studs. 1992. *Race: How Blacks and Whites Think and Feel about the American Obsession*. New York: New Press.

Thucydides. 1982. *The Peloponnesian War*, trans. Richard Crawley. New York: Modern Library, Random House.

Tocqueville, Alexis de. 1969. *Democracy in America*, ed. J. P. Mayer, trans. George Lawrence. New York: Anchor Books.

Trinh, T. Minh-ha. 1990. "Not You/Like You: Post-Colonial Women and the Interlocking Questions of Identity and Difference." In *Making Face, Making Soul/Haciendo Caras*, ed. Gloria Anzaldúa. San Francisco: Aunt Lute Foundation.

Uttal, Lynet. 1990a. "Inclusion without Influence: The Continuing Tokenism of Women of Color." In *Making Face, Making Soul/Haciendo Caras*, ed. Gloria Anzaldúa. San Franciso: Aunt Lute Foundation.

———. 1990b. "Nods That Silence." In *Making Face, Making Soul/Haciendo Caras*, ed. Gloria Anzaldúa. San Francisco: Aunt Lute Foundation.

Villa, Dana R. 1992a. "Postmodernism and the Public Sphere." *American Political Science Review* 86(3): 712–721.

———. 1992b. "Beyond Good and Evil: Arendt, Nietzsche, and the Aestheticization of Political Action." *Political Theory* 20(2): 274–308.

Von Leyden, W. 1985. *Aristotle on Equality and Justice: His Political Argument.* New York: St. Martin's Press.

Wallach, John R. 1987. "Liberals, Communitarians, and the Tasks of Political Theory." *Political Theory* 15(4): 581–611.

Warner, Michael. 1993. "Introduction." In *Fear of a Queer Planet*, ed. Michael Warner. Minneapolis: University of Minnesota Press.

Weil, Simone. 1979. *Gravity and Grace*. New York: Octagon Books.

———. 1962. "Human Personality." In *Selected Essays: 1934–43*, trans. Richard Rees. Oxford: Oxford University Press.

Welch, Sharon D. 1990. *A Feminist Ethic of Risk*. Minneapolis: Fortress Press.

Wiggins, David. 1980. "Deliberation and Practical Reason." In *Essays on Aristotle's Ethics*, ed. Amelie Oksenberg Rorty. Berkeley: University of California Press.

Wolin, Sheldon. 1993. "Democracy, Difference, and Re-Cognition." *Political Theory* 21(3): 464–483.

200 REFERENCES

——. 1992. "What Revolutionary Action Means Today." In *Dimensions of Radical Democracy*, ed. Chantal Mouffe. London: Verso.

——. 1989. *The Presence of the Past: Essays on the State and Constitution.* Baltimore: Johns Hopkins University Press.

——. 1983. "Hannah Arendt: Democracy and the Political." *Salmagundi* 60: 3–19.

——. 1981. "The People's Two Bodies." *democracy* 1: 9–24.

Yack, Bernard. 1993. *The Problems of a Political Animal.* Berkeley: University of California Press.

——. 1985. "Community and Conflict in Aristotle's Political Philosophy." *Review of Politics* 47(1): 92–112.

Yamada, Mitsuye. 1983. "Invisibility Is an Unnatural Disaster: Reflections of an Asian American Woman." In *This Bridge Called My Back*, ed. Cherríe Moraga and Gloria Anzaldúa. New York: Kitchen Table: Women of Color Press.

Young, Iris Marion. 1990. *Justice and the Politics of Difference.* Princeton: Princeton University Press.

——. 1989. "Polity and Group Difference: A Critique of the Ideal of Universal Citizenship." *Ethics* 99: 250–274.

——. 1986. "Impartiality and the Civic Public." *Praxis International* 5(4): 383–401.

Young-Bruehl, Elisabeth. 1982. *Hannah Arendt: For Love of the World.* New Haven: Yale University Press.

Zook, Kristal Brent. 1990. "Light Skinned-ded Naps." In *Making Face, Making Soul/Haciendo Caras*, ed. Gloria Anzaldúa. San Francisco: Aunt Lute Foundation.

INDEX